# THE FUTURE OF OUR CITIES

# The Future of Our Cities

DOUBLEDAY & COMPANY, INC., GARDEN CITY, NEW YORK    1961

## Robert A. Futterman

INTRODUCTION BY VICTOR GRUEN

GRAPHICS AND CARTOGRAPHY BY STEPHEN KRAFT

# Introduction

The title of this book is "The Future of Our Cities." The theme is of paramount importance because the future of our cities may be synonymous with the future of our culture and our civilization. Since we are becoming to an ever increasing degree an urbanized nation, the future of our cities will decide our future as a free democratic society.

The very word, civilization, has its origin in the Latin, "civitas," or urban community. Cities have been from time immemorial the cradle of human thought and human progress. In a society like ours, in which the vast majority lives within urban organizations, the question of how we will manage to live and work and communicate within this pattern is of decisive importance.

The bewilderingly rapid technological development which has characterized the last fifty years has not been matched by thorough planning and the implementation of such planning in our urban areas. Instead of *acting* to change or to adapt our cities to the 20th century, we have only haphazardly *reacted* by applying a patchwork of policing and control measures. By our failure to act, we have rendered existing parts of the city unlivable and unworkable. We have made refugees of a great part of their population and have driven these refugees into outlying suburbia. Those who fled were lured by the promise of living in unspoiled countryside; but as the flight became a mass movement, vast stretches were transformed into a disorganized, sprawling, soulless, cultural desert in which the advantages of city living and the advantages of country living have both been lost.

Today central city areas suffer from a loss of population and a loss of economic sustenance afforded by business, social, and cultural activities. Suburbia suffers because of our inability to keep pace with its own growth, our incapacity to supply its inhabitants with roads and utilities, schools and social and cultural amenities. In the last fifty years, distances between our place of work and place of residence have stretched out of bounds.

In some areas of the United States, metropolitan formations around the city have merged—and thus "megalopolis" has been born. Open land, landscape, and countryside are being gobbled up at an alarming rate. As a consequence, the opportunities of the urbanite for recreational activities and enjoyment of nature are lessened daily.

Communication between human beings, the need for which is one of the fundamental reasons that cities came into being, has become increasingly difficult. The automobile, which was originally conceived as an instrument to give man mobility, has promoted the sprawling of our urban areas; thanks to its dramatic birth rate, the automobile has proliferated to such a degree that in vast portions of our urban areas it creates immobility. Public mass transportation, on the other hand, has steadily diminished in efficiency, convenience, and passenger carrying ability. The overall effect is that today, in spite of shorter working hours and in spite of the theoretical speeds available to us, we are forced not only to invest more time in our working day (if we consider going to and from work part of it), but also to take more time to move about during leisure hours, whether to visit friends, attend social gatherings, or participate in cultural, spiritual, or educational activities.

In spite of vast construction activity, we cannot catch up with the destruction of our environment which has been invaded by dangerous, noisy, mechanized vehicular traffic and poisoned by industrial fumes. Slums and blighted areas grow at a much faster rate than our renewal efforts. The latter will remain a hopeless, empty gesture until we realize that patchwork policing measures such as the creation of a few more one-way streets, and the construction of another superhighway, are nothing but poorly and momentarily effective palliatives. Only a complete overhaul of our urban organization can bring it into synchronization with twentieth century technological development.

Planners, architects, and city administrators have realized for many years that decisive action is needed to save urbia. Planning of the highest order and on the broadest basis, addressed to physical, economic, and sociological renewal, and carried forward by creative thought, is desperately necessary. Until a few years ago the very word "planning" sent shivers down the backbones of the largest part of our citizenry. Planning has been regarded as "socialistic" or authoritarian. Only slowly are we waking up to the fact that planning the conservation of our natural and human resources is fundamentally no different than creating a legal system to establish orderly relations in our society.

The question which is so often asked, "Is planning possible in a democratic society?" may be answered by stating that *good planning is possible only in a democratic society* and that a democratic society in this age of rapidly changing conditions can survive only by thorough planning.

What is so important and significant about this book is that it is written not by a planner or an architect or an administrator but by an investor, builder, and real estate developer. The author is a man who because of his widespread activities has participated actively in the shaping of our cities. The fact that he proceeds not just on the basis of economic studies and his company's balance sheet but from a frame of reference which involves the total city and its origins, its cultural patterns, and its social background make the work an extremely valuable contribution.

As a planner and architect, with my own views on each of these problems, I do not necessarily agree with all the findings and suggested avenues of procedure. But I salute the spirit of the book and I greet it wholeheartedly as a valuable ally in the task of re-creating our cities in the image of twentieth-century man.

—Victor Gruen

# Contents

## CHARTS AND DIAGRAMS

10

MAPS

11

# Preface

Though I do not think of myself as an organization man, time has made me a man with an organization. I am deeply grateful to several members of that organization, The Futterman Corporation, for their advice and consent during the preparation of this book, and in particular I thank Harry A. Pollay of my staff for his labors in research and his supervision of the graphic presentations.

I owe a debt of thanks, too, to Martin Mayer (*Madison Avenue, USA,* et. al.), whose article in *Esquire* about myself and my ideas first gave Doubleday thought to the commissioning of this book; and whose persevering editorial assistance made possible a far more orderly and concise communication of my philosophy than I usually achieve in writing.

The principal consideration in real estate is too often cold and simple arithmetic. This practical artifice is seldom creative, and if anything of value is derived, it is purely incidental. Our profession frequently ignores the development of property in relation to the individual and his requirements in our society—it is therefore short-sighted and inhuman, materialistic and self-defeating, as so many of our social institutions tend to be.

Tempting as material success may be to one whose conviction is capitalism, I don't believe a capitalistic society can long exist without a constant awareness that humanity stands uppermost. My hope is that this book succeeds in contributing in some way to this idea.

R.A.F.

# PART I

## 1. The Origin of the Species

Throughout the nineteenth century it was the central tenet of the American Myth that Europe was crowded, urban, urbane, artificial, while America was open, rural, natural, even pioneering. Like most myths, this one mingled important truth and gross error and cooked them together in a single brew. But the brew was satisfying to most Americans, and the myth survived, though the passing of time into the twentieth century made its errors more indigestible and its truths less nourishing. Even today, when more than two-thirds of all Americans live in what the Census Bureau classifies as "standard metropolitan areas," our political and fiscal diet contains large servings of the old myth. Because of the myth and its anachronistic popularity, our cities starve for funds while the farmer feasts on the tax table.

What was false about the myth from the beginning was the notion that cities were ever less important in America than they were in Europe. At the time of the Revolution, the British Isles contained only one city more populous than Philadelphia: London itself. New York was the third largest English-speaking city in the world, and Bristol, the second city of Britain, was scarcely if at all bigger than Boston.

Population density was low in the America of 1790—but even then, 9 per cent of the counties contained more than one-quarter of the population. (Today nine-tenths of 1 per cent of the counties are enough to hold one-quarter of the population.) Industrializing rapidly in the nineteenth century, clearing the Scots off their crofts to make larger hunting preserves and the Catholic Irish off their farms to build Protestant estates, Britain developed patterns of urbanization which the United States will probably—blessedly—never achieve. But Germany over the years has been almost exactly as urban as the United States—and France has always kept a higher proportion of its population on the farms.

The myth was true, of course, to the extent that Europe had no frontier. America was full of land waiting to be tilled for the first time, while the European city dweller could scarcely hope to find himself a farm. "Sixty acres and a mule" was not an alternative open to the Berliner, and the concept of "homesteading" was meaningless to a Parisian. The cities seemed less dominant in the American scheme because their hinterland was free for the asking, and because we needed the mythology of the frontier to form a national spirit.

And the myth was true, too, in the comparison of European as against American cities. The European city *was* artificial. Its growth had been stimulated or constricted but customarily controlled by military and political forces. Its function—as a central market, the home of steam-powered industry and the residence of a dominant middle class—was less influential than its history, whether or not that history was still relevant in the early nineteenth century.

The European city usually was a strong point—a fortified place, where people could hope to be safe during the wars that had ravaged the continent for as long as its history knew. In Italy many of the cities were on hilltops, purely for reasons of defense. Many cities had grown on their sites

16

not because access was easy, but because it was difficult. (Our only such is Salt Lake City.) Others, lying on natural trade routes, had been elaborately protected by encircling stone walls which still stood, even after the artillery to batter them down was part of the conventional armament of all potential enemies.

Walls had not restricted the population of European cities. At the height of the Byzantine Empire, the fortress walls of Constantinople enclosed the homes of at least three million (and perhaps as many as six million) people. Within the walls of Pope Gregory's Rome lay an area about as large as the city of Boston. During the late Renaissance, as the small European bandits were replaced by stronger, more organized, more "legitimate" dukedoms (really enlarged versions of the same), "suburban" communities grew up outside the "core" which the walls enclosed, though it was not until the mid-nineteenth century that such prominent cities as Copenhagen and Vienna decided they could tear down the masonry which had once protected them. The Viennese, in the open space left by the removal of the walls, put up the Ringstrasse, the great street of the city, flanked now by government offices, concert halls, opera houses, churches and tourist hotels. The Danes, less wealthy at the time but more fortunate in the long run, used the space for a system of squares and parks, including the famous Tivoli.

America knew no such walled cities. Not all the American Indians were nomads, but there were never enough of them to build cities. There are twice as many Puerto Ricans in Manhattan today as there were Indians in what is now the United States when Henry Hudson first sailed into New York harbor. Some early American cities had protecting walls (Wall Street memorializes the one in New York), but soon the sheer population of the cities made them invulnerable to Indian attack. An archaeologist might find clues to the development of Pittsburgh's Golden Triangle in the buried sticks of Fort Duquesne, and a city like Colorado Springs might owe its broad avenues to a colonel's desire for streets broad enough to take a troop of cavalry riding twenty abreast, but most American cities grew almost without reference to the wishes of the military.

There were no courtier-ridden petty principalities to distort the realities of city growth. America knew no Ravenna or York, no Aix-en-Provence or Aix-la-Chapelle, artificially inflated by extraordinary political power and then gradually, painfully worn down to size by economic reality after the power had gone elsewhere. A few American cities were established artificially as political capitals—most obviously, Washington, but also Indianapolis, Columbus and others. But American government in the nineteenth century, despite the rush of sinecure-seekers who killed Harrison and depressed Lincoln, was not a big business. Indeed, one of the advantages of a republic was supposed to be that it eliminated the courtiers, the hangers-on, the purveyors and panderers who clustered about a royal court.

The American city, in short, was a natural growth, the result of topography and transportation over a century of time. A few cities sprang up atop the mineral wealth of the rock below their soil—anthracite cities in eastern Pennsylvania; Butte, Montana; the grandiose mining towns of Colorado, Nevada and California. Such metropolitan centers flourished as long as the wealth was real and immediate, and decayed as the mines worked out or demand subsided. Others grew beside the waterfalls which turned the factory wheels—and ran down when more flexible sources of power became available elsewhere. The cities which flourished were more profoundly if less visibly blessed by nature; they had the location, the unique and eternally valuable location.

In all colonial countries the first cities are beachheads—harbors for the ships that bring in the manufactured goods and take out the raw materials. The great American cities at the time of the Revolution—Philadelphia, New York, Boston and Charleston, South Carolina—all had first-rate harbors. Philadelphia, though a river port rather than an ocean harbor, is still the second largest shipping center in the United States. (Philadelphia's river, the Delaware, was level with the Hudson in the minds of the colonials. It was the "South River"; the Hudson, the "North River." Thus the street beside the Hudson in Manhattan, though indubitably on the west side of the island, became "North Street.") New Orleans, the metropolis of French America after the loss of Montreal, was the outlet port for the entire valley complex drained by the Mississippi and its tributaries. The city stood on the sedimentary deposits of the river itself, rather than on the Gulf of Mexico, because the land to the south was still too swampy. Up the river, St. Louis sat at the junction of the Missouri and the Mississippi; Kansas City where the Kansas River met the big bend of the Missouri; Des Moines, "of the monks," on the river first reported by Joliet and Marquette; Cincinnati, beside a natural harbor on the Ohio. The cliché still speaks of Newcastle, but for some years now Cincinnati has been by far the largest coal-shipping port in the world.

The lake ports grew later—Duluth at the tip of Superior near the iron mines; Chicago at the southwesterly tip of the five fresh-water marvels; Cleveland for convenience to Pennsylvania's coal; Buffalo for entry to the system of minor waterways which became the Erie Canal, and which fed into the Hudson and out to New York. Later still came the Gulf area, unattractive in climate, malarial, swampy; but the means of entry to the growing riches of Texas. The port was Galveston—until the great flood at the turn of the century, when Houston, seventy miles inland, took over many of the commercial functions of a port city by constructing a deepwater canal.

The first great city of the West Coast was San Francisco,

19

for the usual reason—the harbor, which ranks with New York and Sydney, Australia, among the world's most magnificent anchorages. Portland grew by the Columbia River, Seattle in the protection of Puget Sound. Los Angeles, like New Orleans and Houston, settled back from the swamps of the ocean front, growing a tentacle of a port at Long Beach—until the mass migrations of the mid-twentieth century stretched the city in all directions. Every West Coast city had the same stimulus to growth—the animal, vegetable and mineral resources of a hinterland that could be reached conveniently only from the sea.

Elsewhere the towns and cities grew along the routes of the westward movement, along streams and rivers (navigable once, at least in part) which had cut the canyons that provided gradual access to the mountain passes. Maps of population density in the United States show the fingers of settlement reaching out toward those passes as the years go by. Again it was the water, wearing the gradual path from the mountains, which largely determined locations.

"If the railroad and the truck had never been invented," Raymond Vernon writes in *Anatomy of a Metropolis,* the first volume in the series containing the results of the New York Metropolitan Region Study, "America's manufacturing centers would have developed very differently. Great multi-storied factories would probably have lined the river banks in order to hold down transport costs."

But the railroad came, and it came early—thousands of miles of it, mostly in the Northeast before the Civil War. The railroads ran to the cities, and because the cities were on the water they ran to the water. Where possible, if the land were not too highly developed, they followed the minor waterways, so that there are places where one can trace overlays of American civilization by changing means of transport. Governor Clinton built the Erie Canal in midstate

New York; Commodore Vanderbilt ran the New York Central Railroad beside the paths; and then Governors Dewey and Harriman built the Thruway, the trucking artery of the state's new industrial giants, over much the same route.

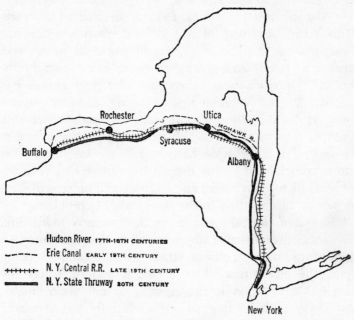

Hudson River 17TH-18TH CENTURIES
Erie Canal EARLY 19TH CENTURY
N. Y. Central R.R. LATE 19TH CENTURY
N. Y. State Thruway 20TH CENTURY

Successive developments in transport often followed the same routes, as in New York State.

The cities which the railroads found were still, by and large, market places and transshipment points, joints between the bones of an agricultural economy. But the same steam that powered the freight engines was turning the wheels of a new nation's new industry. The trains brought raw materials for the factories to process; and, though American industry continued to sell most of its output in the area in which the factory was situated, the railroad made possible a rapid growth of broad trade areas.

21

When Paul Revere rode to warn the citizens of Lexington, he traveled by road. Though the water routes were most influential, because they had the greatest impact on costs of freight transportation, people moved on foot, on horse or by coach—on roads. The mail went by road, which gave even the relatively powerless federal government of Washington's time a strong interest in local conditions affecting transportation. Around the cities networks of roads were leveled so that farmers' wagons could bring food to the center. The roads were wretched. The new nation had fought a war, a revolution against paying taxes, and private enterprise (the builder of most roads before the nineteenth century) was reluctant to risk money on such ventures in the face of a world-wide hatred of tolls. One of the first reforms proclaimed by the French Revolution had been the abolition of tolls on roads, and to this day France will have no part of this solution to the transportation problem.

Still, when the railroads came they crossed roads; and the intersections became stopping points, then communities, then towns and sometimes cities. All other things being equal, the city forms where access is easiest. Today the comparable situation is the crossing of one major motor expressway with another, or with a heavily traveled local road. But where our ancestors would have built a city at the intersection, we put up a shopping center. . . .

Usually, the railroad line did not simply plunge into the heart of the city. Even in the early nineteenth century, land costs and demolition costs were too high to make it attractive for route-builders to bull through built-up areas. Instead, the line customarily swung in an arc about what was then the center of the city, with a terminal as near the core as could conveniently and cheaply be managed. Along the railroad tracks inevitably rose the factories and the warehouses which needed quick and inexpensive freight service—nearer to the center of the city if numbers of workers were wanted every day, farther out if the labor force requirement was smaller.

Of all the arbitrary decisions which are enshrined in the brick and mortar of the modern city, the most important was the one which placed the railroad terminal here rather than there. For around the terminal rather quickly there grew up a second center for the city, competing against and often conquering the center established by the harbor some years before. The original "downtown" had been made by shipping and commodities markets, banking (or what passed for banking), municipal offices and services (if any), and, where feasible, commercial hotels for travelers. In the older cities this area was somewhat decayed by the time the railroad arrived. As the trains took over greater and greater proportions of the passenger traffic, the hotels moved from the waterfront to the terminal area. Businesses dependent on what are now called communications were torn between the need to be near the boats and the need to be near the trains; gradually they moved "uptown," nearer the terminal. Markets, especially food markets, were harder to dislodge; financial, legal and professional centers had less reason to move; and the municipal offices, early encrusted with tradition, usually stayed where they were. But the new building, the "prestige" of the growing city, became progressively more concentrated near the terminal.

Later, spurs would branch out from the main line of the railroad, serving new industry. Rapid transit would become a necessity, to bring people to work in the factories and in the offices (usually the same buildings, before the turn of the century), in the retail shops and the service trades. Still later, the suburban train service, the paved road with its cars and trucks, decisions on the placement of bridges and tunnels would influence the pattern of the city's growth. But all these forces worked on the further development, not the central development, of the city. They came on the scene when the American city had assumed a form, had become an entity as real, as hard to change, as the walled city of Europe.

Given the social history of a city—its distance from other cities, the date of its foundation, the rate of population growth, the first arrival of the railroad, the location of the terminal, the nature of the first major industry and the date when that industry ceased to be overwhelmingly predominant in the city's economy—only one other item of information is necessary to establish the pattern. The missing link is the fundament, the "topography."

Not all coastal or river sites are equally suitable for a city. For nearly a century, until modern flood-control methods lessened (but did not eliminate) the danger, residents of river cities had annual flood worries, and occasional murderous floods. An ocean harbor completely surrounded by a mountain range could be little more than an anchorage, a service to shipping. "The lie of the land" determined where on the waterways the cities would stand, and later acted to invite or restrain metropolitan growth.

Theoretically, too steep a slope up from the water should have inhibited the city, but labor was cheap enough to make short haulage a minor expense. San Francisco's Nob Hill is the most famous example of a built-up impossible slope, but Duluth and Seattle can rival it. What was best in the city usually stood atop the hill, not on the inconvenient slope itself. In Kansas City, for example, the distribution district and poorer residences stood near the river, ripe for inundation, or on the slope; the best homes were atop Quality Hill.

When the hills lay some distance from the water, however, so that they were in the path of the city's expansion rather than part of its necessary center, there was a tendency to avoid them. The city grew, by choice, away from the obstruction. Other natural barriers—a patch of swamp, a wide, deep gulley or a tributary river not easily bridged—would also

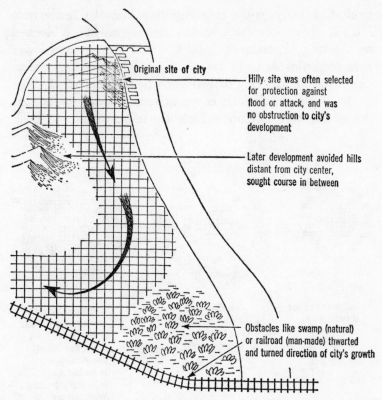

Original site of city

Hilly site was often selected for protection against flood or attack, and was no obstruction to city's development

Later development avoided hills distant from city center, sought course in between

Obstacles like swamp (natural) or railroad (man-made) thwarted and turned direction of city's growth

A city's development was often governed by natural and man-made obstructions.

act to shove the city's growth in the opposite direction. And after the railroad was built its right-of-way formed a similar obstruction; there really was such a thing as "the wrong side of the tracks."

More desirable land near the center of town was quickly taken for residence—though residence and business were not so separate in the early nineteenth century as they are today, and many a flourishing small manufacturer lived above the shop to which his apprentices came for their day's work. Gradually, as the economy grew, industry in the core felt a need for more space. Large-scale expansion was blocked by the ring of residences, and the land they occupied was then too valuable to be bought for industrial use. Business "leapfrogged" the ring of residence to an outer ring.

Meanwhile, small-scale commerce and industry, squeezed out of the core but not sufficiently self-contained to push

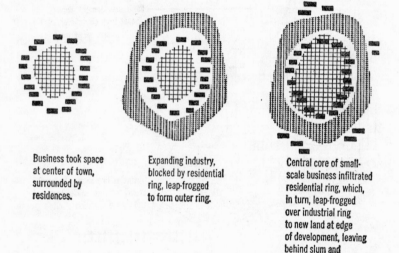

Business took space at center of town, surrounded by residences.

Expanding industry, blocked by residential ring, leap-frogged to form outer ring.

Central core of small-scale business infiltrated residential ring, which, in turn, leap-frogged over industrial ring to new land at edge of development, leaving behind slum and "gray belt."

The "leapfrogging" development of cities was coupled with the decline of the central core.

to the outer ring, infiltrated the old residential areas and made them less desirable. Those who could afford to move made their own jump, "leapfrogging" the outer ring of industrial building to new land near the edges. With the middle classes went the stores, "uptown," away from the established core. The old residential ring became a residential slum and a home for marginal industry, and we have it with us still in the form of the notorious "gray belt," the inner-ring blight which the city planners must demolish and reconstruct to permit the expansion and proper insulation of the core.

Every American city shows these alternating bands of glory and garbage, and often the garbage has been what it is for a long, long time. New York by-passed the area between Chambers Street and Washington Square, which has been a slum now for over a century; Philadelphia jumped from the Delaware frontage to Independence Hall, to Penn Square, where City Hall stands and the terminal stood until 1953, and then again to Logan Circle and out to Thirtieth Street. Boston leaped west from Beacon Street to Harvard Square, Dallas from Commerce Street all the way out to the airport region and Southern Methodist. Louisville is the classic case: from Main Street south, its development can be drawn in a series of neat rectangles, most of them today relatively undesirable places to live or work.

Moving from one residence to another—which in the nature of things meant "leapfrogging"—became an American tradition. "At the end of three or four years we'll move," says a character in Henry James's novel *Washington Square*. "That's the way to live in New York—to move every three or four years. Then you always get the last thing." Today's pattern of suburban housing developments and "industrial parks" fits an American tradition; but now the distances are greater and the land more precious, and wherever the frog leaps he is powered by an internal combustion engine.

Once built, cities are hard to remake. Archaeologists digging into the great cities of Asia Minor have found as many as nine different cities built, destroyed, rebuilt on the same land, each rising from the rubble of its predecessors. But with all the efficiency of bulldozers, all the horrors of our atomic weapons, we are amateurs of destruction beside the erosive sands and the roving tribes of antiquity. In taking Jericho, the Book of Joshua says, "the Israelites utterly destroyed all that was in the city, both man and woman, young and old, and ox, and sheep, and ass, with the edge of the sword. . . . And they burnt the city with fire, and all that was therein. . . . And Joshua adjured them at that time, saying, Cursed be the man before the LORD, that riseth up and buildeth this city Jericho." In the next campaign, according to the same chronicle, "Joshua burnt Ā-ī, and made it an heap forever, even a desolation unto this day." The almost incessant warfare of the last millennium in western Europe produced no such devastation, and when the archaeologists come to explore the remnants of what we now call modern times they will find few fresh starts.

In the United States, especially, cities have grown by accretion. The city of antiquity was built atop the ground, and could in theory disappear from one day to the next, leaving only some brick and mortar in the approximate form of walls. Modern cities exist above and beneath the ground. The patterns of water mains, sewage tunnels, gas lines and cables fix the places that must be public streets or squares. Once established, the pattern exerts its influence over the actions of generations unborn and unconsidered.

All this is not theory. For the practical real estate investor on a large scale, it is the frame into which he must set his thinking and his work if he hopes to grow rich. To build, or to buy intelligently, an investor must start with a belief about what is going to happen to the city of which his holdings form a part. For this belief to be more than a hunch, one aspect of a congenital optimism, the investor must understand the city, its individual pattern and the relation of that pattern to the prospect of national growth.

We are, as everyone knows, in the middle of a great tide of population increase, and most of that increase will make its home within what the Census Bureau defines as a "Standard Metropolitan Area." But not all cities will prosper in the years to come. During the last decade, which saw in terms of absolute numbers the greatest increase of Americans ever registered over a ten-year period, many of our cities actually lost residents. Downtown jobs declined, downtown stores made fewer sales, downtown services lost volume and, too often, quality.

For the American city was the creation of steam power, as employed in the railroad and in what historians like to call the Industrial Revolution. For nineteenth-century purposes, the American situation was ideal: open land and a market town, ready for expansion. Industry could be efficiently located, markets efficiently placed, transportation created at low cost to service profitable growth. While the Europeans struggled to eliminate their walls, to fit the cramped patterns of old cities to the transportation needs of new industry, America simply rolled ahead behind the steam engine.

Now our cities are as firmly patterned as their European forerunners, and the steam engine is no longer a force for growth. The age of the automobile is upon us, and the age of the airplane draws near. In the current period the European city, which developed perforce the workers' suburb and the outlying industrial plant, seems more functional than the American metropolis. No one can pronounce firm verdicts, because the evidence points in many directions. The automobile and the truck come into conflict with city patterns at some points but not at others. Properly planned, the federal highway project must stimulate our cities. Roads, like railroad tracks, need terminals and routes; the cheapest routes are those already used by the trains; nationally, perhaps, the road builders will not radically change the directions of growth.

The city reacts like an organism. When the body is damaged, antibodies are created. But cities must have vitality to react successfully—to use (since they cannot destroy) their own patterns, to clear their blight, to conserve and restore the variegated culture which makes agglomerations of humanity attractive rather than frightening. And meanwhile they must keep their gaze on the sky, for the airplane does not need a route; it needs no more than a big flat place on which to lie down. The question of how well our nineteenth-century cities can adjust to the age of the auto has not yet been answered. The question of whether they can adapt to the coming age of the airplane has scarcely been asked.

And in all this search for answers there is no escape from history. The sociologists and their allies can improve their "methodology," but the potential of any city is a function of its existing pattern and the economic feasibility of working within it—and every pattern is the product of history. You cannot take current statistics and project them forty years ahead; such procedures look like science, but they are actually alchemy. To predict the future of anything, you must know the rationale of its past.

# 2. People and Jobs

When Premier Khrushchev visited the United States in September, 1959, he spent several days at the home of an Iowa farmer named Roswell Garst. The chief of the ardently industrialized Soviet offered no explanation of why he wished to spend so much time at a single farm (however successful), but Mr. Garst made the matter clear: he told newspapermen that Mr. Khrushchev wanted to find out why only 7 per cent of the American working force could produce enough food for the entire nation, when it took almost one-third of all the Russians to feed the Soviet Union.

All cities are vassals of farm technology. Unless the farmers can produce many times what they need to feed themselves, the population of the hungry cities will melt back to the countryside. What has made possible the rapid growth of American cities is the growing scientific efficiency of farming, which gave the cities not only food but—increasingly with the years—a surplus population no longer needed in the fields.

Our mythology holds that our cities were "un-American," populated largely by "the dregs of Europe," while the farms enshrined the sound old stock. But the immigrants before

1880 were as likely as not to settle on the farms. The foreign-born never formed as much as a third of the population of any state with a big city in its borders; but they were 40 per cent and more of the population in Wisconsin in 1850, in Arizona, Minnesota, Nevada and Wyoming in 1870, and in North Dakota in 1890. By then the land frontier was closing quickly; instead of a fertile quarter-section of grassland in Iowa, the new immigrant was offered an arid half-section on the plateau to be served by the Great Northern Railroad, and the opportunity to starve in a cold climate. Especially if he had no tradition of land ownership behind him—if he was a Jew, or an Irish laborer, or a refugee from the Sicilian *padrone*—he went to the cities, where he found communities of people in much the same situation as himself.

These communities were visible. They clustered in ghettos —often several communities to a single ghetto—in the oldest and least habitable sections of the city. Decent people never saw them, and therefore exaggerated their presence. It was assumed that the cities were growing because Europeans were pouring through Ellis Island. But a high proportion of the newcomers to the city (less visible because less concentrated in a single neighborhood) were farm boys no longer needed on the farm. The period of greatest immigration, 1880–1910, was also a period of great internal migration by native-born Americans. The population center of the country continued to shift west—but only because the western cities were growing more rapidly in sum than those on the eastern shore. Today, what with the Los Angeles area to San Diego, the six counties of San Francisco Bay and the sprawling Texas cities, that center is west of Chicago.

The unsuccessful farmer and the European immigrant, then, populated the American city. Logically they would seem to be unpromising human material, but here as elsewhere the logic would be historically inaccurate. Farming, like the purchase of real estate or the writing of a book, requires specific qualities, the absence of which need not imply general incompetence. Many an incapable farmer has, like Ulysses Grant or Henry Thoreau, performed brilliantly on a different stage. Nor was the European immigrant likely to be, in fact, the "dregs" of his community. The nineteenth century fortunately came before the time of travel on credit, and those who made it to America had both the initiative and the competitive habits to be something better than what despairing Marxists later called the *Lumpenproletariat*.

Moreover, the supposedly superior economic opportunity of America was not the only, and perhaps not the most important, reason for emigration from Europe. The idealistic view is far closer to the truth than cynics admit. America was colonized to begin with largely by members of a deviant religious sect worried about King James's intentions in religious matters. The revolutions in western Europe in 1848 were as important as the crop failures in propelling Germans to America; the Jews left Russia not to get rich but to escape pogroms. The Irish came in greatest quantities not (as is usually believed) during the famines of the mid-nineteenth century, but during the political persecutions of the 1890's and 1900's. Not the least of the reasons why Italians flooded in from Sicily in the late nineteenth century was the monarchical shift from the House of Bourbon to the House of Savoy. The minorities which leaped the ocean were vulnerable rather than weak; one need only look at modern Israel to see the caliber of people who will migrate when necessary.

Without economic opportunity, to be sure, many of the immigrants would not have come; South America as a whole attracted only a small fraction of the immigration that came to the United States, and Canada, economically exploited by Britain until the turn of the century, exerted almost no pull at all. No one can understand American cities who believes that the immigrants were impelled solely by hopes of financial betterment. They brought to the cities a spirit of high hope rather than a low taste for money-grubbing. If one *must* relate to money, the worst that could be said is that the uprooted specialist, as a normal instinct, wished to keep his earned possessions. Settlers whose background was middle class, whatever their creed, were the ones who most strongly displayed acquisitive instincts.

That the immigrants were often disappointed is a matter of record. The cities of the late nineteenth century did not want the talent of the disappointed farmer or the hopes of the European refugee; they simply needed cheap labor. The American city was and is more thoroughly a creature of economic development than any other such entity in history, and when labor was needed it reached out for the cheapest and nearest supply.

Thus, by 1900, the East European was preferred to the resident of the more highly industrialized western Europe, because he would work for less. The cities of California, despite cultural and "racial" objections, were willing to cart in quantities of Orientals, over the violent protests of Samuel Gompers and his American Federation of Labor. Pressure for the exclusion of immigrants, from the "Know-Nothings" of pre-Civil War days to the labor unions of today, was always strongest near the bottom of a business cycle, when the cities did not need laborers. California decided it could do without Chinese after the completion of the Panama Canal had lowered the cost of transporting Europeans to San Francisco to the point where Caucasians could come almost as cheaply as Orientals from across the Pacific. (Not to mention the Mexicans, and Indians and Easterners of all sorts flooding in via the Union Pacific which the coolies built.) The nation as a whole decided to close the doors when the depression of 1920–21 demonstrated the staggering amount of unemployment that had become possible in an urbanized America.

It was not an accident that the nineteenth century saw the spawning of revolutionary movements on the left, and on the right a sentimental nostalgia for the past. What the cities wanted from their new inhabitants was muscle power, plain, ignorant, religiously oriented; and they deliberately brutalized their laborers to keep them that way. There can have been few periods in human existence when the life of the free man was so miserable as it was in the cities of the industrial revolution all over the world—and beyond the conventional misery lay the worse horror, the threat of unemployment. Earlier societies had not known the problems of profitable capital goods investment. As Lord Keynes pointed out, two cathedrals in a medieval town were twice as good as one, but of two railroads from London to Canterbury, one might well be superfluous.

Starvation was a possibility on the American farm, but usually those who lived on the land could, even in the worst crop years, scrape together a subsistence. And if produce could not be sold, and the children had to go without shoes —well, the children had gone without shoes before. Such alternatives were not possible in a city, where disaster could be entire. Marx and Henry George, Ruskin and Morris, were not fleeing from imaginary demons; they were reacting to what they saw in London and New York. Their mistake was merely in projecting the trend, forgetting that a coming generation could benefit from the sacrifices of the present, that there were cyclical tides in the affairs of man, even in the lower classes. The thesis of capital investment and the antithesis of detestable poverty were capable of synthesis into a much different society and a dynamically happier community.

For the farm boys and the immigrants built their cities well. By their sweat they dug the subways and the streetcar lines, the sewers and the water mains and the railroad gradings which made possible the rational social organization

35

of the metropolis. Cities which came later, after the disappearance of the great mass of cheap labor on which nineteenth-century economy rested, lack many of the resources which guarantee the continuing vitality of the older cities. Popular legend has it that New York, Philadelphia and Chicago are in grievous trouble, while the new cities of the West are unencumbered by major municipal problems. In fact, it is the Los Angeles, the Houston and the Miami—the city without adequate rapid transit, worrying about the next generation's water and power, never more than a step ahead of sewage pollution—which has the most to fear from the accelerating movement of urban growth. Maturity need never again suffer the agonies of adolescence.

The older cities are sounder, despite their dilapidated look, because of the work done by the sweaty immigrants and the bewildered farmers of seventy-five years ago. And the new migration today, which seems to threaten the cities, the great labor surplus of partially civilized rural Negroes, poor southern whites and harassed Puerto Ricans, is only a continuation of the old economic pattern—the sole distinguishing features being color and/or country of birth. The cities want such residents (and whatever isolated judges or newspaper editors may say, the cities *do* want them) for the same old reasons, to supply the endless demands for cheap labor. New York has Puerto Ricans, not because they love New York—most of them don't—but because the flood tide of Negro migration turned to California and the North Central cities. If the Negroes had gone in such numbers to New York, the "Puerto Rican problem" would be centered in Los Angeles and Chicago.

In the long run, we may be sure, the contribution the new immigrants make to the cities will exceed the pain they cause and suffer when they first appear. Today, only a dozen years after the first waves broke on the shores of New York, the Puerto Ricans are already clearly following the paths marked out generations ago by people who came directly from Europe.

Some of the jobs that awaited the farm boy and the immigrant were the same in all the cities. All cities needed hod carriers and ditchdiggers, chimney sweeps and sewer rats, blacksmiths' assistants and (later) streetcar conductors, dishwashers, policemen, firemen and ward heelers. The industrial jobs available, of course, were a product of the city's economic function, which meant again its location.

Steel *had* to grow in western Pennsylvania and in Birmingham, Alabama, where iron ore and coal and limestone deposits were found near each other. Finance was inevitably concentrated in New York, because the American money market was so closely oriented to the British money market, and New York was the major port of entry from England. Because it costs less to ship the raw fiber to a single plant than to ship the resulting textiles to many separated markets, the cotton mills had to be near the community which bought the cloth; which meant, originally, New England: nowhere else was the necessary power source, the falling river, so convenient to the places of major consumption. Michigan held one of the great hardwood forests of America, set just north of the enormous grasslands—so, furniture became the staple product of Grand Rapids.

At two points—one fairly early in the process, the other fairly late—a growing specialized industry in a city seems to reach what the physicists have taught us to call a "critical mass." The first of these points comes when an industry achieves the experience and *expertise* (the "know-how") which makes that city the natural place for any new business entering that particular field. The market is here, the special services which the industry needs, the skilled labor force, the people who will buy out the entrepreneur if he wants to sell or find him weaker rivals to purchase if he wishes to expand.

The city develops, for this industry, a gravitational pull. Companies in the same business elsewhere find themselves at a disadvantage simply because they are not in the "right" city.

Once established, this gravitational pull may outlast the circumstances which gave it birth. St. Louis was a center of the fur trade in early nineteenth-century America because it was the river city nearest the Rockies. Later Kansas City set itself up athwart the natural path into St. Louis, but the fur trade did not move. The fact that all the garment showrooms are within a quarter of a square mile in New York means that buyers can make their rounds most efficiently, and any dressmaker whose showroom is out of New York must pay the costs of attracting buyers away from natural paths. (As recently as fifteen years ago, more than half the garments sold in the United States were produced in the New York metropolitan area. In this respect, by the way, as in some others, an exception must be made for Los Angeles, which has grown in dry goods and hard goods to the point where it is destroying an American tradition: the price tags, "Slightly higher west of ———.") The motion picture industry wound up in Hollywood because the warm, dry climate permitted the maximum number of days of outdoor picture taking. Television never goes outdoors unless absolutely necessary, but the very existence of the movie-making community dragged much of TV to the West Coast within a decade of the industry's foundation.

Usually, any industry within a city will eventually grow beyond its most efficient size, finally achieving a "critical mass" which produces dispersion if not explosion as marketing methods change. Industries which were set up near markets, like the textile industry, lose their favored position after population shifts. Outlying firms with cheaper labor and power supply can compete more efficiently because they are, in terms of the national market, no longer "outlying"; and if progress in machinery has occurred, the high-priced expert labor of the district becomes a force as centrifugal as once it was centripetal. In outline, of course, these are the annals of a dozen New England cities, but such dispersion is visible everywhere, in almost all major industries tuned to a locale where they originally thrived.

Detroit, for example, no longer makes as much as half the nation's automobiles. Its predominance in cars and trucks was, from the beginning, largely a matter of luck plus critical mass. In the early years of the business, Indianapolis seemed as likely an automobile center as Detroit: as close to Pittsburgh's steel, and with the highways coming through (finished autos could transport themselves) more centrally located in relation to the market. But Henry Ford was in Detroit and liked it there, while his Indianapolis counterparts never developed techniques of mass production. The Stutz Bearcat was no match for the Model T in the middle-class market. (More recently, Indianapolis has become a major assembly area for automobiles, and its earlier loss of the volatile auto industry has come to seem a blessing in disguise. A few other cities had "luck" similar to Detroit's to push their growth: Dayton, Ohio, in the inventor of the cash register; Washington, in Franklin Roosevelt.) By the mid-1920's, Detroit became the home of the "know-how," and Walter Chrysler never seriously considered an alternative location for his growing business. But the cost of shipping finished automobiles is heavy, and in the years since the war assembly plants have sprung up closer to the markets —in southern California, now second only to Detroit, in Kansas City and St. Louis, Buffalo, Atlanta.

Again, Pittsburgh's dominance of the steel industry is solidly based on the quantity of coal in the nearby West Virginia hills—to say nothing of the soft coal deposits in western Pennsylvania, Kentucky and along the northern tier. The smelting and forging of steel require enormous heat,

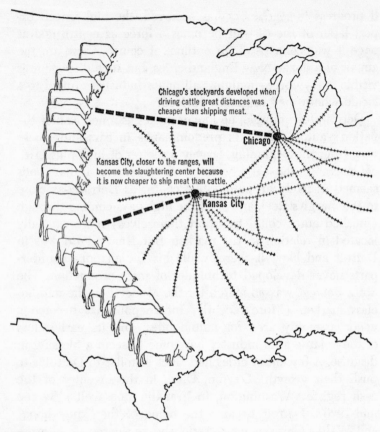

Chicago's stockyards developed when driving cattle great distances was cheaper than shipping meat.

Chicago

Kansas City, closer to the ranges, will become the slaughtering center because it is now cheaper to ship meat than cattle.

Kansas City

Changes in marketing costs can affect economic fortunes of cities.

and coal is still the cheapest way to make the necessary little hells. But coal can be shipped cheaply along the rivers and lakes, and most of the iron ore now comes from Minnesota and Canada, rather than from Pennsylvania itself. New processes in steel manufacture have made it possible to substitute electric power for some of the coal heat, where electric power is cheap enough, which means that steel can now be produced economically in California. (When Kaiser

Steel settled with the union in the fall of 1959, breaking the industry's previously united front in the great strike, Pittsburgh's leaders proclaimed that Kaiser's West Coast plant was more efficient than anything in Pennsylvania; and even if it isn't, the Kaiser monopoly on the Pacific Coast is more than enviable.) This desire to get the production near the market where possible has led to the construction of the world's largest plant, U. S. Steel's Fairless works, between Philadelphia and Trenton rather than Pittsburgh and Youngstown. The economic and topographical advantages of Pittsburgh persist, but their force is lessened; the gravity that pulled in Carnegie and Frick is gone. Even the basing-point system of steel prices, which charged the customer freight from Pittsburgh even if the steel he used was made across the street, has disappeared.

Chicago became the world's largest butcher of beef because it was the last major railroad terminal to which steers could be driven. Even after the cattle had to be loaded on trains to get to Chicago, the gravitational pull of the grain pit and the stockyards kept animals rolling to the market place. But as it was cheaper to drive cattle to market than to ship them, it is now cheaper to ship meat than cattle—and Chicago, never very convenient to the range, must lose its leadership as a slaughterer. Still the biggest butcher in the country, though its production is now only a small fraction of the nation's total, Chicago will presently fall behind Kansas City, which is nearer the beef if not the hog, and almost equally well served by railroads.

Not all concentrations of industry reach this second critical point. Where the value of the item is very high by comparison with shipping costs (in electronics, for example, an industry of miniaturized products), the plants can be anywhere at all—even in Phoenix, Arizona, where a warm climate and cheap Mexican labor have built an industry in the desert. The aluminum industry needs macro-watts

41

of electric power, and will tend to cluster near the great dams, whatever other factors intervene. Atomic energy, of course, could radically change the distribution of aluminum plants, but history indicates that artificially produced power will tend to locate near natural power to serve existing plant facilities and labor pools.

The advantages of the port city must continue, because the airplane can never become inexpensive enough for more heavy, low-value items; Memphis will handle vast quantities of cotton as long as cotton is an attractive commodity. And some values which would seem ephemeral prove lasting. East Coast dominance of the money market, for example, was dictated by the importance of European capital in financing the American industrial expansion of the nineteenth century. The native financial market grew enormously and became wholly professional, but the role of London in the reinsurance of large risks, and Geneva in the world of international banking, still forced the money market to concentrate heavily in New York.

A city's dominance of an industry may strongly promote its growth, but an industry's domination of a city almost guarantees eventual municipal agony. No city (except Washington) will do very well in a massive depression, but the ordinary tides of a balanced local economy see one industry losing ground while others gain. If the city has a variety of employment in its area, those who lose jobs in the declining industry merely cross the street and help other industries expand. If one industry predominates, its layoffs will exert a multiplier effect, creating hardship in retail trade, services and local industry catering to the shrinking local market.

Eventually, then, disaster comes to all cities which stand on a single economic base. Sometimes—if the base reflects mineral resources rather than location advantages—the disaster can be total: Central City, Colorado, simply shut down.

If the city has other situational benefits, however, over a period of time an alert and ambitious citizenry can repair the damage. Grand Rapids and Utica are far better off than they were a generation ago, because their industry is now highly diversified and their transportation advantages enhanced by truck routes, but not many people in either city would care to live through the last thirty years again. Seattle, on the other hand, is no better off than it was, having made up the losses from a departing lumber industry by concentration on aircraft, thereby inviting a second "critical mass." The struggle to keep a city going after the dominating industry has shrunk (or, as sometimes happens, disappeared) is the most noble of activities available to the modern businessman. Such struggles are now plainly and admirably visible in cities like Providence, Scranton and South Bend.

Among the apparently prosperous cities of mid-century America, the observer can find candidates for such disaster within the near future—plus a few which are sliding gently down right now. Detroit, for example, has found nothing to replace the automobile industry, and will almost certainly drop farther in share of total national production. Seattle suffered a bad recession in 1957–58 because of overdependence on the aircraft industry (you'd think their past economy would have taught them). It is instructive to compare the population gains of one-industry Seattle as against diversified San Francisco during the last decade. Charleston, West Virginia, is booming, but the boom is so heavily concentrated in coal-based chemicals that there must be trouble in the future. Sixty-five per cent of Miami's population depends on the tourist industry for its income (manufacturing takes only one-eighth of the working force, and much of their production is for local consumption), and jet travel brings the hot–dry southwestern deserts and the balmy Caribbean closer to the North Atlantic cities every year. Akron is saved only by the fact that the rubber companies are not dependent

on new car production and have diversified their own operations. Even so promising a city as Baton Rouge would be
endangered by the dominance of petro-chemicals if the state
government and the very popular state university did not
provide stabilizers for the local economy. Tulsa has been
lucky: its staple product, oil, is practically exhausted, but
natural gas and an established white-collar market place
made the transition almost painless.

Most American cities have enjoyed and then suffered a
dominant industry in the early stages of their development.
To lay out the "grid" of any city, one must know what that
industry was, how long its dominance lasted and when the
city achieved diversification. Cities, like animals and plants,
grow in cycles, and no city's present situation can be under-
stood without reference to its cyclical pattern in the past.
From a real estate investor's point of view, the current stage
of the cycle is a fundamental consideration. Many a declining city offers good buys—if one can be sure, from a study
of the history, that business will turn up again. In the declining state, cities suffer a flight of capital, and prime
properties sell for cheap. On the other side of the wave, many
an ascending city is a bad place to put money. The herd is
buying, prices are high—and trouble is just ahead. Current
information, once again, is only part of what the investor
must know; trends project to the future only from the logic
of the past.

The nature of an industry determines, to a large extent,
its location within a city. If the plant must ship in and out
great quantities of bulky material, it must be near the water
or the railroad—or, today in some cases, the superhighway.
Very large installations can be self-contained or nearly so,
provided only that the workers can get to the site from
elsewhere. (Thus the "company town," which rarely flourished for psychological reasons. Old man Hershey built

44

solid, livable houses near the chocolate factory and then had to rent them to outsiders because his workers obstinately insisted on living some distance away, costs or no costs.) Small establishments, on the other hand, must draw on the services of a central city, renting part of a building, hooking into existing power and water lines, calling repairmen as needed, sending workers out into the neighborhood for lunch or a haircut, drawing employees to the job via the general transit facilities that converge on the "core."

Some industry is noisome. The stockyards could not have come much closer to downtown Chicago than they are without raising bellows of complaint from everyone else who worked in the city. Chemical plants and oil refineries are almost equally smelly; drop-forge works are unbearably noisy; paper mills pollute the water and the air. Such plants will locate, by popular demand, away from the center of the city.

Other trades, especially those in which "communications" play a major role, must be near the heart of town. The newspaper must have a relatively central location to get its product out all over town quickly. Corporate executives who do business with each other want to be near the same restaurants; advertising agencies want to be near those restaurants, too, as do lawyers and accountants. Any business that lives on fashion, which would include the garment industry, live entertainment, children's toys, retailing and perhaps finance and real estate, must be located where it feels (or thinks it feels) the heartbeats of the public. Every seasonal business must be downtown, where its labor force can find other work in slack times. Major retailers must locate where the transit lines converge, which means near the jobs of the office workers whom the transit lines serve. Railroad companies, of course, are over the railroad terminals, and shipping companies on the docks.

On the whole, people do not enjoy the time it takes them

to get from home to work and back again. All other things being equal, they would rather live near the job. But other things are almost never equal. The atmosphere of an industrial area tends to be sooty at best, and positively injurious at worst. (The agitation has been all about cigarettes, but industrial and automotive exhausts are unquestionably a greater menace to health, and no advertising agency could possibly convince people that they soothe the nerves.) Land near office jobs is almost by definition prime land, too expensive to waste on the limited income-producing possibilities of residential use. The leapfrog growth of our cities has made the "ring" around the core highly unattractive for those who can afford to get out of it. Only a small fraction of the American urban population can walk to work, though, as we shall see later, this situation may be about to change.

Residential areas inevitably stand in *some* logical relation to jobs—and, again, such relations are created by transport. The question is not one of distance, but of time (many a near suburbanite on a commuter rail line is effectively closer to his job than the central-city dweller afflicted by inconvenient transit or crowded streets). And time, as Calvin Coolidge is believed to have observed, is money.

The transport of people is as important to the city as the transport of goods, but the two elements are very different. A crowded, very densely built downtown is murder on deliveries of any sort (especially by truck), but it makes possible rational patterns of housing and residence. High-density housing itself is not necessarily so barbarous and degrading as the medievalists and the "garden-city" folk always claim. Residential density usually helps people get to work faster, always makes possible the economical provision of many necessary and pleasant services and saves money at every turn. (You don't have to bus children to school in the central city.) Density creates a variety of retail stores, different occupations mingled together, an interesting social life and—usually—a tolerant community. Most important of all, density frees poor people as well as rich from the restrictions of their immediate environment, by providing the ground condition of inexpensive rapid transit, the circulatory system of the successful city.

# 3. *Transit and the Automobile*

In the history of mankind, settlement meant immobility; and settlement in cities, except for those rich enough to own a horse or ambitious enough to trudge long distances, meant immobility in a crowded place. The farmer, by and large, was stuck with his farm, unless he was unlucky enough to strike the big boss as a plausible soldier, and serfdom, for most people in the Middle Ages, merely confirmed the inevitable. The city dweller, too, could go only as far as he could walk, which was usually no great distance—though the Crusaders walked behind Peter the Hermit clear across Europe to be massacred by the Turks on the other side of the Bosporus, and any attack or pillage or plague always sent people fleeing afoot to try and get away, as they did under the German dive-bombing of 1940 or before Pharaoh's avengers thirty-five hundred years before.

Up to the nineteenth century, a man born in a European city was likely to spend his entire life not only within that city, but within the neighborhood where he was born. Anything else was too much work, and too likely to prove disappointing. When Johann Sebastian Bach heard that the great George Frederick Handel was visiting a town only twenty miles away, he got on the road and walked all day in hopes of meeting so eminent a composer; but Handel had gone before he arrived.

It is a point of argument whether the size of the nineteenth-century city created public transit, or mass transit made possible the astonishing growth of the cities. Similarly, men argue about the interrelated causality of the chicken and the egg. But one fact is certain: the growth of "mass transit" was a by-product of the increasing cash income of the population. Before he will be willing to spend anything to avoid walking, a man must have at least a pittance of what economists call "discretionary income"—he must have something left over after he has paid his rent, bought his food and clothed his body.

Despite the implications of the name today, then, "mass transit" was obviously first created to serve the middle classes, who could afford to pay for it. The workingman of the mid-nineteenth century lived near his work and walked to it; often, indeed, he lived *at* his work. Small manufacturers put apprentices up in their shops where "portal-to-portal" could be under one roof. The "gray belt" areas around the core of the early nineteenth-century cities were blighted not only by the leapfrog of industry, but by industry's tendency to carry with it whenever it moved the housing of the poorest sections of the community.

America's first transit system was a "public stage," which carried New Yorkers from as far north as Bleecker Street down to Bowling Green and back for a fee. The stages made their first runs in 1830, and they were, of course, private enterprises. They catered neither to the rich, who had their own horses and buggies, nor to the poor, who could not afford such frivolity, but to the growing middle class. A few years later the first railroad lines crept to the edges of the cities, and began taking people out into the country (all the way to mid-Manhattan, in the case of New York) for picnics and

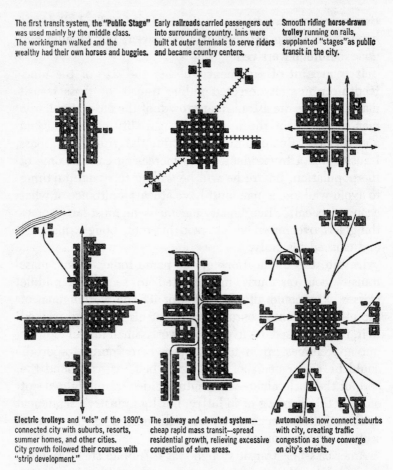

The first transit system, the **"Public Stage"** was used mainly by the middle class. The workingman walked and the wealthy had their own horses and buggies.

Early **railroads** carried passengers out into surrounding country. Inns were built at outer terminals to serve riders and became country centers.

Smooth riding **horse-drawn trolley** running on rails, supplanted "stages"as public transit in the city.

**Electric trolleys** and "els" of the 1890's connected city with suburbs, resorts, summer homes, and other cities. City growth followed their courses with "strip development."

The **subway and elevated system**— cheap rapid mass transit—spread residential growth, relieving excessive congestion of slum areas.

**Automobiles** now connect suburbs with city, creating traffic congestion as they converge on city's streets.

City development has been influenced by changes in modes of transportation.

a day's excitement. By and large, they carried a better class of people than the stages. Inns were constructed at the country terminals to serve the iron-chariot trade.

Often enough, the new inns became country centers, headquarters for farmers, but they did not develop into settlements for people who worked in the cities, though the trains ran as frequently as every ten minutes, fares even for longer trips were under ten cents, and speeds as high as twenty miles an hour were not uncommon. The trains did not come near enough to the business district to justify commuting, and after a series of accidents in the 1850's led state legislatures to ban steel locomotives from city streets, the chance of the railroad as a transit medium disappeared. (Railroads do serve certain marginal transit needs within the big cities, the Illinois Central linking the University to the Loop in Chicago, and the New York Central carrying some traffic between Forty-second Street and Fordham Hill. And in a sense, of course, the railroads are the "rapid transit" of the metropolitan area where suburban lines still function.)

Instead, the horse-drawn trolley appeared, to compete with the stagecoach. Like the train, the trolley rode on steel rails, which was a great luxury in that time of foul, cobbled streets. Passengers received a smoother ride, and the horses had less work to do because the friction between wheel and roadway was greatly diminished. The trolley lines were profitable, and their proprietors paid "franchise taxes" to the cities for the right to lay tracks on the streets.

Meanwhile, planners were dreaming of ways to take transit traffic off the streets entirely—underground trolleys, or great suction tubes drawing trains full of passengers through the city at high speeds, or elevated railways. The first "els" came in the 1860's, exempt from the rules against steel locomotives because they were not actually on the streets. Among the most charming illustrations of Old New York are the crowds riding the el above the Bowery, still the city's restaurant and theater street in the late 1860's. They are not working-class crowds; the men are dressed in frock coats and the ladies in crinolines. At a time when many men worked for a dollar a day and less, there were few working-class nickels to be wasted on transportation.

As the city grew, however, its sections tended to become

51

increasingly specialized. Land near three carriage-making shops was worth more to a carriage maker than to anyone else, because he knew that potential customers would be in the neighborhood. Though the immigrants crowded into the gray belt ring, usually within walking distance of work, more and more men with better jobs moved out to more comfortable surroundings—to bridgeheads conveniently near ferries or along the slowly lengthening trolley tracks.

The great expansion came in the 1890's, when rising wages for more highly skilled work increased demand for transit at the same time that rock-bottom wages for the laborers who laid track made transit facilities cheap to build. Every American city, and most American towns, suddenly grew shining lines of trolley track, extending to even the most remote clusters of "suburban" homes, into the immigrant slums, out to the lake or the beach and the summer homes of the well-to-do. The old public stage which ran on the public street was not entirely supplanted, and horse-drawn omnibuses with curtained windows still carried that part of the population which mistrusted the trolleys and their passengers. But the electrification of the trolley systems, which made them cleaner and more exciting, seemed to doom the flexible bus. The pattern of trolley tracks began to influence the directions of city growth, as the financing of transit lines influenced the development of the capital market. Eventually the overcapitalized trolley systems went broke, and some echoes of the crash are still heard: James Gould Cozzens' *By Love Possessed* drew its plot from the aftermath of such a disaster.

It is hard to realize these days how much trolley track there was in America only fifty years ago. New York City alone contained 683 miles of it, within the city limits, and it was possible to ride from Brooklyn up Manhattan to the Bronx and out through Westchester, Bridgeport, New Haven, New London and Providence, all the way up to Boston, on trolley tracks alone, paying forty-eight five-cent fares. "Megalopolis," the giant city stretching for hundreds of miles up the Atlantic Coast, may be a new concept to some analysts, but this much of its reality was present more than half a century back.

Trolley lines inevitably produced strip development, and homes and then stores, and even small factories, made borders for the streets on which the trolley ran. But the trolley was slow, if only for safety's sake. (Before 1910 a German-made trolley sped a measured mile at a speed of almost 125 miles per hour.) And especially after the introduction of the automobile in the early years of the century the streets were crowded. In 1907 the first gasoline-powered busses made their appearance (the bodies were English, and the motors French), further cluttering the streets. New York, consistently ahead in transit development, already had a flourishing collection of elevated lines, and in 1904 the first subway was opened for traffic all the way north to the tip of Manhattan Island and into the Bronx—Interborough Rapid Transit, not solely for the old carriage trade, but inexpensive and extensive enough for the "masses."

Some notion of what subway lines were worth to the owners of the real estate they served can be gathered from a report by the City Club of New York in 1908. The Club claimed, after a survey of valuations, that the rise on the stretch from 135th Street north amounted to a grand total of $80,500,000, *after* deducting the "normal" rise which would have occurred without a subway. The cost of the entire Interborough subway system, about seventy miles of track, most of it underground, was only $43,000,000. In other words, property owners in the northern section of the city alone gained almost twice as much from the building of the subway as the system cost to build.

In its report the City Club was arguing that real property owners who would benefit from transit construction should pay at least part of the necessary subsidy through special assessments. (There was never any hope that the subways would pay for themselves through fares; even in the best years, the profits on operations could not come near the interest and amortization on the cost of digging tunnels through rock.) Unfortunately, however, the subway had been built out of the city's general fund, the real estate tax on *all* property, whether near the subway or not. The bad precedent prevailed, as bad precedents will; the idea of a special assessment never conquered the violent objections of the owners who desired the "something-for-nothing" edge that prudent businessmen don't depend upon but never throw away. (Some of those who opposed such special assessments in the 1920's now pay out every day to support the "Park-and-Shop" garages.)

All over the country, the success of New York's subway raised a desire to emulate, but only a few other cities ever did anything about it. Boston, which did not have so high a downtown density, solved its worst problems by running key trolley lines underground through the most crowded parts of town, and finally added a pair of conventional subway lines for the most traveled routes. San Francisco, in 1914–17, dug a two-and-a-half-mile transit tunnel through Twin Peaks; Philadelphia started a series of projects, one of which took the better part of half a century to complete. A few cities, notably Rochester and Newark, had abandoned canal beds which could be used to drop the main trolley line below the level of conventional traffic, achieving the gains of a subway system without the costs. Chicago and Cleveland found space beside the railroad rights-of-way, already graded and convenient to the important terminal areas. Sandy soil made subway construction even more difficult in Chicago than it was in New York, but the elevated lines went up in quantity. Els were cheap. The Northwestern Division of the Chicago transit system, 57.33 miles of four-track elevated line, cost only $1,635,738 per mile to build in the 1910's. By contrast, Toronto's subway, completed in 1954 cost nearly $60,000,000 for four and a half miles—and New York found $250,000,000 would be inadequate to build a six-mile subway line and its associated spurs up the East Side in the later fifties.

The theoretical purpose of rapid-transit facilities in those days was to *avoid* undue density in downtown residential districts, and many rapid-transit supporters were crusaders who hoped to give the poor a Better Life. In the absence of such facilities, the newcomers to the cities had been crowding into their ghettos to a degree hard for the mid-century American to imagine. They had to walk to work, and because sweatshops were clustered they clustered near the sweatshops. In 1900 the most densely populated residential area of Manhattan, the lower East Side, contained almost half a million people in its most crowded square mile; today, thanks largely to the development of the city's rapid-transit system, no square mile of New York has as many as two hundred thousand residents. Urging Los Angeles to build a subway or elevated system as soon as possible, the consulting firm of Kelper & DeLeuw in 1925 stressed that rapid transit "enables the city to expand [geographically] and prevents undue concentration of great masses of people in a small area."

By then, of course, the automobile was on the streets in fairly great quantities. (Kelper & DeLeuw observed that "the number of vehicles operated into and out of the congested district of Los Angeles during thirteen hours has reached the approximate total of 334,000. . . . Similar counts for the central business district of Chicago made in 1923 show a total of 330,000 for a 24-hour period. This is very remarkable when it is considered that Chicago has a population two and one half times that of Los Angeles.") City planners were already worried about what the automobile was going to do to the motion of traffic on the older and busier streets of downtown. "The great increase in the use of automobiles in recent years," economist Leslie Vickers wrote in a report for the Committee on Rapid Transit of the American Electric Railway Association, "has emphasized more thoroughly than ever the desirability of creating subway developments in the busy districts of large cities. . . . It is perfectly evident that electric trains must furnish transportation to most people traveling to and from the business district, and the larger the city the greater the percentage who must use public transportation service. . . ."

The lesson was already plain. Density can be served only by mass transit, preferably rapid transit. Otherwise . . . chaos.

It was already apparent that busses and trolleys would not be enough for the job. Their slowness was customarily exaggerated—Vickers spoke of busses moving through the cities of 1925 at "two or three miles an hour," while a survey done by *Fortune* magazine a few years ago showed that there was no major American city where public transport averaged less than eight miles an hour at rush times. (The two cities *Fortune* ranked at the bottom were Pittsburgh and San Antonio, both completely surface transit systems. Pittsburgh could have built a full-scale subway for $40,800,000 in the 1920's, and finally did nothing. What price city planning?) But even thirteen miles an hour, *Fortune's* average for "transit" speed in twenty-five major American cities, is far too slow to deter the building up of great residential densities near the heart of large cities—if those who work near the center must rely on busses and trolleys.

As the 1920's projected the future, then, the failure of the cities to produce adequate rapid transit for their workers could have only one result. The small minority of upper middle class and wealthy would be free to live where they wished, because they owned automobiles and could exert enough political pressure on federal and state subsidies and autonomous "authorities" to build decent roads near their houses. Other middle-class people would be able to escape the congestion near the center of the city by moving out to one of the suburban communities which clustered around the commuter railroad stop—strung out, as Raymond Vernon recently put it, like beads on a string. The rest would be restricted by their economic situation to homes in a dangerously overcrowded center of town. The 1920's failed to build its rapid-transit systems: New York, Philadelphia, Cleveland, Chicago and Boston remained the only cities where something quicker than surface transportation but cheaper than the commuter railroad was placed at the service of the moving masses of the city.

The thirties came, and the world had bigger worries than rapid transit.

It does not seem to have occurred to anyone, except perhaps Henry Ford, Herbert Hoover and Robert Moses, that another time might come when nearly every American family would own a car, and that this simple fact would make the rational organization of cities infinitely more difficult.

Contemporaries such as architect Edward Duell Stone call it the Mount Vernon or Monticello complex; historian Oscar Handlin finds it an eternal manifestation of the emerging middle-class American city dweller; but wherever its roots there can be no doubt that most Americans with a drive to attain a certain economic position want the social equivalent: their own house with its own plot of land. Apartment houses are indigenous to France and Germany, not Britain and America, and it was fairly late in the nineteenth century before anyone built such a structure to house Americans who might have the means to own their own home. Even then, as the gallivanting streetcar lines poked out into relatively unsettled areas, many who could not afford their own house in the center, but did not wish to live in a tenement, happily rode the trolleys and the double-decker busses out to the less developed edges of town.

By the mid-1920's, all the areas conveniently served by rapid transit were already built up in the row or small-lot manner, and speculators were starting apartment houses near the streetcar stops or even near the commuter railroad stations. Much of the area between the commuter stops or in the wedge between the streetcar spokes was vacant or farmed; its inconvenience made it implausible for housing.

Then the automobile and Mr. McAdam's embellished successors opened up all the vacant countryside within the circle, and Americans reverted to tradition. Without the depression and the Second World War, the heavy movement to the suburbs would doubtless have occurred much earlier. As history unfolded, the opening of immediate suburbia to intensive settlement waited until the late 1940's—by which time twenty years of poverty or shortages, coupled with the rapidity of wartime population flux, had created deficiency and dilapidation in urban housing. Stymied and smoldering for two decades, what might have been a relatively gradual movement became an explosion. In the decade of the 1950's, virtually all the net growth of population in most metropolitan areas came in the sections outside the boundaries of the central city.

In many cities 1947 was the year of greatest population density in the area served by the transit lines. Then the middle class, the original source of transit income, went elsewhere. As riders fell off, city after city replaced its streetcars with busses, which were less expensive to buy and to maintain and which could prowl the streets away from the trolley tracks to pick up new business. Subway and el service deteriorated as revenue decreased.

Theoretically, the transit lines' loss should have been the

commuter railways' gain, but the philosophy was wrong again. For most of the new suburbanites, a trip to work on the train involved a drive to the station, the train ride itself and then a trip on public transit from the railroad station to the job. Driving was more convenient and, despite all curses at traffic, usually less time-consuming.

As more and more cars came on the streets, the busses moved more and more slowly. Commuting by bus from the outer areas of the city itself became difficult, and the rise in average incomes allowed virtually every employed family to purchase a car, and even to pay for it over a period of time. Parking charges downtown, except in the largest and oldest cities, were rarely a great deal more than the transit fares, especially if the trip involved a transfer, and some companies could even provide their own parking lots for employees. Greater and greater proportions of the people who worked downtown began to drive to work. *Fortune's* 1957 survey found only seven large cities in America (New York, Chicago, Philadelphia, Cleveland, St. Louis, Pittsburgh and Boston) where more than half of those who entered the Central Business District arrived by public transit, while there were thirteen cities (Los Angeles, Baltimore, Washington, San Francisco, Milwaukee, Houston, Buffalo, Minneapolis, Cincinnati, Kansas City, Dallas, Denver and San Antonio) where 65 per cent or more came in by private car.

The problems caused by this flood of cars have been discussed *ad nauseam*, complete with photographs of central city at rush hour. (All those photographs are essentially ludicrous: nobody's moving.) It takes sixteen lanes of superhighway to carry into town in an hour as many people as can ride on a single track of subway, and incredible numbers of garages to get the cars off the street after they arrive. (If the cars remain on the streets, the city clogs; "No Parking" regulations are most rigorously enforced in the cities which have the greatest proportional inflow of automobiles.)

59

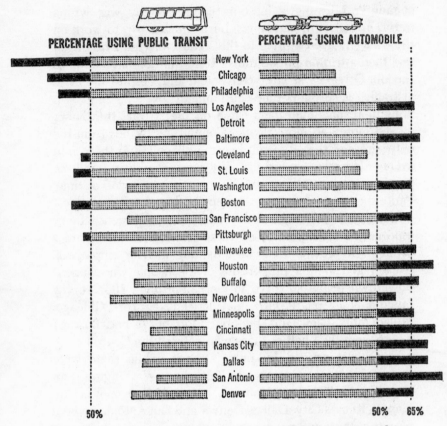

PERCENTAGE USING PUBLIC TRANSIT          PERCENTAGE USING AUTOMOBILE

New York
Chicago
Philadelphia
Los Angeles
Detroit
Baltimore
Cleveland
St. Louis
Washington
Boston
San Francisco
Pittsburgh
Milwaukee
Houston
Buffalo
New Orleans
Minneapolis
Cincinnati
Kansas City
Dallas
San Antonio
Denver

50%                                         50%  65%

*Fortune's* 1957 survey found only 7 large cities in America where
50% or more of the people who entered the central business district
arrived by public transit, while there were thirteen cities where 65%
or more came in by private car.

At present, thanks to an excellent transit system, high parking
costs and a still substantial number of unskilled workers too
ill-paid to afford an automobile or learn to drive, only 17
per cent of those who come to New York's Central Business
District arrive in private automobiles. *Fortune* has estimated
that if everybody who worked south of Fifty-ninth Street

in New York wanted to drive in, the entire area would have to be covered with multistory garages to the exclusion of all office buildings, shops, homes and so forth. Moving and standing still, the automobile takes space and plenty of it, and the one thing no mature city ever has is space.

Roads eat space, too. Most cities have been able to move through their streets greater numbers of automobiles than would have seemed possible thirty years ago. Parking restrictions and one-way movement have effectively widened streets without construction work; staggered lights have pushed a greater flow through the artery; left-turn lanes and similar gimmicks have cleared traditional traffic blocks. But streets alone cannot move the volume of cars necessary to transport people into a healthy downtown of a modern city without strong rapid-transit facilities. Washington has tried everything, including a thorough staggering of working hours, which can be done more effectively in Washington than anywhere else because there is only one major employer. Instead of heading home at five, the government worker finds himself assigned to a time between four and six, and the assignments are planned to scatter the traffic. What happens is that traffic backs up between four and five, and from five to six it backs up farther. The painfulness of movement in Washington at rush hours has already blighted a large part of the city's downtown and prevents the planning of a sensible core for the capital.

Los Angeles, which is three times Washington's size with equivalent transit facilities, reacted more vigorously to the challenge of the automobile, built scores of miles of six- and eight-lane expressway feeding directly into what passes for central city in this fantastically spread-out agglomeration, supplied upward of fifty thousand off-street parking places. The result is little more encouraging than Washington's failure to do anything. Both cities, of course, were handicapped by building codes which restricted the height of any new structure to thirteen stories, thus prohibiting really high density in the core. (Los Angeles in 1957 finally bowed to the skyscraper.) And without high density in the core, rapid-transit systems cannot be maintained economically, let alone built from scratch at today's prices.

However, the building of freeways and garages cannot continue forever. The new interchange among the four Los Angeles freeways, including the grade-constructed accesses, occupies by itself no less than *eighty acres* of downtown land, one-eighth of a square mile, an area about the size of Rockefeller Center in New York. It is hard to believe that this mass of intertwined concrete constitutes what the law calls "the highest and best use" of centrally located urban land. As it affects the city's fiscal situation, such an interchange is ruinous; it removes forever from the tax rolls property which should be taxed to pay for city services. Subways improved land values without taking away land; freeways boost valuation less (because the garages they require are not prime buildings by a long shot), and reduce the acreage that can be taxed. Downtown Los Angeles is already two-thirds freeway, interchange, street, parking lot and garage—one of those preposterous "if" statistics has already come to pass.

The freeway with narrowly spaced interchanges concentrates and mitigates the access problem, but it also acts inevitably as an artificial, isolating boundary. City planners do not always use this boundary as effectively as they might. Less ambitious freeway plans may be more successful—especially when the roadways and interchanges are raised, allowing for cross access at many points and providing parking areas below the ramp.

Meanwhile, the automobile and its friend the truck have cost the central city some of its industrial dominance. In ever greater numbers, factories are locating in the suburbs or in "industrial parks" removed from the city's political jurisdiction. The appeal of the suburb is particularly strong for heavy industry, which must move bulky objects along a lengthy assembly line and wants enough land area to do the entire job on one floor. To light industry, the economies of being on one floor are much slighter, but efficiency engineers usually believe in them, and manufacturers looking for ways to cut costs cannot be prevented from turning to efficiency engineers.

This movement of industry away from the central cities is not so catastrophically new as some prophets seem to believe. It is merely the latest example of the leapfrog growth which formed the pattern of virtually all American cities. The big factories which are relatively near the centers of our cities—the rubber factories in Akron, Chrysler's Detroit plants, U. S. Steel's Pittsburgh works—often began on these sites at a time when *that* was the edge of the city, yet close to transport (river), storage (piers) and power (river). The "leapfrog" was a phenomenon of the railroad and the steam turbine, and the time when the belts of residence surrounding the old factory area were not yet blighted.

The truck and the car gave the manufacturer a new degree of freedom in selecting his plant site. Until internal combustion became cheap, he had to be near a railroad siding and a trolley line or an existing large community of lower-class homes. The railroad siding is still important—it is usually, though not always, true that long-haul shipment by rail is cheaper than trucking. But anybody who promises a substantial volume of business can get a railroad to run a short spur to his plant these days, and many businesses can live without the railroad. And there are now many millions of workers for whom the factory with the big parking lot, which can be reached by driving across or against the usual pattern of rush hour traffic and grille-route bus lines, is actually more convenient than the walk-to factory.

Willow Run, General Electric's enormous installations at Louisville and Syracuse, the Pentagon, Boeing in Seattle, Douglas and Lockheed in Los Angeles, the new automobile assembly plants everywhere—none of these is substantially served by any sort of conventional mass rapid transit. They are all suburban plants, relying on the roads to keep them supplied with workers. And wherever the new thruways go up their banks are lined by neat glass and metal and colored brick light industry. The drive along Massachusetts' Route 128, the by-pass which makes an arc about twenty miles from downtown Boston, may be a vision of the future.

The future could be worse. The plants along Route 128 are mostly well designed and nicely set against the New England rocks and trees. They can even be rather grand, like Edward Land's monument to the astonishing success of Polaroid. But they deny the values of the city—the crowded, competitive, tolerant city, the "melting pot" which gave off so many of the most admirable American qualities. They are segregated businesses, combining again on one site the factory and the office, drawing their work force from segregated communities. It is interesting to note how many of the plants on Massachusetts' Route 128 draw most of their income either from the government in non-competitive cost-plus arrangements, or from the exploitation of patents which grant at least a partial monopoly.

While the factories were always the center of the labor market, they were often on the city's periphery. In spreading the factories even farther, the automobile may not have changed to any great extent the growth pattern of the cities. Even the loss of hotel business to the outskirt's motel has been relatively painless; the hotel-motel demarcation is becoming harder to find every year. What hurts most is the damage the automobile has done to central-city retailing, especially in those cities where public transit is feeble.

64

Some retailing, of course, always spreads with the population—grocery stores, drugstores, local haberdasheries and dress shops, candy stores and the like. But whenever a major purchase was contemplated forty years ago—a new bedroom set or a winter coat, an Easter bonnet, a bicycle for Junior— the family set off for the downtown department store, where the selection would be greatest. Department stores congregated in the "one hundred per cent location," where all the transit lines converged. The stores are still there, but the volume of the "downtown store" has been on a relative decline, while in many cities the suburban "branch" sells more and more dry goods. If the retailer and hotelman's downtown unit sales have been decreasing, however, his dollar volume continues to rise, and it is dollars which you put in the bank.

In most discussions of this phenomenon, the figures are substantially inflated. No suburban shopping-center branch —not even Hudson's vast Northland outside Detroit—does anything like the unit volume of business or carries anything like the variety of merchandise to be found in the home store. Telephone orders distort the picture: the suburbanite naturally calls a local rather than a central-city number if both are listed in an advertisement, especially if the local call eliminates city sales tax. The suburban branch is thereby credited with a sale which would have been made even if its glass doors had never opened. Accounting procedures which continue to charge a disproportionate overhead and warehouse expense to the main store make the branches seem more profitable than they are. In many cases the statement "We break even on our downtown operation and make money on our branches" would be turned around if the cost analysis were recalculated on terms less prejudicial to the old store. Fear of the competition—always a great motivating force in the American economy—makes retailers who do *not* have suburban operations exaggerate both the volume

65

and the profitability of their rival's shiny new branches. The fact seems to be that very many large branch stores are uneconomical, that the choice of location in the suburbs is as important as it was downtown, and that even highly suburbanized cities will support only so many big branches. Moreover, the cost of operations is always high in *any* new store, as the conservative bankers who act as controllers for retail giants are beginning to discover.

When all has been said, however, the big branch store remains a major break with history in the development of American retailing. Just as the suburban factory may be more convenient than the downtown plant to the worker with a car, the trip to the shopping center may seem far easier than to the downtown department store, though both are the same distance from home. Indeed, there are some cities where the suburban shopping pulls customers who are geographically much nearer to downtown. Raymond Vernon reports that residents of East St. Louis have been driving across the Mississippi, through the heart of downtown St. Louis and out to the western suburbs for major shopping, simply because parking is easier at the big branches than it is in the heart of town. To the extent that the problem is merely parking, an aggressive downtown management, like that of Lazarus Brothers in Columbus, Ohio, can fight back successfully by building a garage on the lot next door. If the distant patron of the suburban branch has been frightened away from downtown by traffic problems, however, the city store can only pressure the politicians to do something about the highways or await the completion of the federal highway program. And if the affection for the suburban branch reflects a desire to shop with "nice people," rather than with the indiscriminate urban mass which supports the downtown department store, the central location may be in serious trouble. Today, according to land economist Homer Hoyt, shopping centers and their associated parking lots cover some 46,000 acres of land, which is almost exactly the total land area in all the nation's Central Business Districts put together.

The downtown store continues to offer the great inducement of variety, both within its gates and across the street, where other department stores are immediately convenient for the shopper who wants to see what is available before making up her mind. If anything may be predicted in the quicksilver world of retailing, it seems likely that the suburban branch will come to dominate children's clothing (taking the kid downtown is too much of a production), household gadgetry and the discount business in big-ticket items. Department stores were built on dry goods, especially ladies' fashions, and in this area, in the long run, the suburban branches will be hard put to compete against downtown. If this analysis is correct, the suburban branches will turn out to be what management's cost accountants refuse to acknowledge, marginal operations rather than major factors.

Historically in America the appeal of cities has been their color and life, the variety of experience they offered. "How ya gonna keep 'em down on the farm?" was a question that had to be asked long before they saw Paree. Though Americans usually lived in groups segregated by national origin or religious belief, they liked to work and shop in the noise and vitality of downtown. Only a radical change in the nature of the population in the central city would be likely to destroy this preference—and we must now turn our attention to the question of whether such a change, gloomily foreseen by so many urban diagnosticians, is actually upon us.

# 4. Suburbs and Negroes

In their book *American Skyline*, Christopher Tunnard and Henry Hope Reed argue that Franklin Roosevelt's New Deal was what made the modern suburb a possibility—a fine ironical argument, when you consider how suburbanites tend to vote. The first superhighways—New York's Henry Hudson and Chicago's Lake Shore, San Francisco's Bay Bridge and its approaches, a good slice of the Pennsylvania Turnpike—were built as part of the federal works program which was going to cure the depression. At the same time, Roosevelt's Federal Housing Administration, coupled with Henry Morgenthau's cheap-money policy, permitted ordinary lower-middle-class families to build their own homes. Bankers who had been reluctant to lend without better security than the house itself got that security from the U. S. government; householders who had been unable to pick up the burden of short-term high-interest mortgages found they could borrow for twenty-five years at 4 per cent, under government aegis. Neither the works program nor the revival of home construction through the FHA could cure the depression, but between them they cast a long shadow over the residential patterns of the American city.

The depression slowed and then the war stopped home building. When peace returned the American city faced a major decision, though few people realized it at the time. Massive efforts were clearly needed to replace deteriorated urban housing and supply homes for the swollen city population. A big drive for new housing was demanded also by everybody's "knowledge" that once arms production ceased the nation's economy could again be hit by a pile-driving slump. The question, not even asked at the time, was whether the housing effort would be made through urban redevelopment, or through sprawling house-and-lot projects all around the edge of the city. To work over the cities themselves would have required direct federal subsidy, while urban sprawl demanded no more than roads (some of them already provided by 1920's middle-class demand and the thirties' Works Project efforts) and government guarantees behind cheap mortgages ("the least we can do for the GI"). Moreover, the national ethos urged a private house for every family.

Even the apartment houses (which were built with government aid in the years right after the war) went up, almost without exception, on the outskirts of the existing city. It was cheaper to take new land than to clear existing blight. Anyone who believes that successful business meets a public need, that the entrepreneur's profits inevitably grow from the long-run benefits received by the community, must study the racks of garden apartments that sprung out of perfectly good soil in the first half-decade after the war. Did they meet a public need? Perhaps they did—at least that would be the argument from the Congressmen who frantically legislated too much incentive for builders, keeping their blinders in place to avoid looking at the evils of overcapitalization, windfall and random sprawl. But they left a fearful legacy, not to generations unborn but to the very generation that moved out and occupied the new apartments. Herculean as it seems, the job of cleaning up concentrated areas in center city may prove small beside the growing need to restore humanity and grace to our spread-out miles of blighted countryside. If a slogan were needed for the postwar era, it might be "Remember Los Angeles," once a pleasant city of cockeyed but genuine civilization, now an enormous housing tract, mile upon mile of land built upon but not really *settled*.

Again, what was new about the drive to the suburbs was its magnitude rather than its existence per se. Americans have been moving out from the centers of their cities since the beginning; much of the urban blight is seventy and more years old. Center city in the nineteenth century was simply unendurable for those who could get out of it. In the American tradition the newcomer to the city lived at boardinghouses near the job, and the move from the boardinghouse to a real home—always farther out—was a step not merely toward respectability, but toward common decency. When the boardinghouse declined, the "tenement" appeared, and it was scarcely an improvement. One of the large tenements in New York in the 1850's offered twenty-four two-room apartments on each floor of a building measuring 240 by 35 feet—approximately 350 square feet of floor space per family, and the families were usually large. (Toilets, of course, were outside.) Philadelphia and Baltimore developed "row" houses, each sixteen feet wide and two stories high, representing housing for four to six families. Edward Everett Hale described one such Boston wooden tenement in 1869:

. . . in the rear, two closets only lighted from the doors, one of which may be eight feet square; the other is narrower. The front room, which opens on the piazza, is fifteen by thirteen perhaps. This is a suite for a family.

Such housing should have been destroyed when its wretched occupants went elsewhere, but there were always new immigrants ready to take over the abandoned space.

Then as now, slum profits were good. Americans out in the prairie were ruining one patch of land, then moving on to the next, with results that the conservationists are still trying to remedy. In the cities, too, each group of residents despoiled their neighborhood, and then moved on.

Generally, people moved in ethnic groups from neighborhood to neighborhood. Americans talked of "the melting pot," and certainly the image was just. But the pot might have boiled over if the new immigrants, before their absorption into the community, had not ghetto-ized themselves, each living with "our kind." Until the present century, lines were not drawn to the complete exclusion of any ethnic group. Especially in the poorer areas, the failures from the last lot lived cheek by jowl with the newcomers. Thus, the "Big Flat" tenement on New York's Mott Street contained 368 Jews, 31 Italians, 31 Irish, 30 Germans and 4 native-born Americans. Some people remained because the neighborhood was the source of their income and they could not leave it without abandoning their business. There is an old Jewish story about the immigrant who started with a pushcart and rose to owning his own dry-goods store, where he lived in two or three rooms in the rear. The business prospered, and finally he bargained successfully for a cash purchase of Macy's. When the deal had been arranged he began counting out the money from a paper bag, while his wife, who had come uptown with him, looked around the store. He had reached sixty-seven million dollars when his wife came running back and called a halt to the counting. "Jake," she said, "we don't want this. There's no place in the back to live."

Nevertheless, communities usually moved more or less together, as you can verify by studying the street names in what was the edge of the city fifty and sixty years ago. Here one finds the Pulaski Avenues and Calloway Streets, the Athens Boulevards, Masaryk Drives and Mazzini Places. Here the churches are almost all Greek Orthodox; there,

71

Catholic. In some places there are few if any Christian churches, but half a dozen Jewish synagogues. Often the church or the synagogue continues to stand after most of its parishioners have gone elsewhere. Sometimes (though not so often as efficiency might desire) the same building served successive communities as a church, a temple, a movie house and then a church again.

The explosion to the suburbs has continued this pattern of ethnic unity, so that it is reasonable to speak of Italian suburbs and Jewish suburbs and Protestant suburbs—though most suburbs are segregated more severely by income level and "life style" than by ethnic origin. Into the urban housing which these groups have vacated has moved, in the American tradition, yet another ethnic entity: the Negro. But here the ghetto-ing of the newcomer has been less voluntary. The Negro is held in his group less by the group's internal cohesiveness than by the strength of external pressure.

Even today, however, urban segregation is not absolute. There are probably many modern tenements where the proportions are similar to those of the old Big Flat—except that Negroes have replaced Jews as the dominant group. In New York it might be Puerto Ricans instead of Negroes; in Los Angeles it might be Mexicans, living in tenements once occupied by Orientals, who had been imported as coolies to build the railroads and are now dominant in certain middle-class economic functions.

In 1960 Negroes accounted for only 13 per cent of the population of New York City, which was by no means their historic high. Nearly a quarter of the city had been Negro in 1746. In Chicago and Detroit, Los Angeles and Boston, St. Louis and Philadelphia, however, the percentage of Negroes in the city population was at a record high. In Washington half of those who lived inside the city limits were colored. And with the Negro, in the great internal

72

migration of the 1950's, came the poor "white trash" of the South, who share the Negro's economic frustrations but not his color and form an easily agitated neighboring community.

The precise location of the oldest and worst Negro slum in most northern American cities is largely a matter of historical accident. During the 1850's many northerners were more than willing to disobey fugitive slave laws, to help escaped Negroes out of the country before the police could catch them and—bound by Taney's decision in the Dred Scott case—hand them over to their southern owners. Wherever the roads led to Canada and safety, the underground railroad organized its depot; and, as the Civil War provided the prototype for later European stalemates on the battlefield, the runaway slaves and their helpers gave the partisans of the future a handsome example of successful lawlessness for the sake of principle.

In the nature of things, the depot could not be in the center of the city, where too many people might inquire about the appearance of the southern Negro, whose manner inevitably differed from that of the northern freeman. Farms were also dangerous, though they had to be used when the journey from city to city was too time-consuming to be done in a single night. On the edge of the city as it existed in the 1850's, then, some trustworthy conspirator's house was taken as refuge and assembly point. The locations of these houses became known inevitably to quantities of Negroes (and, of course, to a sympathetic local constabulary). Some of the escaped slaves never progressed beyond these refuges, remaining in semihiding until the hue and cry died down, and then joining their fellows as men who were free because it could not be proved that they were not. Often they remained near the house, and about this address there grew up a Negro colony.

It was not, as an ordinary matter, the only Negro community in town. Like other immigrants, Negroes usually chose to live with each other, but there was no pattern of systematic exclusion. Racism as a doctrine in American life, as Oscar Handlin has pointed out, was a creation of the later nineteenth century, born of the bitterness of the defeated South and the decline of the evangelical faith as a source of central moral values. In the northern cities, too, there was no "Negro problem." Not until restrictive laws had completed the structure of discrimination did any large number of Negroes feel a need to leave the South. Not until the First World War cut heavily into the number of arriving European immigrants did the northern cities feel the need to import Negroes to do their manual labor. As late as 1910, the Negro population of New York (the first city to call upon substantial numbers of Negro migrants) was under 92,000. And they were relatively evenly scattered through half a dozen assembly districts of the city, in none of which did they constitute as much as 18 per cent of the total population of the ward. Indeed, more than half the city's Negroes lived in assembly districts where they formed less than 5 per cent of the population.

Like their predecessors, the Negroes tended to move into the lowest level of housing, which had just been evacuated by the more successful of the most recent immigrants. Their presence was noticed immediately, of course—and often they were resented by their new neighbors, men who were clearly among the less successful of their own group, hunting causes for their relative failure. The years just before the First World War were the worst years of labor violence America has ever known. Occasionally, employers brought in Negroes from the South as strikebreakers. One such episode in St. Louis provoked the worst race riot in American history, involving the destruction by fire of the neighborhood where the concentration of Negroes was heaviest.

When massive Negro migration to the North began, in the decade starting in 1910, the worst of the slums were thinning out a little. Building codes and health regulations, though weak and relatively ill-enforced, operated to prevent any renewal of the horrifying overcrowding which had made pestholes of the old slums in the nineties and 1900's. Though the more prosperous of the later immigrants were moving out, their departure did not mean there was ample room for newcomers. The earlier Negro immigrants had moved mostly into Jewish slum neighborhoods. The newer group, especially in the years after the First World War, began to spread into the lower middle-class neighborhoods which had been built for the Jews escaping the slums—New York's Harlem, Chicago's South Side, north-central Detroit. Overwhelmingly Jewish as late as 1925, all these areas had become predominantly Negro before the outbreak of World War II. There is social comment of an odd sort in the fact that the neighborhood where Loeb and Leopold planned their peculiar crime became, before Leopold was well into middle age, an area for Negro laborers.

Why the Negro communities grew up in these relatively new middle-class neighborhoods rather than in the old slums is not an easy question to answer. In New York, according to Oscar Handlin's *The Newcomers*, one of the New York Metropolitan Region studies, the reason was overbuilding by ambitious speculators. Vacant houses in a neighborhood not yet established presented an open invitation to new arrivals in the city. From a nucleus in these few overbuilt blocks, the Negro community spread. In Chicago it may not be entirely fanciful to say that the Loeb-Leopold case itself, deeply felt as a kind of visitation on the Jewish community, contributed to the thinning out of the local Jewish population and helped open up the area for Negro occupancy.

Wherever a Negro group became securely established, other Negroes came to join it. Like the immigrants before them, they looked for their own churches, stores catering to their own tastes, the society of people with similar back-

grounds. And from the mid-1920's on, the Negroes consti-
tuted the largest single group of emigrants to the cities.
Their neighborhoods therefore tended to spread rather rapidly, a situation visible to any passer-by as the spread of
Jewish or Italian neighborhoods was not. The legend grew
up that Negroes took over an area as soon as a few had been
admitted to it, and that in this respect Negroes were different from the newcomers of an earlier day.

It was also widely held that Negroes ruined neighborhoods, a view too violently expressed but not entirely inaccurate when applied to the newest arrivals. All immigrants
had brought with them what the established residents regarded as "filthy habits," but most Europeans had experienced at least some contact with urban living. The southern
Negro—and his poor white neighbor—were entirely unskilled in the arts of urban existence, and on arrival presented
unprecedented problems to the city sanitary and police
authorities. Even today, in a highly urbanized America, the
newly arrived Negroes and the white "hillbillies" make existence hellishly difficult for the streetcleaners, the schools
and the police.

Against the legend, it was fruitless to cite studies of settled
Negro neighborhoods, proving that Negroes can adjust to
city living about as well as anybody else. And in the light of
well-publicized southern segregationist attitudes toward Negroes in other areas of existence, few northerners would pay
much attention to the fact that in many southern cities, such
as Charleston, South Carolina, Negroes and whites lived side
by side (or, rather, back to front, the Negroes occupying
what were once servant's quarters behind the mansions)
without any deterioration of residential neighborhoods. With
Negroes coming up from the South in increasing numbers,
and whites moving to the suburbs in floods, internal pressure
for at least *some* Negro occupancy in established white
neighborhoods became irresistible.

Unfortunately, there were also strong forces at work to make "interracial" neighborhoods wholly Negro within a short period of time. Negroes were welcome in relatively few parts of the industrialized metropolitan centers, and there were more of them to house each year. In the American pattern, the newcomers to the city lived in rooming houses, no great improvement over the boardinghouses of a hundred years before, and wanted out as soon as possible. Conscious of the Negro demand for houses and apartments, real estate brokers specializing in residences went about stimulating a supply from whites. Their methods were often highly antisocial. They could even act as Paul Reveres of racial change: the blacks are coming—sell quick. Deliberately raising a specter of declining property values, they drove the more prosperous away from their homes and roused in the others hatred and fear of a Negro "invasion."

Again it was true that room had been made for the newcomers by the departure of the younger and more successful elements of the community. Those who remained were usually the old folks, who wanted as much as possible of the world to be as it had always been, plus the laborers who feared Negro competition in the jobs which tradition gave to the most recent arrivals to the city. When all elements are added together, the wonder is not that there have been occasional riots and gang wars and pacts of exclusion, but that, on the whole, the transition from white to Negro occupancy has been accomplished as peacefully as it has.

What makes the miracle even more impressive is the fact that the weakening whites of the declining neighborhoods were bolstered by other whites from the South, hardened in anti-Negro attitudes. Religious differences doubtless played a part in easing the transition: the rooted whites, predominantly Catholic and Jewish, found little in common with the "foreign" white Protestants from the South. Purely ethnic civil commotion fortunately could not be aroused; race riots threatened only where color differences were exacerbated by economic competition. Rivalry for jobs creates fear and tension, and social equality promotes such rivalry. For this reason federal imposition of integrated education is producing the first "economic" riots in the South, more than a hundred years after Dred Scott and nearly eighty years after the departure of the carpetbaggers.

Causality in these matters is always obscure. We cannot say whether the failure of mass transit created demand for the automobile, or the automobile killed mass transit; whether suburbanization demanded new highways or new highways produced suburbs; whether the departure of the white community to homes on the greensward invited Negroes to the cities, or the arriving Negroes drove away the whites. More fundamentally, we cannot say whether each wave of immigrants improved themselves and left the dirty jobs to newcomers, or whether the new arrivals forced the immigrants of the generation before up the social ladder.

One of the elements that makes the "Negro problem" so troublesome, however, is our inability to visualize an incoming group that will push the Negroes up and out of the low-paid jobs on which they live. So long as the Negro community in the cities must do the dirty work, there can be little hope of integrating large neighborhoods.

Generally speaking, immigrant communities have risen in the cities by business enterprise rather than by professionalization, and the Negro community, like the Irish, has been somewhat light in the production of businessmen. In both cases it may be because the newcomers spoke English on arrival, which gave them less incentive to do business with "their own kind" than was felt by the Germans or the Russians or the Italians. Whatever the reason, the Negro's failure to prosper in commerce hindered that building up of economic pressure which might shatter the walls of social or residential discrimination.

Professional men and talented individuals in the arts and athletics have sometimes been able to move as though their ancestors were white instead of colored immigrants. There are enclaves of well-to-do Negroes in New York's Jackson Heights, in a decent section of Cambridge near Radcliffe College, in the luxury houses just south of Grant Park in Chicago. But until recently there was no large lower-middle class, of the sort that has populated the suburbs, in the Negro community.

Economically, however, the terms of trade are changing. The path to the middle classes is no longer on the road of small enterprise. The thruway today is the office job, and more and more Negroes are moving into white collars. They qualify economically and by cultural pattern for the suburban life, and they are beginning to push their way into the suburbs.

And the movement of industry to suburban locations has given the working-class Negro his first strong reason to get out of the cities. Traffic studies in New York show that traffic across the George Washington Bridge at rush hour in the morning is almost as heavy to New Jersey as it is to the central city, and that a high proportion of the outgoing vehicles have Negro passengers, going to jobs in Jersey factories.

Elsewhere, too, there seems to be developing a slow but strong movement of Negroes to the suburbs—and the suburban town is less likely than the urban neighborhood to spew forth its white population on the approach of Negro homeowners. In the forty years between 1910 and 1950, the Negro population doubled or tripled in such New York suburbs as New Rochelle, Paterson, Elizabeth and Mount Vernon, with nearly all the increase coming in the last decade. Yet none of these towns experienced any flight of whites. The schools in some of the New York suburbs are now more likely to be genuinely interracial than the schools of many city districts. Similar movements are occurring elsewhere, though they are still infrequent. Perhaps the solution to ghetto-ing will come through the growth of many widely scattered Negro areas—so many that they create an atmosphere of integration. Prosperity leads in this direction, and so does urban renewal, backed by the enlightened self-interest which is producing orderly integration on Chicago's South Side as it will on Manhattan's West Side. Behind these movements are all the influence of billion-dollar institutions like the University of Chicago and Columbia University.

But the Negroes, alone in the history of immigration to the cities, must make their progress themselves. No group now seems likely to come in below them and push them up. For a while it was thought in New York that the Puerto Ricans would form a new lower class, driving their Negro predecessors to a higher status—and, indeed, the recent success of Negroes in office jobs in New York may be traceable partly to their eviction from manual labor by Puerto Rican newcomers. But the Puerto Rican community has shown a strong adaptation to the ways of commerce, and the observer can already find in New York rapid Puerto Rican progress toward middle-class status. Much the same dynamic has been at work among Oriental groups in San Francisco and other western metropolitan centers. Only in Los Angeles and in the border cities of the Southwest have the Negroes profited by the intrusion of a group lower than themselves in the social scale; Los Angeles worries about its Mexicans, legal and illegal, rather than about its colored. Perhaps it is significant that the greatest single stream of Negro migration in recent years has been flowing toward Los Angeles.

I have lived through the trouble of nursing a property in a changing neighborhood to a condition of interracial stability; I own one of the commercial landmarks of Chicago's

South Side. When I bought it the tenancy was entirely white, but the neighborhood was evenly balanced, white and Negro. It was my business judgment that the building could not prosper unless I replaced departing white tenants with whites and Negroes whose profession and personal quality would maintain the high tone of the property.

Some of my white tenants said they would be harmed. Their God is economics; let them compete. If they cannot do so successfully, and I think they can, then let them be harmed. They cannot stop integration by agitating, either surreptitiously or under a flag of white supremacy. The only result of such agitation is panic and disorder.

On the other side, a certain extremist association found fault with my efforts to retain white tenants. Many of these tenants did business largely with the Negro community; it seemed to be the opinion of this association that only Negroes should have easy access to such business—but what price glory? By resisting pressure from both sides, I was able to secure a tenancy which is economically sound and sociologically tenable: Negro professionals working beside their white confreres in mutual respect.

By maintaining the quality of the building, I have been able to lease major areas of it to businesses that need considerable office space—and it is these large, long-term leases that guarantee the solidity of a property. All those larger tenants are white, but they employ Negroes. I look forward hopefully to a time when some of the big proprietors will be Negro, too; but I don't know when that time will come. I would be more confident of the prospect if I could envision the group that will succeed the Negroes in the low-scaled jobs.

But growing social equality should generate economic opportunity. The Negro's capacity to compete may be revealed here on a large scale, without the agitation of extremist groups, through the self-interested spirit of compromise. My own education on the narrow path in this area is largely the work of Abner J. Mikva, a college friend at the University of Wisconsin, later an editor of the University of Chicago *Law Review*, clerk to Supreme Court Justice Minton, partner in a LaSalle Street law firm, and Illinois State Assemblyman. Because of Ab Mikva, the dedicated community boosters of the Hyde Park-Kenwood Conference had my ear directly—and held it by pure economic logic.

# 5. *The Mess in Government*

We live, as everyone knows, in a democracy, which is a form of government we have chosen because we like freedom and not because we want to save money. Democracy, as the history of its development shows, is an expensive procedure. "No representation," said the Stuart King, "without taxation." And so it goes to this day.

Democracy is expensive because it attempts to give a voice to all interests rather than establishing a hierarchy. Nothing can be done by fiat from a central authority. Our Revolution was made against the vested interests of the East India Company and George III. In a sense, however, it was irrelevant that the hated central power was on the other side of an ocean. What made our leaders rebel two hundred years ago was a fanatic devotion to an idea of local authority. Indeed, they had to try a loose confederation of states before considerations of survival forced them to a federal government of the limited powers allotted in the Constitution as written. And to get that Constitution approved, it was necessary to append the ten amendments called the Bill of Rights, now assumed to protect the individual, then regarded primarily as protections for local government and the local constituency against possible encroachments of national power.

Our ideal of local government was, of course, the New England town meeting, where each property owner had his say and his vote. (The idea of universal suffrage, without property qualification, comes from a later period.) Matters involving the co-operation of several neighboring townships could be handled by the officers of those townships acting together as a county board. Really big issues other than those of peace, war, foreign trade and relations among the sovereign federated states—these could be dealt with by the part-time legislators of state governments.

One of the major roles of the federal government in the early years was the establishment of new states; one of the tasks of the new state governments was the organizing of counties and the chartering of cities. States are sovereign; cities are not. Like corporations, they owe their right to exist to the acceptance of their charters by a state government. The degree of state control varies from place to place, but it is generally true that each unit of local government is restricted as to its authority and revenue-raising facilities by state regulation. People who resent restrictions of their liberties are often told to "go fight City Hall," and with much the same connotative cynicism and resignation one might say "City Hall can go fight State House" when it wishes to try some new approach to its problems.

To speak of cities controlling and channeling their own growth is to assume that the cities have governing rather than administrative powers. The city is the center of its metropolitan area, but typically it is only one of the governmental units influencing the development of the area. In 1958, the New York metropolitan area counted no fewer than 1,074 separate governments with taxing power (including school districts, special districts and the like); Chicago had 954. A fractional part of these numbers could be accounted for by the geographical spread of the cities' influence, absorbing into the metropolitan area already existing municipalities which retained their governmental identity. Many more, however, represent simple proliferation—governments specially created to meet needs existing governments cannot or would rather not handle alone.

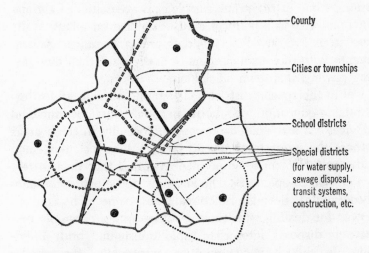

Adjoining and/or overlapping autonomous governmental authorities often prevent proper development of an area.

For example, the school district. Americans tend to be proud of the special relation between schools and the local community in the United States. Elsewhere in the world the governmental unit which runs the schools is larger than the municipality served by the schools; here, the school district is usually smaller. Neither political nor educational theory explains this tinywork pattern. It traces, instead, to the limited powers of municipalities, which were not chartered originally to provide education for their children. When the question of municipal service vs. separate school

85

district was most keenly agitated, in the 1830's and 1840's, those who urged a separate district could point to the discouraging example of New York, which ran its schools from City Hall and consequently involved them in politico-religious wrangling of the most distressing sort. Thus even the newer cities never acquired the habit of operating an educational system; and today, when consolidation of school districts is one of the prime sociological necessities of the nation, the city as a political entity cannot even influence the course of events. School districts are independent governments, with their own charters from the state, their own taxing powers, their own officialdom.

With the special district well established as a way of organizing education, people began to use such governmental devices for less exalted purposes. Especially in those areas where the interests of several communities met, it seemed advisable to form some permanent unit rather than to rely on *ad hoc* co-operation. The large district, crossing not only geographical but also functional lines, came to be conventional for dealing with such problems as water supply and sewage disposal, interurban rapid transit and bridgebuilding. In suburban communities, meanwhile, the *smaller* special district has become an effective tool which older residents can use to make sure that the cost of new streets, street lighting, sewage lines and such falls entirely on the new residents rather than on themselves.

No governmental unit ever entirely disappears, though in some metropolitan areas the wholly non-functional "county" has been withering away in almost Marxist fashion. (A better word than "county" in the usual American pattern might be "shire," which would serve as a constant reminder that the thing itself is dead.) As our cities grow, they beget governments as the biblical patriarchs begat children—and no one of these governments has the responsibility, the authority or the funds to deal with the great problems of the area with anything resembling the efficiency of major industrial companies.

Seeing the inefficiency and confusion, many observers conclude that American local government is falling apart and failing in its central day-by-day duties. In fact, however, everything keeps functioning. "From the perspective of the economic historian," Robert C. Wood writes in his CED pamphlet *Metropolis Against Itself*, "it is hard to conclude that metropolitan governments have, on the average, been insensitive to change, or to judge their response to the pressures for more and better services as abnormally sluggish. On balance, one emerges more impressed with the governments' ingenuity in assembling forces to sustain themselves in their independent roles than expecting the superstructure to crumble."

Even the big problems are handled, more or less well on a short-term basis, by the device of the apolitical authority, the group of genii summoned from the bottle to run the busses or the airport or the harbor or the distant reservoirs. In these matters, where overlapping jurisdictions would make too much mess, municipal governments have been willing to go the whole hog. But in each municipal headquarters the hog remains, insisting on his authority and perquisites and parasitic sinecures, contemptuous of the very notion of a master plan.

Even at best, cities could not control their development to anything like the extent that reformers imagine. It is patterns of economic development, created by factors well beyond municipal control, which determine the direction of the large movements. In two broad areas, however, municipalities and regions can act to regulate the present and influence the future. These areas are tax policy and legislation on land use.

Taxes are most obvious. Traditionally, local government

in the United States was supposed to support itself on the real estate tax—the "rates," as the British call it. But the rate itself is never more than part of the story, because the rate applies to "assessed valuation," and the valuations are matters of judgment rather than fact. Many a city with an apparently high tax rate is actually placing a moderate burden on real estate, because the valuations are only a third of market value or reproduction cost less depreciation. Elsewhere an apparently low rate may represent a burden because it applies against full market value or reproduction cost of the property.

Typically, because householders have more votes than the owners of commercial buildings, valuations tend to be proportionately higher in the business districts. Two per cent of the land area of the city pays 20 per cent of the taxes in Washington, D.C., 27 per cent in Denver, 35 per cent in Minneapolis. In Chicago one-third of 1 per cent of the city's area pays 18 per cent of all the real estate taxes. Such figures can be batted around a little too easily, because much of the disproportion may be justified by the city's investment in rapid-transit facilities to serve the downtown area. Sometimes, however, tax discrimination against midtown can give a company a reason to locate in a suburb—especially if the suburb has suddenly discovered a need to broaden its tax base and is willing to offer tax exemption inducements to the new arrival.

There are two ways of assessing property for tax purposes. Both involve the market value of the land, which can be objectively determined and must not be tampered with lest chaos follow. One method uses market price to determine the value of the building as well as the land (in this context the building is referred to as "the improvements," even if an artist would regard the specimen in question as no improvement whatever over a vacant lot). Washington, D.C., for example, usually works on a base assessment of 60 per cent of market value, with a rate of $2.30 per $100 of assessed valuation. Elsewhere buildings are often assessed at their reconstruction cost, less depreciation. Generally, in these formulas, an attempt is made neither to penalize new buildings by assessing them at their actual cost, nor to reward older structures by allowing them valuation at antique construction expenses.

In addition to their simple revenue functions, real estate taxes can be made to serve planning purposes. In Sydney, Australia, for example, land is valued not on a market or depreciation basis, but on a *potential* basis. Generally, areas are homogeneous with respect to the quality of the structure built on the land. Slum land is reduced in value by the fact that slum buildings stand on it, and the slum buildings themselves are obviously worth little. Thus our real estate taxes fall only lightly on the slums, though the slums require the most expensive services from the cities. Many American slums, however, are located near the center of town, on land with a very high potential value if only the slum could be removed. On the Australian system, such land would be taxed rather heavily, to penalize the owners for their failure to make the highest and best use of their property. Whether such valuations would be constitutional in the United States is an interesting question; whether they would function as desired if imposed is equally dubious. There is danger, at least, that the "slumlord," stung by higher taxes, would merely crowd his residences further and suck more blood from his tenants to maintain his profits.

Rather than hit the slum owner for failure to improve his land, American cities have been rewarding the man who does clear blighted areas by giving him a reduction in his tax bill. The Quality Hill apartments in Kansas City, for example, have a ten-year exemption from taxes on "the improvements"—that is, they will pay real estate taxes only on the land value as it was before the new buildings went up. For another fifteen years, the development will be taxed only on one-half the value of its improvements to the land, and not until a quarter of a century has passed will customary valuation procedures be applied to the project. Even more generous tax allowances from the City of New York enabled Metropolitan Life to build its enormous Stuyvesant Town housing project beside New York's East River.

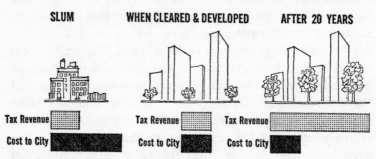

A tax allowance to an urban renewal project area will eventually result in permanent advantage to the city.

This urban generosity to the developer has been criticized by various city planners, among them Lewis Mumford, but in fact such arrangements are hard to abuse. From the land as it stood the city was receiving only the tax on slum valuation, and without the developer the prospects of higher revenues from the area were dim to the point of invisibility. The same taxes continue to be paid by the new development, even at the beginning, so there is no loss of revenue to the city. The services required by the new tenants are if anything cheaper than those needed in the old slum. And eventually the city tax rolls do rise by the value of the improvements. Unfortunately, it is rarely the slum owner who plans or builds such housing, and the sale price he receives for his property when the developer takes it over may represent an overly charitable estimate of the real value of his land. Nobody likes to see the slumlord make windfall profits, but it is more important to build the housing than to haggle over moral principles, especially when insistence on morality is likely to produce expensive, time-consuming lawsuits, and perpetuate the earlier immorality.

Typically, the positive use of real estate taxation for planning involves only housing. In the chapter on urban renewal we shall have occasion to consider whether such policies might not be applicable to problems of commercial blight, as well.

In the days when city government was restricted to maintaining law and order, putting out fires and establishing *ad hoc* ordinances, the real estate tax produced enough revenue to carry the burden. Franchise and licensing operations paid for themselves, and the maintenance of potters' fields for the burial of the unimportant dead was an activity in which charities could be expected to help.

Functions multiplied, even within the limited charters of the cities. Water supply came first, then street-cleaning, sewage disposal and garbage collection, then clinics and hospitals for the indigent poor, street lighting, road maintenance, rapid transit, welfare—on and on, a list that never shrinks and rarely stops expanding. Clearly the real estate tax could not pay for everything, even if valuations grew steadily; and in many cities they do not. Depreciation may run a close race with inflation, even in easy money periods, and the new buildings may rise in the suburbs. Highways and parking lots proliferate. Government buildings and educational institutions, both tax-exempt, take up larger and larger fractions of the city's space. The values to be taxed in the city of Boston actually declined from 1930 to 1951, though the value of tax-exempt land and buildings rose by nearly 50 per cent.

Today taxes on real property provide cities with less than

two-fifths of their total income. Another quarter comes from federal and state aid—not so generous as it looks, because the money came out of the pockets of the city dwellers in the first place. The rest—three-eighths of the total—derives from nuisance taxes and charges for services. The sales tax as a device in municipal finance goes back less than thirty years, but it is now common. Taxes on admissions to theaters and sporting events are standard; taxes on restaurant meals are routine. The state of Pennsylvania alone can boast no fewer than 415 local income taxes. Cigarette sales taxes are almost unavoidable, as are taxes on liquor, gasoline and electricity, telephone bills and assorted services. Gross receipts taxes are not uncommon either—you can lose a million dollars in your business, but if you handled ten million in the process you pay full tax on the ten.

Such taxes do not greatly affect city development, as an ordinary matter, though some of them are dangerous. When New York City suggested a tax on stock transfers, the New York Stock Exchange threatened to move to New Jersey. The state of Kentucky has driven some whiskey warehousing out to Indiana by taxing liquor aging in barrels, and Indiana has meanwhile driven some industry the other way through its gross receipts tax. Local income taxes might seem particularly dangerous in this respect, driving wealthy residents to homes in the suburbs, but in fact such taxes are customarily collected at the source rather than at the residence, forcing commuters to make at least some contribution to the city where they work. According to Mabel Walker, St. Louis draws as much as a quarter of its municipal revenue from taxes paid by commuters.

Another source of funds is available to the cities—borrowing at relatively low interest rates assured by the exemption of the interest payments from federal income tax. In the long run, of course, the city does not make money by borrowing; but by refunding the city can postpone lump-sum repayment forever, and meanwhile the cash is being spent. Experts argue at length as to whether cities should attempt to meet expenses out of tax revenue, or should sell big bond issues to finance capital improvements; the truth of the matter seems to be that a preference for one or the other procedure is largely a matter of taste. Self-financing authorities, of course, must sell bonds. They are created for the purpose of constructing capital plant which the city cannot finance on its own resources or credit, and as fee collectors they are forbidden to poach on tax revenues.

There is much dispute over the planning aspect of city tax policy as a whole, argument as to whether industry flees high-tax cities and moves in on low-tax cities. In extreme cases, when "tax enclaves" have been carved out near cities, forming "industrial parks" where municipal government has little to do and thus little reason to tax, the tax pattern has undoubtedly determined the location of factories or even office space. But it seems unlikely that tax rates are as great a factor as the general health and soundness of the community. Low taxes and lawless slums will not draw companies away from areas with high taxes and well-ordered communities.

It is an error to believe that a city which needs, for example, a rapid-transit system, can save money by not building such facilities. The choice is merely between the financial cost of building and the social cost of failure to build. In many cities today, the failure to plan and build will cost much more than the expenses of intelligent urban renewal.

Historically, the specific planning function of the cities was customarily restricted to building codes and zoning laws. Both were usually written as the result of a hue and cry, to meet some immediately pressing problem, and neither necessarily served the long-term interests of the city. Some spectacular examples of bad judgment are on record. One of the sources of the traffic horror in Los Angeles and Washington is the zoning ordinance, which prohibited buildings of more than thirteen stories in either city (in Los Angeles for fear of earthquakes; in Washington to make sure national monuments would continue to dominate the skyline. London until 1958 similarly guaranteed the primacy of St. Paul's). The result was a failure to develop downtown density to the point where rapid transit would be feasible. More recently suburbs which zoned against all industry and even apartment houses, to maintain themselves as green communities of homeowners, have found themselves beaten and bruised by school taxes. Their representatives are to be found everywhere, hunting for investors or businessmen planning to erect multiple dwellings or factories.

Most cities, of course, were "laid out" by somebody at some time or another. Not until the period after the Second World War were "developers" willing to spend their own money on streets, and when new land was being opened up everyone had to know where the streets were going to be. Virtually every city in the United States was founded with the idea that it would grow to be a metropolis, and in the city's earliest days someone made a "plan" covering the area for miles around. William Penn's plan dominated the purely physical layout of Philadelphia for many years. Oglethorpe designed Savannah so well that the city's center has never deteriorated entirely. The famous L'Enfant plan for Washington was inevitably imitated all over America. August Woodward got his name on a street by laying out Detroit in a similar manner. The major influence on Seth Pease, who surveyed Cleveland in 1797, can be judged by the name he gave his main street—Euclid Avenue.

Unfortunately, nobody ever paid too much attention to the original plans for the cities when "practical considerations" interfered with their execution. Rectangular grid patterns were the most inexpensive to establish, and the national pattern was irrevocably set by the famous New York State commission of 1811, which divided New York into the grimmest of endless right angles. Most early plans were too good for the cities as they later developed, but the state plan for New York was so bad that it was eventually improved. Before the city had spread to that far north area, Central Park was removed from the grid and preserved by William Cullen Bryant and Frederick Law Olmstead.

Meanwhile, the Pennsylvania Railroad had run its tracks and built its station on L'Enfant's Mall in Washington; Chicago had grown up in haphazard rectangles around river channels, Philadelphia had made a rabbit warren of Penn's original project, and Boston had built up every possible yard of downtown, reclaiming land from the harbor when new yards were needed.

The original designs for American cities mostly predated the railroad, which quickly made hash of them. For the rest of the nineteenth century, there was little talk of planning. Theory held that economic forces were uncontrollable, and that any interference with the "natural" development of a city would produce disaster. New "subdivisions" were created to promote the profits of the subdividers. It was not until the last years of the century that civic leaders began to worry about the blight that natural development and the natural leapfrog had created. L'Enfant's original plans for Washington were restored, more or less in order, though the southeast and southwest quadrants were allowed to continue in squalor. In New York the Park Avenue railroad tracks were covered for nearly three miles, allowing the development of the city's swankiest residential street. Boston created the belt of parks which still works to restrict the size of the blighted inner ring; Kansas City and Cleveland renewed or built boulevards. The destruction of downtown San Francisco by earthquake allowed Daniel Burnham to create the charming layout of America's most popular city as late as

1906; and in 1909 the same great architect proposed for Chicago the first fully developed city plan, never achieved but partially realized in the preservation of Grant Park, the widening of Michigan Boulevard and the creation of the Wacker Drive.

Except for Burnham's superbly imaginative Chicago plan, however, none of these turn-of-the-century proposals could be related to the economic forces which were shaping cities. Moving Washington's railroad station out of the Mall was necessary; placing it where Union Station is today set an artificial eastern boundary on the city center and virtually guaranteed the northward spread of the southeast blight. Similarly, the placement of Grand Central and Pennsylvania stations in New York assured the unbelievable congestion of midtown Manhattan between Lexington and Seventh avenues. Even at their best, these American imitations of Baron Haussmann could do no more than beautify a small section of center city, while the rot spread out the ring.

The possible effects of zoning were grievously limited by the constitutional and practical prohibitions of legislation *ex post facto*. If the slaughterhouse was there, it would do no good to zone an area for residence. Zoning in already developed areas became an infiltrated Maginot Line, a desperate effort to prevent further deterioration. Only recently have cities moved the next step, writing zoning laws so that existing exemptions apply only to existing tenants, whose eventual removal from the property must restore the land to higher uses.

Building codes come with zoning, but except where frivolities like height and bulk regulation become causes of uneconomic sprawl the code tends to influence architecture more than development. Where different areas have developed at different times, however, the changes in building codes can make fascinating changes in vista. The Wall Street area, midtown Fifth Avenue and Park Avenue between

Grand Central and Sixtieth Street were developed under different codes, and an experienced man could write the codes from looking at the buildings, the way a conductor can sketch a score from hearing a piece of music.

Today such piecemeal devices are history. The flies can no longer hope to conquer the flypaper. Central city is not the metropolitan area, and acting by itself cannot even approach a solution to urban problems. Taxes, zoning laws, building codes, local improvements—all must be co-ordinated to meet the needs of the area as a whole. The argument is painfully obvious, so obvious that nobody argues back. But, except in isolated places like Miami, Baltimore and Toronto, nobody seems to be doing much about it either.

Some of the horrors perpetrated by the absence of central jurisdiction are beyond the power of description to add or detract. We have towns which dump their sewage into the river used for water supply or recreation by towns downstream. One city closes its parks to residents of another. Public hospitals stand underoccupied beside boundary lines across which sick people are sleeping in hallways. Highways peter out suddenly into lanes. Adjacent small school districts run inefficiently small schools with inefficiently large administrative staffs, and cannot be persuaded to amalgamate. (In both California and New York, state governments have been forced to rewrite their aid-to-education formulas to force school consolidation.) Sales taxes apply in one part of a metropolitan area, but not in others. The same house on the same acreage of land may receive radically different valuation for tax purposes in different parts of the same metropolitan area.

As suburbanization proceeds, the wealth of the area tends to move from the crowded, slum-ridden central city out to other political jurisdictions. The other political jurisdictions need money, too, of course, but central city needs it worse.

Police, fire, welfare, traffic problems are overwhelmingly severe in low-income, high-density areas, and the central city almost by definition has the monopoly on those. Taxes pile on taxes to pay the city's necessary expenses, urgent matters are patched together (most of the time successfully, as Professor Wood points out), and little is done about long-term problems. Indeed, some of the taxes, in the outer municipalities as well as the cities, operate to make the prospect more desperate. Everybody taxes the railroads, as a matter of tradition and habit, and when new money must be found it seems easiest to hit the railroads once again. Trains are dropped, sometimes tracks torn up and rights-of-way sold, and the absolutely necessary "rapid transit" of the metropolitan area sinks into bankruptcy. Thank God the railroads had a lot of fat on them when the slicing started, or most would have disappeared already.

The apolitical public authority, set up across municipal lines to handle a single aspect of the city's problem, often compounds the over-all confusion while doing its own job adequately. The bridge-and-tunnel authority makes money while the local transit goes broke. The highway authority looks for new ways to spend its profits while the traffic authority wonders how it can move and garage the cars entering the city, and the railroad schemes to eliminate passenger service. Each authority sells its own bonds, often with no more backing than its own credit, and thereafter by the terms of the bonds (the "preclusions") it must act as a private enterprise rather than as a part of metropolitan government. Nobody can make a rational accounting of the city's resources and needs, because too many different entities drain the varied resources and meet the different needs.

Cities today are too large to be governed "from the grass roots"; we lose infinitely more than we gain by clinging to the concept of the small political jurisdiction where people vote as neighbors on matters of common interest. All such people have other neighbors they ignore. Policy must be made for the area as a whole, reflecting the political sentiments of the area as a whole. In each metropolitan area, government must be strong and centralized. (Significantly, the most thorough recent research job on the sort of government a city should have, which produced the new charter of Philadelphia, came down strongly on the side of a very powerful mayor, with responsibility and authority reaching into the nooks and crannies of administration.) Cities today are big, highly diversified service industries, and must be run as such.

Metropolitan area government is inevitable. The sooner it comes, the better the cities our children will enjoy. It is a great mistake to look upon "Metro," as the Miamians call their new experiment with the form, as a way of saving money. The salaries that might be eliminated by reorganization are an infinitesimal part of the cost of government, and the possibilities for planning opened by Metro will more than absorb any savings. But the money will be well spent, which is the sole criterion of real cost. Nearly two hundred years ago, the conservative leaders of the United States found that the Articles of Confederation did not work and wrote a Constitution. It is up to the conservative leaders of today, with their deeper understanding of practicalities, their well-developed self-interest, to promote the metropolitan area government of the future.

# 6. *The Balance Sheet*

It is hard to avoid a gloomy tone when speaking of our cities as they are today. The only future which the present can envisage, unless extraneous assumptions are introduced, is a future in which the known trend lines are extended out toward the horizon. And the trend lines in our cities, as an endless stream of critics keep pointing out, all seem to point outward and downward.

Our cities were built to a pattern of single-core-and-rings development, with density gradually decreasing but always high. For a generation the density of central city has been diminishing, and metropolis has been sprawling all over the countryside.

Our cities were built by and for sweated labor. A more humane age will not tolerate such working conditions, and demands a more decent home life to boot.

Our cities were built around the railroad and the river. Today a majority of the population and a rising proportion of the goods travel by road.

Our cities were built at a time when planning was something that emperors did in France; at a time when space was no problem, the country was full of it. Today we are approaching a time when there will be no sensible place to which a community can move on, once it has fouled its current environment.

Our cities were built in days when government served only a housekeeping function, which could be chopped into any number of convenient pieces. Now municipalities must succor the sick and feed the impoverished, maintain the flow of traffic, deliver water and remove wastes, educate everybody to the end of adolescence, and plan for the future of entities far larger than themselves.

The balance sheet as the critics see it—not without reason—shows a few depreciating assets against a list of rapidly compounding liabilities. With a few brave exceptions, who call attention to horrors in hopes that a St. George will be summoned up to stab them, the critics promptly retreat into Utopias, the making of ideal models which could come into being only after a war had destroyed everything else (and everybody else, too).

Yet there are few liabilities the cities suffer that could not be overbalanced, and rather quickly, too, by the application of intelligence and money. Both are now available in quantity for the sane reconstruction of our cities. Often the intelligence employed is that most effective variety—angry intelligence, which insists that things must be done however the committee votes, and bullies the worriers into action.

Many of the trend lines which lead to slums and stagnation can easily be reversed; some of them, in fact, will reverse by themselves during the next decade, even if little effort is put into saving our cities. Apart from the famous examples of death and taxes, every problem bears the seeds of a possible solution. What has made so many people so gloomy about the future of the cities is the fact— always true, into antiquity, and not surprising—that problems are easier to see than solutions.

Let us look, then, at what can be done, with confidence that much of it will be done. We may not be very bright, but we know enough to come in out of the rain.

First things first: obviously, the population growth. We do not know how considerable the population gain will be; we can be relatively certain only that the official projections are wrong, because they have always been wrong in the past. Unfortunately, they have not been consistent; sometimes they understate, sometimes they overestimate.

But all the people who will form households during the next fifteen years are already here. We can say with some certainty, barring war, that 1975 will see at least ten million more American households than we have today. With farm technology still improving, and small towns losing their function, it seems clear that the entire net gain will settle in and around the cities.

Everybody knows about the "population bomb." Indeed, the critics who see an unholy urban sprawl on the face of America build their trend lines on the numbers of new households. But the households in being ten years from now will not come in the same sizes and shapes as today's households. The key fact for the next decade is that an actual majority of the additional households will consist of adults *without* minor children. During the next ten years, then, there is a guaranteed growing demand for urban housing, convenient to work and recreation, from families whose children have grown up and from new families which for one reason or another have not yet produced offspring. And demand creates supply.

"Other than our population growth," writes H. Bruce Palmer, president of the Mutual Benefit Life Insurance Company, "the most explosive force in our economy is the federal highway building program." Bull's-eye. Fifty billion dollars is to be spent by the federal government in the next ten years, to build some forty-one thousand miles of superhighways. There has been a great deal of argument about whether or not billboards shall be allowed beside these roads, but not nearly enough discussion of what we wish to do with this enormous addition to our national resources.

Mr. Palmer has put the matter precisely. "In industrially mature areas, surrounding our urban centers," he writes, "the new highways will generate renewal of whole sections of cities. In new and virgin routes, highways cutting through the countryside, acting as huge conveyor belts, will also cut across every preconceived idea we ever had of 'grassroots' America. If future America is built to a width of two to five miles each side of the conveyor belts, we will have a new national main street carrying with it an ever-deepening mixture of motels, filling stations, garages, carhops, outdoor theatres, and creating in its wake a new kind of community which would have no mayor, no ordinances, no sewage disposal plants, and perhaps no civic pride.

"With all this at stake," Mr. Palmer continues, "we have not yet answered some simple questions:

1. Should the interchanges of the new federal highway program be planned inside or outside of our urban areas?

2. How can the great national programs of urban renewal and highways, working simultaneously in many areas, be coordinated so that the local economic usefulness of existing urban centers is enhanced? Certainly both of these national programs should not be carried out in opposition to each other.

3. In our urban redevelopment planning, how can we compensate in both the public and private sectors for a potentially successful highway program as contrasted to a dismal outlook for mass rapid transit?

4. How will local communities finance terminal facili-

ties for the vehicles coming off the new highways into urban centers and provide funds for improvements to local streets and roads?

5. How can urban areas provide for the housing and commercial relocation of people displaced by the new highways?

6. How can we avoid through proper planning, zoning and subdividing control, the undesirable results of land pollution, urban sprawl, and elimination of large areas from the tax rolls with no equivalent tax return possible as a consequence of the highway building?"

Mr. Palmer concludes with a warning: "Once highways are built, they are there for years. We cannot afford mistakes."

This is money talking, not government; this is the private enterpriser. Wise men will pay careful attention to him.

All the questions Mr. Palmer asks are real and important, and must be answered. More important to our present concerns, however, is Mr. Palmer's stress on the enormous motive power provided by fifty billion dollars of construction money and its inescapable impact on the cities. For the new highways, like the railroads, must have termini. Inevitably, they will run, from city to city. And their influence on the future development of our cities will be little less than the influence of the railroad on the city of the nineteenth century.

Some cities have already been revitalized by expressways. Utica, New York, where I own property, was dying on its feet, until the New York State Thruway came by and alerted not only outsiders but natives to the possibilities of the town. Before the Thruway, I had been in Syracuse or over Syracuse many times, on my way west; but the first time I was ever awake in Syracuse and looked around at it was when I turned off at one of the half-dozen Thruway interchanges that serve the city. Think what it will mean to Norfolk when the tunnel is completed under Hampton Roads and the port is linked by expressway along the Atlantic Coast, from Miami and Jacksonville and the Carolinas, through Delaware to Philadelphia, New York and points north!

Federal aid is available to the cities for the construction of access roads, arterial rings to channel highway traffic around or into downtown. Kansas City has already torn down some of its worst slums and replaced them with federally sponsored highway; and, inevitably, along the new highways a better grade of structure is rising on revalued land. Even so stodgy a city as Columbus, Ohio—so conservative a city as Indianapolis—so hideous a city as Gary —will work to get the maximum benefits from the highways which are coming. Miami's new metropolitan area government, all bright-eyed and bushy-tailed, seems to be planning almost a new city around several big redevelopment programs—and the new expressways. Santa Monica's plan for its future rests squarely on the new expressway which will link the city with Los Angeles for the first time (there is no tolerable east-west road in Los Angeles today). And the new road to O'Hare and beyond may free Chicago's northland from its crowded clinging to the lakefront.

Political prediction is much trickier, but even here there are grounds for optimism. It is true that local sentiment tends to run against the idea of metropolitan area government, to cherish the small, inefficient municipal unit—"a poor thing, but mine own." What has held back the cities, however, is less the attitude of the local voters than the attitude of the state government. And the coming decade will surely see a great reform in state legislatures.

Typically in America today, the city dweller pays taxes to support public services for the rural family. Virtually all the state governments are gerrymandered to give rural areas at least veto power over all expenditure of money. (In the extreme case, Georgia, three counties with a thousand inhabitants each cast as great a vote in the election of a governor as the city of Atlanta.) For the last generation, the pattern of representation in state legislatures has been demonstrably unjust. It becomes more unjust every year, and pressure for change accumulates. The 1960 Census should remove the safety valve and set off an explosion which will at the least clear a path for state tax revenues to flow to the metropolitan areas. Unfortunately, central city as well as the farm country showed losses in the Census returns. And unless the suburban areas are willing to accept the fact of their dependence on metropolis the cities may find themselves with even less legislative influence than they have today.

Meanwhile, the obvious need for action has moved businessmen like Mr. Palmer to work in metropolitan area planning groups and committees. Mr. Palmer's city is Newark, and his committee there has put together and built a fifty-million-dollar, sixty-five-acre project involving a factory, public and middle-income housing, churches, a school, a swimming pool and so forth. "The aim," Mr. Palmer writes, "is not to preserve our cities as they are, but to change them to conform to the degree of specialization required in our modern industrial exchange economy."

The employment of such techniques has been spurred by ACTION, a group originally formed in Philadelphia and now operating nationally to encourage metropolitan studies, plans and, of course, action. Regional plan groups long dormant have come to life again, new groups have been formed and in many instances given official status. It is said that these groups are dominated by "selfish interests." Fine. (Though it is true that one must beware the man, especially the politician or the promoter, who has devoted his life to being a crook.) What the cities need is more long-

106

term, intelligent selfishness on the part of the business community.

With the opening of state purses, and the chance of area-wide evaluation and tax policies offered by the new planning groups, we may even see progress in the field of municipal finance. Writing in *Urban Land,* George W. Mitchell of the Federal Reserve Bank of Chicago has proposed a logical division of municipal costs among various revenue sources. The real property tax, he suggests, should be asked to cover only the costs of "general government," which he defines as "paying the mayor's salary, running the court system, and the like; fire protection, which is fairly costly; police protection; and . . . items of this general order." Other necessary metropolitan services, he argues, should be provided on a fee basis. "The obvious candidates are water service, already on a fee basis in a great many communities; sewage service, which can be proportioned to the water charge; garbage service, which even now is often treated on this basis; and provision for the construction of local streets on a special assessment basis. The special assessment was badly abused in the '20's, but there is nothing wrong with it as a financing device."

All other municipal duties Mitchell lumps under a heading of "income redistributing functions . . . health, education and welfare." Mitchell believes that the concentration of these taxes in central-city areas is one of the reasons for the migration of industry to the suburbs—especially where, as in the Chicago area, tax havens have been made available by gerrymandering. "There are many people who pay these taxes who receive no direct benefits. So these 'welfare' type expenditures are of no immediate or positive interest to many taxpayers, who will seek to avoid them if they can." Here, Mitchell argues, the solution "is to pay for these 'redistributive functions' by taxes levied at the state or national level." Locating the bill for such governmental duties in the larger political jurisdiction would assure a more equitable balance of the tax burden. It might also eliminate some of the tax advantage which backward communities now enjoy when compared with the more enlightened northern cities.

"The changes I suggest," Mitchell concludes, "are no doubt radical. No one, including myself, expects them to occur rapidly or on a wholesale scale; but I am convinced they will occur. We are already seeing some of these changes taking place. Adopted in their entirety, I believe they point toward a solution to these very difficult problems."

Amen.

Even the transit situation, the darkest facet on the diamond of our cities, is not entirely hopeless. Everyone knows today that the old central-city pattern cannot be made to work unless something is done to make midtown convenient by some method other than the automobile to the doorstep. Few cities have the funds (or the imagination) to project fully developed new transit systems built on today's cost structure. (San Francisco is an honorable exception.) But at least ninety cities have been working over variants of Victor Gruen's plan for Fort Worth, which places multistory garages and terminals for high-speed busses at the periphery of downtown, and then funnels the crowds to work or to shop on traffic-free plazas via short-run, conveniently slow mass transit.

One possible cure for transit sickness is the combination of the automobile expressway and the transit line. Chicago's new Congress Street Expressway offers eight lanes of highway separated by a pair of tracks in the middle, with access to the transit stations from the bridges over the road. A similar system has been in operation for some years near Stockholm. Even where the highways are already built and their rights-of-way filled from edge to edge, the elevated

108

monorail might take some of the traffic. A monorail down the Santa Ana Freeway would get people from the fantastically growing southeast suburbs to Los Angeles far quicker than they can now hope to travel by car at rush hour. One of the existing Los Angeles freeways has bus stops on special lanes, demonstrating that the needs of the non-motorist were not entirely forgotten. Perhaps the new east-west freeways still on the drawing boards could be planned to offer something quicker, and less dependent on traffic conditions, than the overburdened bus.

Another possible solution for long-haul mass transit is what the planners call "VTO aircraft"—for Vertical Take-Off, meaning helicopters. With the experience of earth-bound traffic jams before us, we are not likely to permit unlimited private use of helicopters into the cities. Helicopters which could carry as many people as a good-sized bus might zip in and out of downtown on continuous operation, carrying thousands every day. So far such helicopters are not feasible technically, but they may be completely practical a decade from now.

Much of our thinking about transit problems is dominated by the visible limits to what can be done here and now. The city is an ancient form of government. The railroad has not been changed greatly in a hundred years; or the automobile, in fifty. Working with the resources of half a century ago is not a promising way to solve today's problems.

How the transit picture will look in the year 2000 is not something that anyone can sensibly predict today. We can be sure only that it is beyond our imaginings. Some time during the next few years we will remember that we are living in the second half of the twentieth century and that technology is no great shakes any more. When our best engineering and organizing minds come to answer the mass transit question, we may find ourselves wondering what we were so worried about back in 1960.

Economic prediction is among the inalienable rights of free-born Americans. It is probably the most common single parlor game played in academic circles, and decades of experience with it have made everyone a little cautious about projecting trends. Unlike some other investors, I think we must suffer in the 1960's a depression more serious than anything experienced in the 1950's. I believe in the inevitability of cyclical movement, and I cannot see how a mankind rational enough to avoid war can avoid the natural cycle of economic events. Whether the economy booms along or rides a roller coaster, however, the cities must benefit.

Continued prosperity will take the sting out of the current arguments about the extent to which the national wealth should be devoted to producing private consumer goods or public capital assets. Our over-all level of consumption is now so high that a proportion of increased production from continued prosperity could be diverted to solutions for urban problems without any consumer feeling a personal pinch. Indeed, the last decade has seen a process of this sort in motion: state and local budgets have risen far faster, in proportion, than either the federal budget or the national income—and will doubtless continue to do so.

A slump, on the other hand, will demand rapid action by the government to avoid or reduce unemployment. We no longer hear so much as we used to about the backlog of school projects, highway programs, hospital plans, conservation and antipollution projects which the government supposedly has filed away against the day when vast public investment might be required to maintain the base of the economy. But there can be no doubt that governments would react quickly in the 1960's to any radical deterioration in the market place. Because more than two-thirds of the population now live in metropolitan areas (and the metropolitan areas would be hit worst by a slump, the farm community having been well squeezed out by technology during the boom), most of the money for public works would go straight into urban construction and reconstruction.

Isolated economic influences, of course, will help or harm specified cities and areas. The St. Lawrence Seaway will grow in importance during the decade, stimulating still further growth in the industrially dominant North Central States. Chicago and Cleveland especially must benefit from the increase in Lakes traffic; and Detroit may make up its losses from the decline of local automobile production through gains as the port of access to a developing peninsula. Predictions that the Seaway would hurt New York and Boston have already proved false; but Philadelphia and Baltimore, caught between the Lake ports and the inevitable great growth of Norfolk, may suffer more than anyone has yet guessed. (It is interesting to note in this connection the Norfolk and Western's recent acquisition of the Virginia Rail Road and its attempts to absorb the Nickle Plate. Note also the efforts of the Chesapeake and Ohio, centered in Norfolk though corporate headquarters are elsewhere, to gain control over the Baltimore and Ohio.)

Other port cities are sure to benefit by the gradual redirection of American trade. Miami and New Orleans are inevitable centers for growing trade with South and Central America; Seattle will be the natural port of entry from Alaska, and San Francisco from Hawaii. Silly as it may seem from a logical point of view, the admission of these territories as states guarantees the expansion of their economies.

Mid-continent is the sure bet. Here, in the great belt running Houston-Fort Worth-Dallas-Tulsa-Kansas City-Wichita-Omaha-Des Moines-Tri-City-Minneapolis-St. Paul, America still has wide-open spaces. Here the new highway program will open up areas near cities which have been handicapped by inadequate local transportation. Their location makes them natural centers for the airlines, and most of them are already railroad hubs.

Growth of river traffic, too, will build older cities into new metropolises. The decade after the Second World War saw a fantastic rise in traffic on the Ohio. The decade following the completion of Chicago's deep-water canal from the Great Lakes to the Mississippi must see a similar expansion of traffic on that Mother of Waters. Others will open up in turn, from the Mississippi west—the Missouri, the Arkansas, the Red—when the flood-control people and the Corps of Engineers have done their work.

Finally, the South, unless it permits its peculiar notions on race relations to strangle its economy, must firmly join the twentieth century during the next decade. Atlanta has already done so, establishing itself as the service station for the enormous area between Memphis and the sea.

Even the drain to the suburbs seems likely to assume different forms in the decade to come. As noted earlier, the predictable change in household composition will create greater demand for urban housing rather than tracts in the suburbs. Even those whose demographic position would indicate a *drang nach suburbia* may decide to remain within city limits rather than move out to the edges as those edges recede farther and farther from downtown. The open spaces near the cities are rapidly disappearing, and civic pressure, one hopes, will reserve some of the few remaining unsectioned areas for human recreation. In new housing, then, the choice is likely to be among city apartment houses, near-suburban apartment houses, or private homes way out in left field. The swing back toward apartment construction has been in progress for half a dozen years. Even in Los Angeles, the balance has already tipped, and more than half the new housing units fall in multifamily dwellings rather than on individual plots of land.

112

Greater density of residence in the suburbs will be matched by rising business density. As Raymond Vernon has pointed out, many smaller businesses have remained in central city simply because central city offered relatively cheap loft accommodations. In the years ahead older suburban plants will be abandoned by their present owners, seeking larger or better facilities, and will become available in pieces to urban small business at something resembling city rents. Meanwhile, a number of the older city lofts will be destroyed in the course of urban renewal and highway construction programs. The tide of small business runs out toward the suburb.

As their populations increase, the major metropolitan areas will *need* subcores in the suburbs. New York is generally taken as identical with Manhattan, but much of its industry has been scattered across the three rivers for many years—and its business section has developed independent centers in Brooklyn, Jersey City and Newark. No one downtown can serve an area as large as the New York metropolis. Even smaller cities have long-established subcore developments—San Francisco, for example, in Berkeley and Oakland; Boston in Cambridge and Brookline; Kansas City in its Kansas twin. Indeed, from a city planning point of view, there is much to be said for reserving the central core to the city's most important operations, which demand the greatest variety of talent and the quickest communications, while lesser enterprises find their homes in subcenters. Economically, New York has the healthiest midtown in America— the amount of construction in it since the war must be seen to be believed—but distant subcenters like White Plains and Hempstead have been thriving, too. The cities which are likely to be in trouble are those which have been growing rapidly without a core, such as Phoenix, where the new "Central Office Buildings," the most imposing structures in town, are going up some eight miles from a decaying central core.

The healthy American city of the future, then, will see a downtown devoted to corporate offices, professional offices, government, retail trade and entertainment; ringed by great expressways feeding into convenient peripheral garages, but also approachable by clean, quick mass transit; and on foot from the great new "middle-income" housing projects which

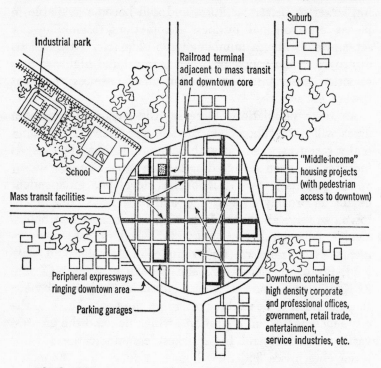

The healthy American city of the future will look like this.

have replaced the inner "gray belt"; surrounded by suburbs clustered about subcores like electrons about a nucleus; governed as an entity, in all important matters, by a responsible "Metro." The vision of this city must be placed on the left-hand side of the balance sheet by anyone who wants to audit the books.

114

Such a vision is like an entry for "goodwill": it may or may not be real. But the trend lines do not necessarily lead to real outcomes either. Blight can always be explained after it exists, but the blight itself was never inevitable. "The fault, dear Brutus . . ." The rise and decay of cities and empires is caused, doubtless, by external forces which cannot be wholly controlled. It is man's reaction to the operation of these forces, however, which determines how greatly they help or how severely they hinder the pursuit of happiness. Dedicated, intelligent, angry men can shape and direct the forces in their own environment. Our history is full of proofs for the proposition.

And all over America today dedicated and intelligent and angry men are guiding the reconstruction of the blighted areas in our cities. It is the persistence, spread and increasing size of urban renewal programs that makes our vision of the healthy city a real asset to balance against the much-touted realities of urban decline.

# 7. *Urban Renewal*

Because so much publicity has been given to so many expensive, large-scale projects, most people tend to regard urban renewal as some new god from the machine of government, riding in at the end of the story on a bolt of lightning, his wonders to work. The most important part of urban renewal, however, occurs quietly, simply as a matter of course. Whenever an owner redecorates the lobby of his building or cleans its outer walls, whenever a householder repaints his porch, whenever the city fills a pothole in a road, the work of urban renewal is accomplished. Cities, like all other capital assets, are kept in working order by routine maintenance; if the maintenance were better, we would need far fewer "urban renewal" projects. In my career as an investor, I have only lately become involved in major building projects, but I consider myself an urban renewer, because I have substantially refurbished, beautified and increased the utility of almost all the other properties I own.

Let the reader beware, then. The tearing down and building up of blockfronts relates to a city's health exactly as surgery relates to the health of a man. It is a dramatic process, and to do it well requires imagination first of all and then great skill, sensitivity and delicacy of touch. But it should be undertaken only as a last resort, after other treatments have failed. Ill-done, or ill-timed, or ill-planned "urban renewal" may do more harm than good. They call it "a slum before the last brick is in place," describing the results of architectural sterility and poor or piecemeal planning.

Once the warning has been entered, it is safe to say that many areas in many of our cities are so badly deteriorated that only major surgery will save them. In some places structures are so old, or were so poorly built, that maintenance expense is wasted money. Again, some neighborhoods have grown so foul that people do not wish to live beside them, and the cancer must be cut away. (With all due regard for the sympathies and opinions of the critics who denounce the "bulldozer school" of urban renewal, most of our cities have neighborhoods with a "character" that *should* be destroyed.) Elsewhere, changes in the city's economy or in industrial technology have made existing structures or patterns of structures obsolete; and the ground must be plowed and planted afresh.

Again, what is new is the magnitude rather than the nature of the problem. Again, too, Raymond Vernon has put the matter most concisely. "Almost from the moment the first house was erected, the first street laid, and the first drainage ditch dug in any of these embryo cities," he wrote in his CED pamphlet, "a process of obsolescence took hold. . . . This obsolescence, one should note, developed not only in the private structures but also in the public domain. It was not only that the first dwelling soon became inadequate by the standards of the people who lived in the city, but also that the street layouts, the sewage systems, and the water supply systems also became obsolescent. Almost from the first, then, there was rebuilding as well as building: a tearing down and reordering of structures and public facilities.

117

'New York will be a great city,' a visiting Englishman remarked a century ago, 'when it gets built.'

"In the course of this building and rebuilding, however, the general tendency was to add to the ossification of the structure: to surface the public streets more permanently and to cram their sub-surface with more and more cables, mains and transit conveyances; to replace wood dwellings with stone, and one-story structures with three- and four-story dwellings and factories. Each rebuilding, therefore, tended to make the next one a little more difficult than the last."

Before this century physical circumstance forced rebuilding of many areas near the center of the city, however expensive it might be. Tied to existing lines of transportation, business and industry could not simply depart their obsolete haunts and set up shop elsewhere. Though the inner-ring residences deteriorated, middle-class city dwellers could not fly too far from the center of town. Leapfrogging developed new areas, but the simple utility of downtown land prevented too wide a spread of the blighted "gray belts."

During the last generation, for the first time, it has been possible for American urbanites to do what the pioneer farmers did: ruin one patch of land and then move on to another. Failure of maintenance during the depression and the Second World War accelerated the decline of formerly decent business and residential areas. And the apparent shift from the "transit city" to the "automobile city" has made a sham of the city's "circulatory" and "respiratory" systems. Actually sound structures *seem* obsolete. Expanded Negro migration jammed the already deteriorated gray belt, the middle classes departed in flocks for the suburbs, industry went out to the ranch-factory *cum* parking lot, business began to wonder whether it might not be possible to draw to an out-of-town site the white-collar workers necessary to man the office machines. Blight spread visibly, and the city

118

fathers began to look around them. What they saw horrified them, and the shiny new projects rising today in dozens of American cities are the first fruits of this horrified exploration of ten years ago.

Today we know that the flight from the cities was a mistake—individually for many of the people who flew, collectively for the nation as a whole. Downtown land is as much a national asset as forest land; both must be conserved and in extremity restored. The first large governmental body to see the problem whole was the state of Pennsylvania, which in 1945 adopted an "Urban Redevelopment Law." Section 2 of the Act is the manifesto of urban renewal, stating the facts and suggesting the remedies with great economy and intelligence, and it deserves to be quoted at length:

It is hereby determined and declared as a matter of legislative finding:

(a) That there exist in urban communities in this Commonwealth areas which have become blighted because of the unsafe, unsanitary, inadequate or overcrowded condition of the dwellings therein, or because of inadequate planning of the area, or excessive land coverage by the buildings thereon, or the lack of proper light and air and open space, or because of the defective design and arrangement of the buildings thereon, or faulty street or lot layout, or economically or socially undesirable land uses.

(b) That such conditions or a combination of some or all of them have and will continue to result in making such areas economic or social liabilities, harmful to the social and economic well-being of the entire communities in which they exist. . . .

(c) That the foregoing conditions are beyond remedy or control by regulatory processes in certain blighted areas, or portions thereof, and cannot be effectively dealt with by private enterprise under existing law without the additional aids herein granted, and that such conditions exist chiefly in areas which are so subdivided into small parcels and divided ownership that their assembly for purposes of clearance, replanning and redevelopment is difficult and impossible without the effective public power of eminent domain.

(c-1) That certain blighted areas, or portions thereof, may require total acquisition, clearance and disposition. . . .

(d) That the acquisition and sound replanning and redevelopment of such areas in accordance with sound and approved plans for their redevelopment will promote the public health, safety, convenience and welfare.

Therefore, it is hereby declared to be the policy of the Commonwealth of Pennsylvania to promote the health safety and welfare of the inhabitants thereof by the creation of bodies corporate and politic to be known as Redevelopment Authorities, which shall exist and operate for the public purposes of the elimination of blighted areas. . . . Such purposes are hereby declared to be public uses for which public money may be spent and private property may be acquired by the exercise of the power of eminent domain.

This law and its imitators grant large powers to the authorities which are to renew the cities. They may determine by fiat, with the consent of the locality, which areas of a city require redevelopment; and then they may decide which structures in the area are to be taken away from their owners and which may be retained; which land is to pass to government ownership, and which to be resold to private parties; what is to stand on this lot, and what may not stand on that one. Recently I purchased a building in Cincinnati, which stands virtually in the middle of redevelopment plans; if that city's planners had decided to incorporate my land in their projects, they could have taken the building away from me overnight, leaving me no recourse but complaint to the courts about the price I was offered.

These powers are constitutional. The owners of a department store in Washington, D.C., appealed to the courts against the expropriation of their property for a District urban renewal project. They won in the District Court, but the Supreme Court laid down against them the law of the land.

120

"Experts concluded," Justice William O. Douglas wrote for a unanimous bench, "that if the community were to be healthy, if it were not to revert again to a blighted or slum area, as though possessed by a congenital disease, the area must be planned as a whole. It was not enough, they believed, to remove existing buildings that were unsanitary or unsightly. It was important to redesign the whole area so as to eliminate the conditions that cause slums. . . . If the Agency considers it necessary in carrying out the redevelopment project to take full title to the real property, it may do so. . . . If those who govern the District of Columbia decide that the Nation's capital should be beautiful as well as sanitary, there is nothing in the Fifth Amendment that stands in the way."

In those states which have adopted urban renewal laws, then (and notice that cities cannot act by themselves), government has all the power it needs to restore the cities. All but eight of the fifty states have adopted such laws, and of the eight holdouts only one, Florida, has a large city within its borders.

The people have the power to build cities in which their children can happily live and work and multiply. What they lack are the plans, and the funds . . . and the recognition that their peril requires a compromise with "self-interest."

The politicians' complaints are all about the lack of funds, but in fact there is a lot of money around for urban renewal, even if not all of it bears this particular label in the budget. New expressways are prime urban renewal projects, but they are labeled "highway." The federal government, not making too much noise about the fact that urban expressways ride over the graves of slum housing, pays 90 per cent of the cost.

Private money is available in quantity. Everyone's ideal of an urban redevelopment project is Rockefeller Center, a wholly private operation. Among the projects considered at

the First International Seminar on Urban Renewal, held at
The Hague two years ago, was New York's Manhattan House
—luxury housing at seventy-five dollars a room per month,
but a major factor in the rapid upgrading of the East Seven-
ties. The apartment house stands on a site formerly occupied
by a streetcar barn, and occupies only 40 per cent of the land
area, the rest being devoted to planting and roadway. As
protection, the New York Life Insurance Company, which
owns the building, bought two of the four facing blockfronts,
and converted them attractively. Obviously, a building like
Manhattan House makes no contribution to solving the problem of housing the poor; but it is urban renewal, nonetheless,
and, like Rockefeller Center, can set off a chain reaction,
controlled, one hopes, within the strong framework of a far-
sighted master plan.

Other life insurance companies have been even more
active than the New York. In the years right after the war,
Metropolitan Life put up apartment developments in New
York and Los Angeles, and just outside Washington. Its New
York contribution, Stuyvesant Town, built with city help in
the form of tax abatements, takes in an eighteen-block area
which previously held more than five hundred antique structures, including slum housing for three thousand families.
Today thirty-five large apartment houses cover only a
quarter of the land area, and house twenty-five thousand
people. Significantly, one of the nearby public schools to
which many Stuyvesant Town children go is widely regarded by educators as the best, or at least one of the best,
in the city.

Prudential, now engaged in an enormous project near Boston's Back Bay, has built one of the nation's great office
buildings over the Illinois Central tracks beside the lake just
east of the Loop in Chicago. This area was by no means
run-down when Prudential began its project, but the
grandeur of the building, and the company's generosity in

supplying a lakeside floral park before it, act as guarantors for the future of Michigan Avenue.

In looking at redevelopment problems, we sometimes tend to neglect the fact that buildings erected for profit or use may serve renewal functions. Large sections of downtown Washington will be restored by federal office projects in the near future—and the fact that the new office buildings are going up because they are needed does not lessen their role as improvements to the land they occupy. In the years since the Second World War, we have averaged more than two billion dollars annually for new school buildings—many of them on blighted urban sites. "Civic Centers" are doubtless more glamorous, but many a post office constitutes redevelopment, too.

Mr. Palmer of Newark's Mutual Benefit Life estimates that the value of new construction during the next decade—counting factories, homes, schools, roads and so forth—will reach six hundred billion dollars. The figure will be all the more impressive for those who know that the total value of *all* existing buildings in the United States is estimated at five hundred billion. Much of this new money would go naturally into projects which serve the purposes of urban renewal—if the cities could make the investment attractive.

The tax money spent for urban renewal purposes—even if it expands to the three billion dollars yearly which is the wildest dream of the candidate for Congress—can be no more than seed corn in the revitalizing of our cities. The urban renewal program cannot have the purpose of "doing the job"; it must be designed to create an atmosphere in which private capital will do the job. Parts of what has to be done—especially those parts which deal with housing and recreation for the low-income third of the population—cannot be made appealing to investors and will require heavy government subsidy. Much of the rest can be done by the exercise of the power of eminent domain; the construction of public facilities which would have to be built even if there were no urban renewal program; and a steady, intelligent dribble of tax money. The "dribbles," of course, will be healthy chunks when looked at by themselves—ten, thirty, fifty million dollars each—but beside the flood of construction expenditure which will occur naturally, barring a depression, they are in truth nothing to get very excited about.

First, however, there must be plans—intelligent, imaginative, *detailed* plans. There is so much to be done in our cities that the demand for action is logical; we must start somewhere. But we are still at a stage where ten million dollars invested in planning would accomplish more than a hundred million in building.

Salvage operations either work or they don't, and when they don't the investment is lost. That the treasure is buried in the cities, often in the most disreputable places, is undeniable. But without a good map, considerable native wit and talent at the dowsing rod, the planning commissioners can dig forever without finding what they seek.

A dozen years ago Philadelphians, dazzled by the prospects opened up in the new state law, thought urban redevelopment would be relatively easy. Everybody knew the areas of town which were worst blighted. Tracts in the center of those areas would be torn up, new housing and associated service structures erected, and, as Redevelopment Coordinator William Rafsky put it in a rueful report in 1957, the "'island of good' would favorably affect 'the swamp of bad' immediately surrounding it. Unfortunately," Rafsky continued, "the reverse has proved true."

Slum clearance from the center of the slum tends to spread rather than eradicate blighted areas. Those evacuated from the project area must live somewhere, and they usually swarm into the already overcrowded houses on the

124

circumference of the project, making conditions in the area as a whole worse than they had been before. (Humane relocation has been one of the touchiest problems in urban renewal.) Because one of the aims of the project is the reduction of density, this added pressure on the periphery of the slum does not diminish when the housing project is completed and the dispossessed are allowed to return. Most of them, in fact, do not return: they have established themselves in what were once better neighborhoods, and are rapidly re-creating the slum the city has just "eliminated."

Many of the housing projects hope to draw middle-income residents; but middle-class people cannot be persuaded to move into the middle of a slum neighborhood, however new and shiny and equipped the project houses may be. If the new project does succeed in drawing a better-off community, that community must usually live in a state of siege. The Illinois Institute of Technology built a remarkably handsome new campus, with Mies van der Rohe designs—and then had to erect barbed-wire fences and patrol its borders with dogs. The neighborhood was that of the near South Side, the worst inner-ring slum in Chicago, and no amount of Mies architecture plunked in the middle of such a neighborhood was going to improve it.

"Slum clearance" in itself, then, was a failure. The new buildings tended to be settled in large part by new arrivals in the city, whose notions of maintenance were primitive. The vitality of the old slum was destroyed, and the mechanical "machines for living" which replaced the wretched tenements offered little of that reason for living which had kept the slum alive. Vandalism was commonplace. The new housing improved little more than the appearance of the tracts on which it was built.

Where slum clearance was successful, it was because the adjacent areas were decent in at least one direction. New

York's East River housing development, from Twenty-third Street to below Houston Street, has been far more successful than the East Poplar or Southwest Temple projects in Philadelphia, because it was not surrounded by slum. The river and its highway provided a pleasant boundary on one side and an easy escape. At the north, where the Metropolitan

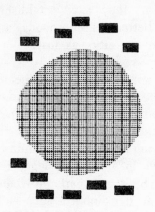
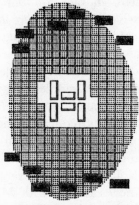

Overcrowding in slum area surrounded by better residential districts

Deterioration of periphery results from evacuation of residents of project area

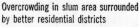

Slum clearance from center of slum may intensify blight conditions in the peripheral area.

Life projects were, the boundary was a hideous but new Veterans' Administration Hospital, Bellevue Hospital (redeveloping itself), and the spanking new N.Y.U. Medical School. To the west, the Metropolitan Life projects were protected by elegant Gramercy Park and the Stuyvesant Square area, which had never entirely deteriorated. Lower down the old East Side slums endangered the municipal projects, but much of the danger was removed by the fine International Ladies Garment Workers' high-rise co-operative apartment houses, which border the development at the south. Here, of course, there was an element of luck:

ILGWU members of middle-class standing could be drawn to the lower East Side without too great a worry about an adjacent slum, because so many of them had sprung from that slum themselves.

Philadelphia, again, was the first to learn the lesson. Rather than working from the inside of the slum out, the city planning commission in 1956 decided to work from the decent borders in. The new program would seek to enlarge the buffer between the good neighborhood and the slum and *prepare* the slum itself for a new life. A thorough survey of the city's housing needs preceded the decision, and left the city fathers hopeful rather than optimistic; the money necessary to do the full job was estimated at a billion dollars. But more than a hundred million dollars was available—two-thirds of it in federal funds—and the planning commission now knew how to spend it.

Reporting to the international conference at The Hague, Rafsky outlined what was to be done. The city would concentrate its efforts on "conservation areas. . . . Slum clearance powers," Rafsky wrote, "will be used to tear out the one or two bad spots in the particular neighborhood. Needed community facilities will be installed, and city services will be stepped up where necessary. The Housing Code will be used to put a floor under housing conditions. In addition, the government will use the various available aids to stimulate voluntary rehabilitation of houses to above-standard levels. . . . Business interests, both those within the neighborhoods and those concerned with investment anywhere in the city, will be encouraged to participate in the improvement effort in any way they can. . . .

"The work done will be 'anchored' to stable neighborhoods. It will not, as formerly, be surrounded by as yet untouched substandard conditions. Starting on the outskirts of the problem will protect the changes brought about from adverse influences. . . .

"In . . . conservation areas, an improvement here and there may be enough to do the job. Such improvements might be getting rid of a factory which is fouling a residential section with smoke and odor, or clearing up a traffic problem which is making living unpleasant for people there, or taking care of an isolated run-down house which is causing residents to think the neighborhood is not perhaps as good as it once was. Eliminating such problems may well save neighborhoods that are good but old. It can replace incipient blight with something that is good. . . .

"Meanwhile, the dilapidated or near-dilapidated areas, although not receiving full-scale treatment until later on, will not be wholly neglected. . . . Code enforcement will be stepped up, with concentrated enforcement campaigns scheduled successively. . . . The city plans to initiate a program of taking over tax delinquent property, clearing it, and making the land available for such use as a parking lot, or a playground, or perhaps a small park or play area. This latter device will minimize the impact of eventual redevelopment, spread the relocation of families over a longer period, and reduce the eventual cost of property acquisition. At the same time, creation of desperately needed open space will make the areas more livable right away."

Will it work?

Maybe.

*Can* it work?

Certainly. The Philadelphians know what they are doing. The new projects under the conservation program are being started adjacent to "stable neighborhoods or large parks or solid industry or something similar." And "every effort is being made to relate the program, where feasible, to the highway construction program." If Philadelphia can succeed in making a hundred million do the work of a billion, it will have shown the nation how to accomplish what has been too often described as an impossible job.

But lower-income housing and slum clearance must be no more than one part of the urban renewal effort. Fine residential areas do not guarantee the greatness of a city, though severely deteriorated housing can obviously harm its prospects. The activity downtown is the determinant of the city's health, and any urban renewal program must be based on an assured stimulus to downtown.

All the activities clustered together in the heart of town must figure in the renewal plan, and each must be supported separately.

The commercial function is probably the most important: downtown must be the place where local business has its offices and out-of-town business has its branches. To support this side of downtown, the city must supply enough good transit (preferably mass transit, though thruways and garages will do in smaller cities) to make sure that nobody will be too unhappy about going "into town" to work. Any urban renewal program which did not include ways and means to speed people into and out of downtown would be a waste of money.

Beyond transit, the city should not have to put money into the office building side of downtown. Income-producing properties are supposed to pay taxes, and can afford to pay a share of the cost of *good* transit. Where a building makes a contribution to the amenity of the area, however, by using only a fraction of its lot, some tax relief should be available. And temporary tax relief is legitimate as an inducement to a company to build in an area marked for redevelopment in the master plan. Moreover, where urban land is held in tiny parcels, which is the case in many large cities, government aid ought to be available for the builder who wishes to make an improvement in downtown. Condemnation proceedings are legitimately brought against the newly entrenched speculator or old dog-in-the-manger who holds out for an exorbitant price for his subsection of a large parcel, thereby endangering a project which will benefit the entire city.

Retailing needs even less help than general commerce. Transit, of course, is vital—and here, too, government help ought to be available in putting together parcels for projects which serve a community need but can be privately financed. A store which wants to build a garage for its customers ought to feel that the city planners are on its side.

Public office buildings, to house state, city and federal bureaus, should not be planned to occupy prime commercial space. Their role in the master plan should be as buffers, protecting the heart of downtown from any rot in the inner ring—convenient to transit and to retailing, but not the heart of a neighborhood. (They should elongate rather than square off downtown, because the long, narrow downtown permits easier handling of the automobile problem.) As Los Angeles experience so vividly demonstrates, the "Civic Center" so-called does not necessarily improve the area around it. Perhaps the new Los Angeles Civic Center, being constructed as part of a planned development, will exert a more beneficent influence. Such buildings, it must be remembered, do not pay taxes and should not take land which might otherwise produce great amounts of municipal revenue.

Cultural facilities, too, must fit into a plan, and cannot be relied upon to create good neighborhoods by themselves. Even universities, which represent a far greater concentration of cultured population than a museum or concert hall can hope to attract, have seen their surroundings deteriorate drastically in the last quarter-century. Chicago and Columbia have been the most advertised sufferers, but many major schools in older cities sit in the water in the same leaky boat. Again, planning can help: Westwood Village and UCLA have supported each other brilliantly, to give Los Angeles credit as well as blame.

Television has hurt downtown entertainment more seriously than most critics are willing to admit. There is little advantage to be gained by being the first on your block to have seen the latest Hollywood extravaganza, when everybody else is talking about last night's television special. Still, there is a large audience which wants to get out of the house; the moviemakers are complaining but, in fact, they're not starving. And, like any capital plant, downtown should be used continuously. There should be movie theaters in the new downtown—and restaurants, and legitimate theaters, and concert halls, and even honky-tonks and night clubs— if only to keep the roads and the garages and the transit system working when the office staff goes home.

Finally, the plan must leave room for people to *live* in or next door to downtown. The housing that clears the slums is essential to the sanitation of the city, but the new housing and easy walk from the office buildings feeds the city's growth. Future generations will find it hard to believe that there was once no major residential use of Kansas City's Quality Hill, Norfolk's Golden Triangle, New York's Coenties Slip, west-central New Haven. Not the least admirable aspect of the Bunker Hill Redevelopment in Los Angeles, the nation's largest single integrated urban renewal program, linking downtown with the new Civic Center, is its intelligent, attractive provision for middle-income housing smack in the middle of the area.

But there must be a plan—indeed, there must be many plans, all fitted to a master plan. Any major project anywhere in a city sends ripples of change through the surrounding neighborhoods; a major project downtown may influence the lives of everyone living in the city, not always for their foreseeable betterment.

Three and a half centuries ago John Donne in his *Devotions* urged all to remember that "no man is an islande," that we are all part of a mystic unity, and that anything which

131

damages one man damages all. In fact, however, man can usually regard with relative equanimity anything that happens to people far away. It is when the trouble comes to his own doorstep that he recognizes, in anguish or annoyance, the interdependence of the species, the poison that is another man's meat.

Slum clearance sends the slum dweller roaming the town in search of new lodgings, making his presence felt where it was not felt before. New highways debouching on downtown create traffic jams, unless someone has been foresighted enough to build garages. (And if the garages are built before the highways, they may draw new cars to downtown along the old streets, changing traffic patterns in such a way that the highway plans become outdated. Thus the Business Executives' Research Committee of Dallas complains that "with more parking facilities new problems have been created, such as the sudden jamming of the streets as the parking lots disgorge the vehicles at peak periods." And New York refused to adopt an ordinance requiring garage space in new office buildings, on the grounds that the garages would simply draw more cars into an already overcrowded downtown.) New buildings must have transit to service them, and new transit is inconceivable—as the "spread-out density" cities, Los Angeles and Washington and Phoenix, know to their sorrow—unless there are enough buildings about the transit stops to draw heavy traffic.

To make plans which recognize all the complex patterns of interrelation within the city is a job which requires a large staff, time, brilliant leadership, and—probably—the most modern data-processing equipment. The single master plan is not enough, however good the surveys on which it is based, however sound the projections of the future. To avoid dislocations which can wreck the projections, there must be what Stanley Pickett of Canada's Community Planning Association has called "an intermediate level of planning, which will take into account the complex interrelationships, the subtle shifts in habit and emphasis, the radiating secondary effects of the renewal proposals as far as they can be anticipated. . . . The concept of boundaries to a renewal scheme," Pickett added, "must be eliminated, for no matter how large an area is involved in the project, it will have a periphery somewhere and it is around that periphery that planning must anticipate change, if renewal action is to prosper. . . ."

Within Pickett's "planning districts," someone must make "horseback" or "windshield" surveys, determining the nature of the neighborhood as it exists and what should be done to improve its functioning. In many cases, conservation—a slight stepping up of maintenance expense—may remove the problem. Elsewhere, active rehabilitation is required; still elsewhere, everything must be razed and built anew. Wherever buildings are razed, the character of the neighborhood inevitably changes. If the land is to be cleared for highways, the planners must know the effects of these man-made topographical dividers upon the area as a whole; for housing, the sort of residential community that may reasonably be expected to live here; for industry, the economic and social impact of the plant to be built; for downtown, the traffic patterns which will be created. Perhaps no one but a seventh son of a seventh son should be encouraged to enter the work.

We should not have to guess at what the new Prudential development will do to Boston, or the Central Business District plan to Cincinnati, or the civic center to Seattle, or Saarinen's arch to St. Louis. We should know much more than we do. Funds for urban renewal have not been so great as the lover of cities might wish, but the shortage of building money has been far less severe, so far, than the shortage of planning money. We need enormous data files and precise analyses, the stuff of judgment. With all the information in the world, we would make mistakes, and certainly much of the money put into planning work would be wasted. But the mistakes would be far fewer, and the waste of money far less, than now seems likely.

Still, much information is already available. On the basis of the information we have, let us now look at nineteen American cities, one at a time, to assess their strengths and weaknesses, and try to tell their fortunes.

# PART II

# 8. Chicago

A deep love for the city of Chicago is not something everyone can achieve. In all countries, it is the secondary or inland metropolis (the Moscow rather than the St. Petersburg, the Lyons rather than the Paris, the Manchester rather than the London, the Berlin rather than the Hamburg, Chicago rather than New York) which concentrates and distills the national ethos and displays in glaring simplicity whatever faults the national character may have. When Fort Dearborn became Chicago, not much more than a hundred years ago, America was still a pretty raw country. Chicago grew up as a raw city. Seventy years of conscious cultivation by some of the nation's richest and most able men (cultivation which began, essentially, with the Columbian Exposition of 1893) have not entirely covered over the rawness.

Part of the problem is that the city grew so rapidly. In 1870, when Mrs. O'Leary's cow was practicing her kicking, Chicago had a population of less than 300,000. A decade later, when the postconflagration cleanup was about complete, the population was over 500,000. By 1890, it had passed the million mark.

Inland city for the nation that spanned a continent: little

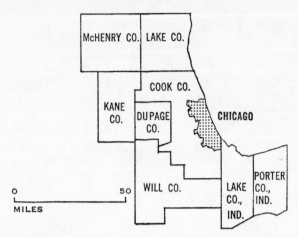

Chicago, Ill.-Northwestern Indiana Standard Consolidated Area.

more knowledge than that is needed to find the scale of
Chicago's growth or to confirm one's confidence in the city's
future. The city stands on Lake Michigan astride a river
which has been made to link the Great Lakes and the Mississippi, between the iron ore and the coal deposits, between
the granaries of mid-continent and their markets in the eastern cities. The importance of the site was recognized as early
as the 1830's, when the canal between the lake and the river
was projected, but it was the railroad building of the period
just after the Civil War which gave Chicago its commanding
position. The city became, in the eyes of virtually all the
builders, the natural terminus for the profitable long haul,
the junction point of eastern and western roads. Indeed,
until Robert Young's campaign of the 1940's, passengers from
New York to points west had to change trains at Chicago,
because it was here that the western routes began. Until the
big planes appeared in the 1950's, the quickest route from
New York to the West Coast always involved a stop in Chicago. So important is Chicago's situation (and so strong the
force of habit) that disgusting little Midway Field, the

138

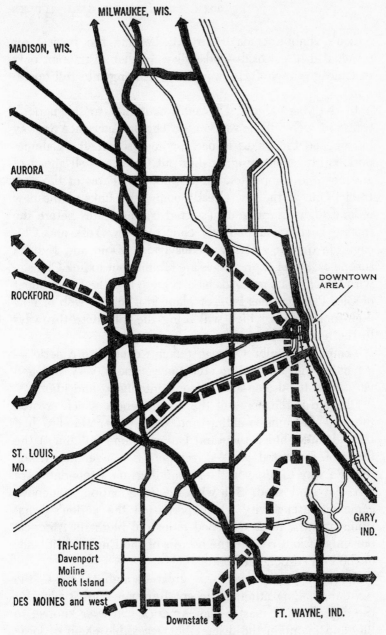

MILWAUKEE, WIS.

MADISON, WIS.

AURORA

ROCKFORD

DOWNTOWN
AREA

ST. LOUIS,
MO.

GARY,
IND.

TRI-CITIES
Davenport
Moline
Rock Island

DES MOINES and west

Downstate

FT. WAYNE, IND.

Highway Arterial System.

139

nation's shabbiest major airport, became the busiest air terminal in the world—and will yield that distinction only to Chicago's own O'Hare, just now coming into full operation.

In the years ahead, Chicago's centrality to the nation's transport web will be reinforced. The St. Lawrence Seaway has opened the Lakes to ocean-going freight, the Calumet port improvement program has put Chicago well ahead of any possible competitors in the race for shares of the new traffic. One of the few already completed links of the new federal highway program (started by the states before the federal government moved) connects New York and Chicago via the New Jersey, Pennsylvania, Ohio and Indiana turnpikes. Other expressways are fanning out to link Chicago with the cities its railroads have served; and the Department of City Planning has built or planned a superb web of new high-speed roads which will bring the interstate thruways to the heart of Chicago.

Temperamentally, Chicago remains central to America— a baffling and fascinating study in contrasts, very rich and very poor, handsome and hideous, intelligent and idiotic.

Chicago is the home of the inventiveness which created the balloon-frame building and then (after the fire had burned up eighteen thousand balloon-frame buildings) the fireproof structural steel skyscraper; the ingenuity which found a way to rest very large buildings on a foundation of soft clay and sand. But with the imagination, somehow, came an insensitivity which permitted the nation's worst slums and the most wretched industrial blight in America, our only serious rival to the horrors of the English Midlands or the Franco-Belgian frontier.

Chicago's civic fervor was great enough to create the Columbian Exposition; to accept Burnham's great plan for the city, the first master plan America had ever known; to buy and maintain the distant but accessible chain of large

140

parks in the Cook County Forest Preserve. Its dominance as a distribution center emboldened it to cover the railroad yards with the Merchandise Mart, still the largest commercial structure in the world, containing more rentable office and showroom space than can be found in the entire city of St. Louis. But a pit of civic indifference left the Burnham plan unfinished and preserved a tradition of municipal corruption which produced machine-gunning on the streets in the 1920's and an infested police force helping with burglaries (for a cut of the proceeds) in the 1950's. And the vision which created the Merchandise Mart was so self-centered it could not see the blight so huge a structure would bring to all the other areas in Chicago which had once housed wholesale activities.

Chicago is ambitious, and until Los Angeles took a little of the heart out of its publicity aimed to displace New York as the nation's first city. But meanwhile an unrealistic zoning law virtually prevented the construction of skyscrapers after World War II, and abdicated to New York all the city's pretensions to home-office status for the nation's industry.

Chicago, perhaps more than any other large city, enshrines that spirit of the West which accepted a man on the basis of what he did rather than what he was, which welcomed an original, free-wheeling approach to both commercial and private problems. But cosmopolitan it is not. The city has insisted on a pose of manly stupidity, still reflected in the editorial pages of its largest newspaper, drove from the city the great artistic and literary talent which came to it in the early years of the century, allowed itself to become the home of public prudery and private vice, surface respectability over gleeful barbarism, the nation's strictest movie censorship law and most degraded night clubs. Its insulation against all things "foreign" narrowed the base of its civilization and keeps it even now a follower rather than a leader among American cities.

I do not like Chicago, personally, despite my respect for some unusually self-aware people who live there. But, professionally, I can't resist it.

They call downtown "the Loop," because of the ring of elevated lines which encircles it, but in fact the *shape* of Chicago's downtown was not much influenced by rapid-transit facilities. Once the swamps were filled, the city's center inevitably grew within the right-angle bend which turns the south branch of the Chicago River to Lake Michigan, less than a mile away. The river, though small and easily bridged, formed the northern and western boundaries of downtown; the lake, the eastern boundary. The fantastic collection of railroad lines, with their associated yards, made a virtually impassable southern barrier. Chicago pioneered the skyscraper because it had to function from a highly restricted, relatively small downtown. Not until the 1920's, when the big bridge was thrown over the river to carry Michigan Avenue north and the Tribune Tower and Wrigley Building went up on the far side, did the city's office and shopping center expand out of the Loop. Generally speaking, the city's elegance has been moving north ever since, though the financial district is still happily within the Loop on LaSalle Street, and State Street south of Randolph is still the most remarkably concentrated retail street in the world.

In theory, Chicago's downtown south of the river is a long rectangle with its major axis north-south. In fact, time has squared off the Loop. Once one gets south of Congress Street, downtown, except for a narrow strip on the park at Michigan, is merely a collection of old and decaying buildings, a spectacular example of inner-ring blight. And the area just north of the river along State and LaSalle is pure and simple slum, complete to rooming houses, brothels and cheap bars (a fit companion for New York's far West

142

Fifties). The good commercial area north of the river is still largely restricted to a relatively narrow strip on both sides of Michigan, with a bulge in the direction of the lake. (Grant Park, which runs from Michigan to the lake, has its northern border at the Illinois Central Railroad yards just south of the river. It was over these yards, incidentally, that Prudential built its masterpiece, buying the air rights over much of the area to fit its skyscraper into the artificial zoning laws, guaranteeing its primacy virtually forever by its position at the top of the park, where nothing can ever be built to keep customers on Michigan Avenue and riders on Lake Shore Drive from seeing the sky-high Prudential sign.)

North of the North Michigan commercial district the lake bends west, and in the triangle formed by the lake and the northern border of the elegant shopping area the city has planted its most expensive apartment house and luxury hotel development, including the famous Mies van der Rohe Lake Shore apartments, the Drake and the Ambassador Hotels. North again, an upper-middle-class apartment and town house development parallels the lake and Lincoln Park, culminating in the Edgewater Beach area just south of Evanston. The strip of luxury is a relatively narrow one, however, and what lies west of the elegance is deteriorating or worse.

Due west of downtown is mostly industrial and low-grade commercial, with slum housing for spice. Here the Congress Street Expressway was brought in from the intersection of the Tri-State Tollway and the East-West Tollway out at the Cook County line. Officially, the Expressway is Route 90, one of the most impressive of the federal highway projects, brilliantly used for city planning purposes. Down the middle of the expressway, separating the two strips of concrete, runs a new rapid-transit line feeding directly into the Loop at the LaSalle Street station. (Recently, the transit authority purchased some eighty-five-mile-an-hour trains for this strip, to show the drivers there's a faster way into downtown.) So far, unfortunately, the expressway has failed to stimulate any great amount of private building along its route, though a dozen or so public housing projects have been completed and more are on the way. The city's master plan calls for predominantly industrial redevelopment north of the expressway and predominantly residential development to the south—if ever there were a road which made a natural divider, this one is it.

South of downtown is the home of the city's greatest problems and greatest urban renewal activities. The exit south from the city's center is unusually restricted: only two city blocks separate the railroad yards on the west from Grant Park (which itself contains the tracks of the Illinois Central). Directly south of downtown, most of the land area between the river and the lake is occupied by tracks, and the area just west of the river is used for the same purpose. The near south, seventy-five years ago the city's number-one residential area but leapfrogged long ago, is thereby insulated from the brisk and busy and potentially upgrading air of downtown. Its future will be determined by the success of plans to tear up some and build over other railroad yards between State Street and the river.

As though the railroad horror were not enough, the stockyards stand at the southern edge of the inner ring, blighting a large area around. South and east of the stockyards, however, Chicago built its first high-quality outer-ring residences. Great apartment houses rose in a cluster at the southern edge of Lake Shore Drive, and behind them, enjoying the luxury of Jackson Park by the lake and Washington and Hyde Park to the west, there grew up the great residential and institutional complex associated with the University of Chicago. Here the first great transit lines were developed, here the Rockefellers made the largest of their educational endowments, here the gigantic Museum of Science and Industry stands as the permanent memorial to the Columbian Exposition.

Here Chicago suffered its disaster. Depopulation through the drive to the suburbs was met by the great influx of Negroes from the South, many of them unaccustomed to city living. South Side became a slum—and a Chicago slum, which is the worst of all. The patches of good residential area shrank. Slum threatened to jump the Illinois Central tracks and destroy the apartment houses by the lake.

The University of Chicago has told the story dramatically in its booklet *Saving Our Cities,* part of a successful fundraising campaign run not to build for the university itself, but to salvage its environment. The pamphlet reads:

One by one the mansions and show places of the wealthy were abandoned, and former owners became suburbanites. South Side houses and apartments were taken over by ever present speculators for exploitation of workers who demanded living quarters.

Multiple-family firetraps instead of homes became the rule in a large part of the South Side.

As one area after another was abandoned to the exploiters, resulting problems became more and more difficult to solve.

Poor enforcement of housing and zoning laws left the way open for speculators to crowd more and more families into more and more run-down and unrepaired buildings. And, because the need for any kind of off-the-street shelter was so great, many landlords grew fat on exorbitant "take-it-or-leave-it" rents.

Overcrowding, with too many families sharing mean and inadequate cooking and toilet facilities, created unhealthful and often filthy living conditions.

Inadequate police protection made possible and even encouraged the spread of vice, crime, vandalism, and juvenile delinquency.

Closer and closer to the University Community came this pressure of lawlessness, poverty, blight, and decay. . . .

The original idea of the University was to have an integrated campus for scholars *living with their work.* It is most important for faculty to reside *in* the University Community. Teaching and graduate work require seventeen to eighteen hours a day; doctors are on call around the clock in University hospitals. Danger, especially at night in the slum areas surrounding the campus, not only interferes with hours given to the work but with the quality of work.

This danger to families has frightened some faculty members away and given grave concern to others. That so many have remained in the community is evidence of their dedication— dedication that has been thoroughly tested.

The Chancellor decided it was up to the University to take the responsibility for leadership in meeting this condition head-on. . . .

Urban renewal is a responsibility of an urban university.

With the university's assistance, and often under the leadership of university people, the Hyde Park-Kenwood community organized itself as a neighborhood planning its own future. Because I purchased and modernized the most important commercial building in the area, I have been a witness to much of this planning, and I find it all most impressive. As matters stand today, the renewal area includes about 170 acres, and the projected expense is in the neighborhood of two hundred million dollars, of which the university will put up fifty million. City government is cooperating via the Land Clearance Commission, the Community Conservation Board and the intelligent Mayor's Commission on Human Rights, which has successfully handled the extremists on both sides. This is not a public housing project, though there will be a modicum of low-income housing to justify federal subsidies. Instead, it is an effort to make a middle-income neighborhood rise on the debris of a slum—a neighborhood with good housing, its own local shops, professional and subcore commercial offices, all built about the nucleus of one of the nation's great universities.

146

Some twenty-five thousand of the area's seventy thousand inhabitants will have to be relocated before the project is finished (fortunately, they don't all have to move at once), and there are more than twenty public housing projects built or building just north of Fifty-first Street. There is no avoiding the fact that most of those who will be evicted are Negroes. But the planners have neither the hope nor the intention of creating a lily-white neighborhood. Their goal is an integrated middle-class community, a demonstration to the nation as a whole that neighborhoods can save themselves. With the political and financial power of the university behind them, and professorial and business intelligence in the leadership, the project seems at present to have something like a four to one chance of success.

South Side is one among many deteriorated Chicago neighborhoods, but with the big advantage that it started good and went bad. Great stretches of Chicago started bad and got worse, and require drastic action very soon. Equally serious is the absence of neighborhoods which exist to fill a single need. Zoning laws or no zoning laws, most of Chicago has grown up haphazardly. Across the Chicago River from downtown, for example, the north bank of the Chicago River presents (reading from west to east) the Merchandise Mart; a garage; the City Office Building; the Central Cold Storage Building, a hole in the ground which will shortly be, under the capitalistic sponsorship of a labor union, a group of large middle-income apartment houses; the new glass-skinned Chicago *Sun-Times* offices and printing plant; the Wrigley Building; a very large parking lot, and the Admiral electrical appliances factory. Mish-mash. Except for the housing tracts (and even those are often broken up by strip development of light industry along the radial roads), Chicago as it stands is a planner's nightmare. But projects are in construction or on the drawing board which would transform central Chicago—and this term, in the Department of City Planning's definition, includes very much more than the relatively healthy Central Business District.

The radial highway projects, most of which are either completed or assured by federal money, are the most elaborate of any city in America. Congress Street and the Northwest Expressway (which will also, eventually, have a rapid-transit line running down the center), tie Chicago to the western and northwestern suburbs and to the circumferential Tri-State Tollway; South and Southwest Expressways, which will be more conventional roadways, are both authorized and in the land acquisition stage. South is the strongest external factor boosting hopes for the success of the Hyde Park-Kenwood project. Meanwhile, Lake Shore Drive will be improved (saving wear and tear on the hydraulic system which lifts and depresses the line dividers, adding to the number of in-lanes for the morning, out-lanes for the afternoon). And Wacker Drive, an admirable two-level legacy from the Burnham plan, will be extended to join south and southwest, closing the Loop around downtown. Meanwhile, far to the south, the Calumet Skyway is open, carrying express traffic twelve miles over industrial parks and mean residences to the great port development on the Cal-Sag Channel.

No area downtown is untouched by the Department's proposals. The riverfront is to be made a pleasure dome, like the "Nizza" in Frankfurt, a marina with foliage. Just north of the river, in the old Fort Dearborn section, there are to be cultural centers and inner-ring middle-income residences. (The city could certainly use some new theaters and a new concert hall, even though the old one no longer appears to be falling down, as it did for a perilous couple of months while the new Borg-Warner Building foundation supports were being sunk next door.) North and northwest of the middle-income residences the plan foresees a very large collection of public housing projects and lower middle-income apartment houses. Due west of downtown and just across the river, where there are now only a few fine buildings, a transportation center is proposed to centralize the railroad passenger traffic, supply a heliport more convenient than Meigs Field and give the city its first downtown airlines terminal. At the edges of the existing business district, north and south, government office buildings would improve deteriorated blocks of the Loop. The air rights between the Prudential Building and Lake Michigan would be built up with major office buildings and perhaps some luxury apartments on the shore, and something would be done to rehabilitate the slum of Navy Pier, poking out into the lake beside the outlet of the river, currently used mostly by the University of Illinois for its two-year program in Chicago.

The University of Illinois, which wishes to start a four-year full-status college inside Chicago, would move to a very large new campus just south of the Loop, built over the railroad tracks that now pinch downtown from expansion southward. And beside the new campus, in the now badly deteriorated near South Side, private construction, aided by public condemnation and perhaps land clearance support, would put up the city's largest colony of middle-class apartment houses, restoring what was Chicago's best residential area in the long-ago days before leapfrogging began. At the moment, unfortunately, the state seems unwilling to put up the money for the university project, and the railroads are complaining of possible inconvenience. A fair reapportionment of the state legislature, removing some of the parity-grabbing downstaters so horrified at "wasting" public money, might turn the tide.

Well west of the river, large areas on both sides of the Congress Street expressway would be selectively redeveloped, with major conservation efforts to keep what is salvageable. Along the shore to the east, the plan calls for

149

redesigning Grant Park, creating several islands in the lake, and filling in land to make a new park in the area between Navy Pier and Lincoln Park where Lake Shore Drive now runs along the water's edge and there is no greenery. Perhaps the horticulturists could find some way to grow sturdy trees there, too, forming a screen against one of the most penetrating bitter winds in the temperate zones. To the south of Grant Park, where Burnham Park begins, Chicago has already built McCormick Place, the inevitable exposition center which is part of all city plans, getting the conventions out of the stockyards and Navy Pier, neither of which is exactly what a city wants a visitor to see. The new structure includes an auditorium with more than five thousand seats, plus ballrooms and restaurants large and small, all overlooking the lake.

This is the nation's biggest urban renewal plan, projected at a cost of one and a half billion dollars. And even if the entire plan becomes reality, much of Chicago will remain very dreary. Typically American from the period when Americans aggressively did not care about aesthetic considerations, Chicago is a painfully ugly city. But the new roads, and the kind of civic awakening that would be forced by so large an improvement of the area around downtown, might create highly productive dissatisfactions. A great deal will depend on the city's ability to hold its middle-class and lower-middle-class white population, and here the projection is not good: half a million whites left Chicago for the suburbs in the 1950's, and the University of Chicago's Community Inventory estimates that white migration from the city will accelerate during the next decade. Losses in that direction might be balanced if educators could develop new techniques to speed the acculturation of southern Negroes to city living. The success of the Hyde Park-Kenwood project would help immeasurably; not the least of the Negro's problems in adjusting to northern city existence

150

has been the precipitous flight of the more established elements of the white community on the first appearance of a dark face down the block.

Even if the Planning Department programs fail, and little is done to prevent the spread of physical and spiritual ugliness in Chicago, the city's future is relatively secure. Its economic position is impregnable and its vitality enormous. Chicago is still America in microcosm. Perhaps in Chicago we will find the answer to the question of whether America will use its unique resources to create a greater civilization—or will condemn itself to a meaningless, soul-destroying proliferation of goods, comforts and waste.

# 9. *Los Angeles*

Mission headquarters for Spanish Jesuits; trading center for a good farmland; minor Pacific port; major railroad terminus; oil town; old-folks town; movie paradise and dream capital. Eventually a minor industrial center, where the inhabitants of a relatively isolated metropolis took in each other's washing.

Then the Japanese struck at Pearl Harbor, and in Los Angeles history became almost irrelevant. This was the war town *par excellence.* Here was good transportation, cheap, plentiful electric power and vacant land by the mile for the construction of factories. The city faced the Pacific, across which fantastically long lines of supply were necessary to maintain the war effort in Australia and New Zealand, in Hawaii, on the exotic atolls. Men and materiel flowed through the city and the nearby port Long Beach; and in the valleys the aircraft factories covered over the farms forever. Soldiers' wives came to Los Angeles because it seemed nearer their husbands, and that nice Jones girl from normal school became Rosie the Riveter. The First World War had brought unsophisticated Americans and the air of sophistication to the cities of the eastern sea-

152

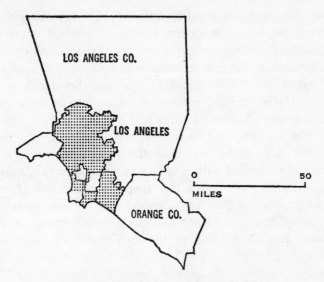

LOS ANGELES CO.

LOS ANGELES

ORANGE CO.

0            50
MILES

Standard Metropolitan Statistical Area.

board; the Second World War drew millions to the Pacific shore, and splattered Los Angeles all over the landscape.

They stayed when the war was over, though economically it seemed touch and go during those first years of peace, when the military aircraft factories were no longer needed and nothing seemed likely to take their place. That was the time when depression was expected momentarily all over the country; might as well be in Los Angeles, where there were no heating bills and a state government wearily experienced in these matters would take care of the unfortunate. A virtual monopoly of the commercial aircraft business (both Douglas and Lockheed are Los Angeles companies, and between the DC's and the Connies they had the airlines sewed up in the late forties) helped tide the new giant over the reefs of apparent peace, and then the Korean War put any thought of economic trouble in the background.

153

But the weakness persists economically; Los Angeles is a war baby, and real peace, should it descend upon us, might blight the city. Nearly a quarter of the manufacturing employment of the Los Angeles area is in aircraft and aircraft parts (including missiles), and another tenth is in metals fabrication and machinery related to aircraft construction. Few American cities had a worse scare in 1957, when the Air Force cut back heavily on procurement schedules. Yet it must be said that the conversion to missile-making was handled with greater ease in southern California than anywhere else—and the area's recent rapid growth in electronics, textiles and apparel, automobile assembly and heavy machinery (not to mention government, which accounts for 10 per cent of the area's total employment)

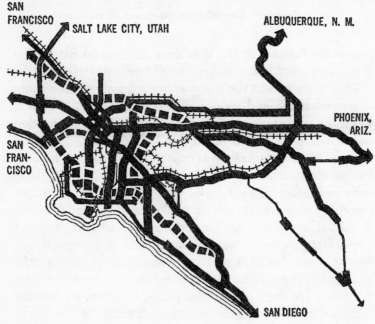

Highway Arterial System.

may provide the local economy with a far less shaky foundation.

Given continued prosperity, Los Angeles will become the first megalopolis, stretching down the Pacific Coast until it meets San Diego coming up. The direction of its growth is topographically controlled. Though the war spilled the city over the hills into the San Fernando Valley to the north, real mountains inevitably block any great expansion in that direction. Any attempt to advance west or southwest meets the insuperable barrier of the ocean, and due east the terrain is semi-arid, bleeding off to desert. Off to the east lies the Ontario-Riverside-San Bernardino complex, already California's fourth largest market, and some day, despite topographical difficulties, the land between Los Angeles and this threesome may be filled in with housing. The roads— and what roads they are, some of them—are open most easily to the southeast, to Orange County and thence to San Diego. In census terms, the Los Angeles, San Diego metropolitan areas are all contiguous right now, and a matter of a few years will make reality of what is still a statistician's fiction. Orange County, the southern section of the Los Angeles metropolitan area, nearly tripled in population in the last decade, and the trend lines are still up.

Yet Los Angeles, as everyone outside its Chamber of Commerce seems to know, is a city in trouble. New York *Times* reporter Harrison Salisbury returned from a trip there and paraphrased Lincoln Steffens to say, "I have seen the future—and it doesn't work." Megalopolis may be assured, but its health and happiness are much in doubt— and there is more than a slight danger that what was once central city will die disgustingly while the developers hack up the southeast countryside.

Downtown Los Angeles sits back about a dozen miles from the Pacific Ocean, comfortably inside a bend of the

Los Angeles River. The river is not so prominent a topographical feature as it was a hundred years ago, but it is still enough of a barrier to make dead ends of two-thirds of all the streets running from downtown to the east. The early development of the city naturally followed the lines southwest to the port (past the oil fields in the Baldwin Hills), and due west to the established oceanside community of Santa Monica. There was also some development to the northeast, where the three railroad lines—Southern Pacific, Union Pacific and Santa Fe—ran perforce between the Puente Hills and the San Gabriel Mountains. Here, suitably separated from downtown by a range of hills cut by a dry canyon (Arroyo Seco), grew up one of America's first successful upper-middle-class suburbs, Pasadena. The continuing importance of the name Huntington in the Pasadena area testifies to the role of the railroad in its development.

Indeed, Los Angeles as a whole, though notorious as the city of the automobile, has been a major railroad town for many decades. Rail lines cut up and down and around all over the city, which probably has more unguarded level crossings than any other municipality in America. Los Angeles at the turn of the century even developed a first-rate surface-level electric-railway rapid-transit system, parts of which still function in a Toonerville Trolley manner. The tracks for this system run mostly west and southwest from town.

When the war came, there were few flat open spaces remaining in the square formed by the mountains to the north, the river to the east and the ocean to the west and south. The city expanded in a seemingly impossible direction—north into "the Valley." Roads were driven through the few gaps in the Hollywood Hills (themselves a lower connecting link between the nearly impassable Santa Monica Mountains and San Gabriel Mountains), and the

156

factories sprouted in Burbank and Van Nuys, North Hollywood, Encino and Sepulveda. Even today, there are only four roads capable of carrying through traffic between downtown Los Angeles and the San Fernando Valley; but, then, there are only two roads which go all the way from downtown to Pasadena, so traffic bottlenecks were no novelty.

The postwar expansion—more practical, cost-plus opportunities having departed—burst the bounds of the river instead of fighting the mountains. The new industry and the housing developments spread a wide swathe between the dry hills and the ocean, marching southeast, overwhelming the old farming suburbs, Montebello, Pico, Whittier, and the like; through Downey and Norwalk and Lakewood; and across the county line to Buena Park and Anaheim (where Walt Disney placed his pleasure dome), down to Santa Ana itself, more than forty miles from Pershing Square in the heart of Los Angeles.

By and large, the areas which had been developed earlier were left to rot. An inner ring of Mexican slum crowded downtown itself, and in the southwest quadrant Negroes took over what had been third-rate housing to begin with. The roads running due west became the first battleground against encroaching blight. A "Miracle Mile" was put together on Wilshire Boulevard a few miles out of downtown, to offer convenient shopping and office space for those living in the Hollywood section between Wilshire and the hills. One of the most successful such projects, the Miracle Mile, not only preserved its own immediate area but stimulated a rash of commercial construction along the Wilshire strip all the way back to downtown. Along Wilshire rose four of the first five over-thirteen-story buildings to be erected after the city repealed its antique height limitations in 1957. Past the Miracle Mile, Wilshire runs west into Beverly Hills and Westwood Village, residential suburbs of the highest quality, as far removed from the danger of blight as any neighborhoods in America. Between these two, as added protection, lies the projected "Century City," bordering on Wilshire, a planned collection of skyscrapers and high-rise apartment houses, which the joint developers, Webb & Knapp and ALCOA, estimate at five hundred million dollars' worth of buildings before the job is done.

But the area north of Wilshire near the center remains in danger. It is the most thickly settled non-slum neighborhood in Los Angeles, consisting mostly of small houses, now thirty and forty years old, crowded onto relatively small plots of land. Palm trees are not much good for disguising obsolescence. And Hollywood itself, of course, stands for the one industry in the area which has suffered a general decline since the war, though, of course, television production has picked up an ever-increasing part of the slack.

Before Hollywood or the inner ring or the near southwest can become attractive again, downtown must become a magnet. These neighborhoods (aside from the hillside parts of Hollywood, which are guaranteed de luxe) offer as special inducements only their nearness to the center. And the age of the auto damaged downtown Los Angeles even more severely than other city centers, because so much of the early expansion occurred in areas across the hills, wretchedly inconvenient to the heart of the city.

Hope lies in two possibilities—that the success of the Wilshire strip development, still proceeding, will create sufficient density to support a subway line, and that downtown can be revitalized by a series of major efforts. The first such effort, already under way, is as major as anyone could ask—the Bunker Hill Urban Renewal Project, in which an estimated $315 million will be spent to rebuild a section of the inner ring nearly half a mile square on hilltop and hillsides just north of the Central Business District. Exceedingly well thought out, the project is to be financed largely from private funds, though federal, state and city governments are all putting up pieces of the cost. What remains will be supported by the sale of Redevelopment Agency bonds, backed by the difference between the real estate taxes now paid in the area and the taxes which will be due from the new owners when the project is completed. The site will be shared by office buildings, motels, apartment houses and garages (this *is* Los Angeles, after all: the plans call for at least one parking space for each apartment dwelling unit and for each four hundred square feet of rentable commercial space).

A great deal more will need to be done before Los Angeles can claim an established downtown. Transit is essential from all directions, not just the west, and some of the time now put into dreaming of a downtown with raised pedestrian malls and sunken truck arteries might well go into practical scheming for monorails and helicopter service. At present the Los Angeles Metropolitan Transit Authority owns only 1,736 busses and rail cars—as against more than 1,500,000 privately owned automobiles. And something should certainly be done to provide greater quantities of middle-brow entertainment in the city's center, so that middle-class Angelenos might find it more difficult to say that they "never go downtown."

For the rest of the area, the basic needs are the usual conservation and rehabilitation, plus the construction of viable subcores around the edges of the city. Not much can be said for the quality of construction in the San Fernando Valley or in the new southeast suburbs, but most of what exists is too new to collapse in the near future. Among the subcores, Santa Monica is plotting an urban renewal program of its own. Many of the suddenly inflated southeast villages have managed to retain a center and a character, though none of them is entirely free from the shopping-center chicken pox. Excellent models of what can be done to establish such subcores on a prosperous and durable basis are to be found in the area, especially in Beverly Hills and Pasadena.

Los Angeles has no serious governmental problems. The city itself occupies some 450-plus square miles, extending way out into the Valley and down a strip to the port area of San Pedro. The boundary lines are peculiar—not to say crazy—with Culver City, Beverly Hills, Santa Monica, Inglewood and such forming separate municipalities surrounded by Los Angeles. Nearby suburbs like Pasadena, Glendale and Burbank also retain their independence. But municipal liaison is relatively good under the auspices of Los Angeles County, and in the California structure the county has more than the usual political authority.

As yet there is nothing approaching a master plan. Relocation of those displaced by the Bunker Hill project is being done on a strictly *ad hoc* basis. The rapidly deteriorating east-west arteries north of Wilshire—especially Beverly Boulevard, Santa Monica Boulevard and Third Street—are being allowed to slide where conservation might arrest blight. There are no plans to control the operation of parking lots, which give a Swiss-cheese texture to downtown and to the development along the Wilshire strip. The city is obsessed, not unnaturally, with the problem of keeping the cars moving. Some 250 miles of freeway are already in existence, and despite the lack of a master plan the authorities have already mapped a thousand miles more to be built in the next two decades. The projected cost for roadways alone runs something like four *billion* dollars, most of it, of course, federal money. Oddly enough, nobody believes that the new roads will solve the city's problems.

With this sort of money budgeted for placebo concrete, it seems silly to say that Los Angeles cannot "afford" to build a rapid-transit system. The most recent survey of transit

160

possibilities in Los Angeles was a minor affair, involving an outlay of only $175,000, an insignificant fraction of what San Francisco is spending for similar engineering studies. But, as the director of the Transit Authority points out, there have been fifty such surveys in the last thirty years. Perhaps the time has come for action.

Finally, the advertised menace: smog. The climate that built the city now threatens to destroy it. Recurring patterns of temperature inversion in the lower atmosphere hold fumes near the ground, poisoning the air. The condition is worse downtown, though no part of the area has been entirely free of smog. Nobody knows which fumes are the most severe irritants. Some authorities hope that exhaust burners on the automobiles, which will presently be required by act of the state legislature, will remove the worst source of air pollution, but one school of thought holds that even then industrial gases would continue to make breathing painful on days when nature misbehaves.

Eventually, for self-preservation, the city and the state will take whatever steps are necessary to stop smog; it requires only a few deaths to create irresistible political pressures. These necessary steps, however, may shift the economic patterns of the city in unforeseen directions. Downtown redevelopment in Los Angeles, therefore, requires more courage than similar projects elsewhere in the country.

Prognosis: uncertain. Despite my admiration for Bunker Hill and Century City, and for the directing intelligences of the new Metropolitan Transit Authority (which recognizes the need for rapid transit facilities and has drawn a subway system on the most recent Los Angeles Metropolitan Map), I feel that the resiliency of this get-rich-quick paradise has yet to be tested. There are two questions to be answered:

1) Is the automobile city functional without a downtown core—and, in the case of Los Angeles, without really suc-

cessful subcore development? I think the answer here must be, No.

2) Can a decaying downtown be revitalized to such a degree that it will act as pumping station for so vast a circulatory system? The answer here lies in the solution to the transit problem. Given adequate transit, I think the answer may be, Yes.

# 10.  Washington

Europeans always feel more at home here than anywhere
else in America (they *think* they like San Francisco, but
that's only because they never get to know it). Washington
is essentially a court city, plunked down where it is as artificially as Versailles. It was laid out by a European and—
thanks to restoration work at the turn of the century—the
original design is still visible. In Washington, more than
anywhere else in America, the visitor is amidst history, however much the history may be bowdlerized by monstrosities
like the Jefferson Memorial, which Frank Lloyd Wright
once described as a public comfort station. Most of all,
Washington does not stink of sweat the way the other
American cities do. Its growth was not a function of economic development, but of court patronage.

Topographically, the city is dominated by its river, a
broad boundary which has only recently been crossed in
force (though politically the District of Columbia line runs
a few hundred yards in on the Virginia side of the Potomac).
To the east a lesser river, the Anacostia, cuts into one edge
of the district, separates the city from eastern Maryland, and
with its associated swamps (now parks) makes an almost

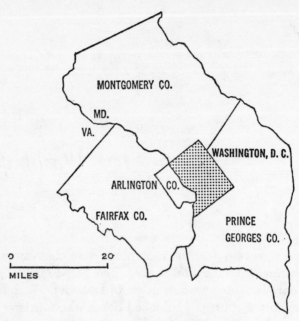

Standard Metropolitan Statistical Area.

equally ponderable barrier. The joining of the two rivers creates the larger Potomac which ambles through Virginia from Washington to the Chesapeake and on to the sea. North and northwest, the land stretches away from the river as a rolling plain, with only a few smoothed-over and lived-on hills plus an occasional granite outcropping. Running northwest, the avenues must bridge the canyon cut by Rock Creek, which holds several pleasant roadways, bridle paths and a park, and forms a neat permanent boundary to any major commercial expansion of downtown.

The original downtown inevitably formed between the dock area and the slightly higher ground where the national monuments were to be built. The Capitol was to be placed on the highest of the local hills, and the city was mapped in quadrants (southeast, southwest, etc.) from the Capitol site.

164

Appropriately named roads (North Capitol, East Capitol and so forth) divided the quadrants. To the west, the north and south quadrants were divided by L'Enfant's Mall, a mile-long stretch of greenery the width of Capitol Hill, bordered by the two patriotic avenues, Constitution and Independence. Access to the Capitol was assured by four avenues running at angles to the quadrant lines—Maryland, Dela-

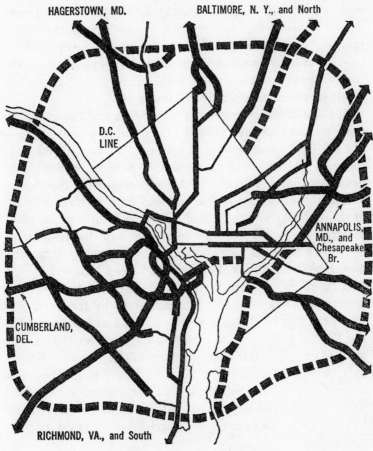

HAGERSTOWN, MD.

BALTIMORE, N. Y., and North

D.C. LINE

ANNAPOLIS, MD., and Chesapeake Br.

CUMBERLAND, DEL.

RICHMOND, VA., and South

Highway Arterial System.

165

ware, New Jersey and Pennsylvania. All four ran to Capitol Hill, were broken by it and then resumed on the other side. Parallel to these boulevards ran other avenues named after original states: Virginia to the south and Massachusetts to the north of Pennsylvania; South and North Carolina to the south, New York and Rhode Island to the north of Maryland; Vermont and New Hampshire to the west of Delaware; and Connecticut to the west of New Jersey. A conventional grid, with north-south streets bearing numbers and east-west streets bearing first letters then words alphabetically arranged, was superimposed to complete the layout, which is—thanks to its combination of order with an endless opportunity for squares and circles at the crossings of the avenues —one of the most attractive in the world.

Because of the swamps, the mosquitoes and the overpoweringly humid summer climate (every bit as bad as Rome— but the Popes knew enough to get out to Castel Gondolfo), the area in the southern quadrants was never a notably healthful place to live. But its convenience to the docks, and to the railroad terminal plunked onto L'Enfant's Mall, made it the inevitable center of the city's life in the nineteenth century. By the turn of the century, the area south of the Capitol both east and west was a noisome slum. Any incentive to rebuild it, however, had been lessened by the transfer of the railroad station from the Mall to the intersection of Delaware and Massachusetts in the northeast quadrant, and by the shift of true power and influence from the Capitol to the White House in the northwest. The new government office buildings went up, in the approved Beaux-Arts monumental style, on the widening triangle between Pennsylvania and Constitution as Pennsylvania nears the White House. The city shifted north, jumping Pennsylvania, leaving the south to decaying warehouses, produce markets and slums.

Downtown Washington established itself in the late years

166

of the nineteenth and the early years of the twentieth centuries along a line between the new Union Station and the White House. Retailing, restaurants, theaters, office buildings all came into this relatively narrow strip. By and large, it was a fairly scruffy development. The typical skyscrapers of the American twenties were forbidden by the zoning laws, designed to maintain the skyline supremacy of the Capitol and the Washington Monument. Most builders felt it would be folly to try to compete with the government buildings in grandeur and elegance, especially on wedge-shaped lots. Moreover, land was available at relatively low prices, which made sprawling economical. The appearance and general atmosphere of Washington's department store district is today a local and perhaps a national scandal, but one doubts that the area was particularly attractive even when new.

The shift west began more than thirty years ago, and as one approaches the White House the level of downtown quality and maintenance rises. Even today, Fifteenth and Fourteenth Streets (one and two blocks from the White House, with Fourteenth running directly to a bridge over the Potomac) are among the most important commercial and quality-retailing thoroughfares in the city. But the movement is distinctly northwest: except for a few large and representative but feudal organizations like the Teamsters' Union, which recently erected its headquarters facing the Capitol across Union Station Plaza, organizations which need Washington headquarters are now building west of Fourteenth Street and north of H. Only a few years ago Washington commerce was concentrated in the diamond bordered by Pennsylvania, New York, Massachusetts and Delaware. Today it is to be found largely in the diamond directly northwest, still between Pennsylvania and Massachusetts, but with Vermont as its southeast rather than northwest boundary and New Hampshire at the northwestern end. As the owner of the District's newest postwar hotel, at the most advanced highly developed boundary of the new diamond, I cannot bring myself to feel unhappy about the trend—indeed, the trend was the reason I bought the hotel.

Residentially, too, except for the drop into Virginia, Washington has moved northwest—way northwest, for the middle-class and upper-middle-class fractions of the population. But for a fringe created by government buildings (among them the Supreme Court, the Library of Congress and the new Congressional office buildings), virtually the entire area east of the Capitol, all the way to the Anacostia, is more or less blighted and more or less Negro. Thanks to its layout and relatively low density, however, Washington presents few slums so frightful as, say, Brooklyn's Brownsville or inner-ring Detroit. A few years back the area just behind the Capitol had the complexion of a *rural* slum, complete to crumbling porches and toilets in outhouses with boards peeling away. The worst of this condition has been quietly remedied, mostly by rehabilitation rather than massive reconstruction, and the new Congressional offices may populate the neighborhood with medium-range apartment houses to give the clerical staffs a home. Major urban renewal is to come.

In the southwest quadrant the city's one active urban renewal project will erect middle-income row houses and small and large apartment houses—plus one subsidized apartment house for poor people, as well as a number of small shops and commercial buildings and even, perhaps, theaters. The development covers virtually the entire quadrant, from Independence down to the Washington Channel of the Potomac, reserves space for expressways and improves port facilities. In concept, it seems to foresee a little suburb, complete to a "Town Center" and a projected hotel and convention hall on "L'Enfant Plaza" just off Tenth Street. A recent "reconnaissance survey of the Downtown Business

168

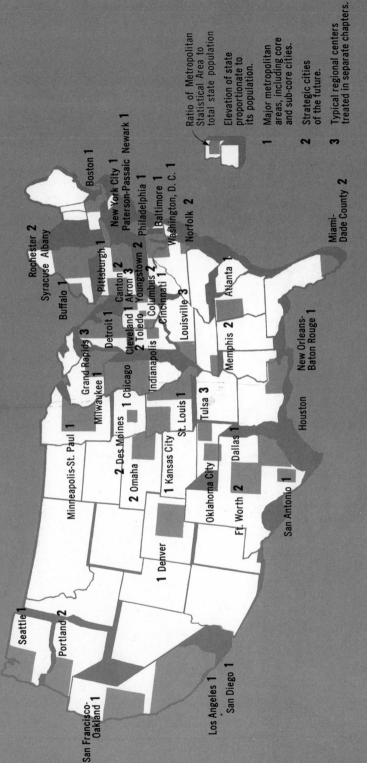

Ratio of Metropolitan Statistical Area to total state population

Elevation of state proportionate to its population.

**1** Major metropolitan areas, including core and sub-core cities.

**2** Strategic cities of the future.

**3** Typical regional centers treated in separate chapters.

Seattle **1**
Portland **2**
San Francisco-Oakland **1**
Los Angeles **1**
San Diego **1**

Denver **1**
Minneapolis-St. Paul **1**
Omaha **2**
Des Moines **2**
Milwaukee **1**
Chicago **1**
Grand Rapids **3**
Detroit **1**
Kansas City **1**
St. Louis **1**
Tulsa **3**
Oklahoma City **1**
Ft. Worth **2**
Dallas **1**
San Antonio **1**
Houston
New Orleans-Baton Rouge **1**
Indianapolis
Cleveland **1**
Toledo **2**
Canton **2**
Akron **3**
Youngstown **2**
Columbus **2**
Cincinnati **1**
Louisville **3**
Memphis **2**
Atlanta **1**
Miami-Dade County **2**

Rochester **2**
Syracuse Albany
Buffalo **1**
Pittsburgh **1**
Boston **1**
New York City **1**
Paterson-Passaic Newark **1**
Philadelphia **1**
Baltimore **1**
Washington, D. C. **1**
Norfolk **2**

**Relationship of Population of Metropolitan Statistical Areas to their State's Total Population**

SOURCE: PRELIMINARY FIGURES, 1960 U.S. CENSUS

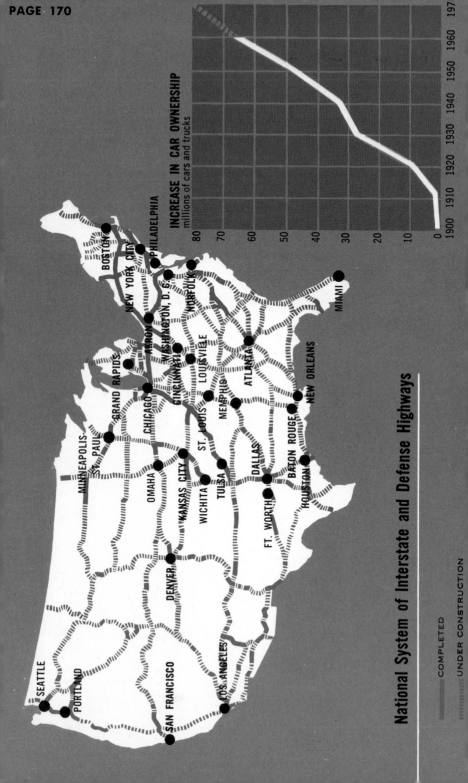

INCREASE IN CAR OWNERSHIP
millions of cars and trucks

National System of Interstate and Defense Highways

COMPLETED
UNDER CONSTRUCTION

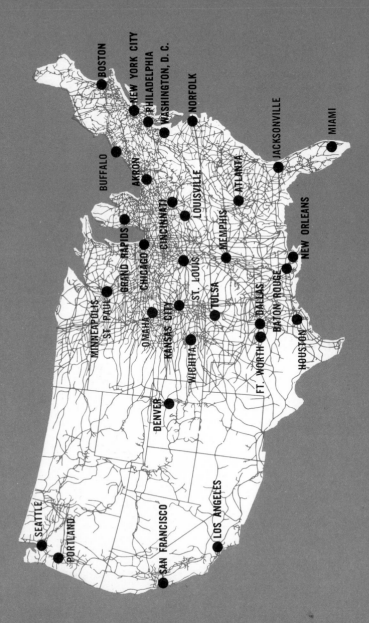

Railroad Routes of the Continental United States

## AIRCRAFT DEPARTURES OF SCHEDULED PASSENGER AIR CARRIERS

| | | |
|---|---|---|
| 1. | Chicago—Midway | 144,353 |
| 2. | Washington, D. C. | 119,644 |
| 3. | New York—La Guardia | 83,270 |
| 4. | Atlanta, Georgia | 77,620 |
| 5. | Los Angeles, California | 71,077 |
| 6. | Dallas, Texas | 63,095 |
| 7. | Newark, New Jersey | 59,263 |
| 8. | San Francisco, California | 56,123 |
| 9. | New York—Idlewild | 53,759 |
| 10. | Pittsburgh, Pennsylvania | 53,228 |
| 11. | Cleveland, Ohio | 52,975 |
| 12. | Miami, Florida | 51,538 |
| 13. | Boston, Massachusetts | 50,378 |
| 14. | Philadelphia, Pennsylvania | 44,987 |
| 15. | St. Louis, Missouri | 44,703 |
| 16. | Detroit—Willow Run | 42,521 |
| 17. | Kansas City, Missouri | 38,016 |
| 18. | Minneapolis, Minnesota | 35,032 |
| 19. | Denver, Colorado | 33,927 |
| 20. | Cincinnati, Ohio | 32,334 |
| 21. | Milwaukee, Wisconsin | 31,686 |
| 22. | Louisville, Kentucky | 29,671 |
| 23. | Buffalo, New York | 29,511 |
| 24. | Indianapolis, Indiana | 29,204 |
| 25. | Houston, Texas | 29,033 |
| 26. | New Orleans, Louisiana | 28,399 |
| 27. | Jacksonville, Florida | 28,140 |
| 28. | Portland, Oregon | 28,100 |
| 29. | Fort Worth, Texas | 27,937 |
| 30. | Charlotte, North Carolina | 26,315 |
| 31. | Detroit—Metro. Wayne Co. | 25,557 |
| 32. | Tampa, Florida | 25,225 |
| 33. | Columbus, Ohio | 25,030 |
| 34. | Dayton, Ohio | 24,737 |
| 35. | Memphis, Tennessee | 24,219 |

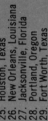
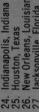
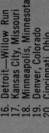

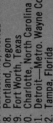

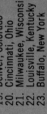

## Major Continental United States Airline Routes

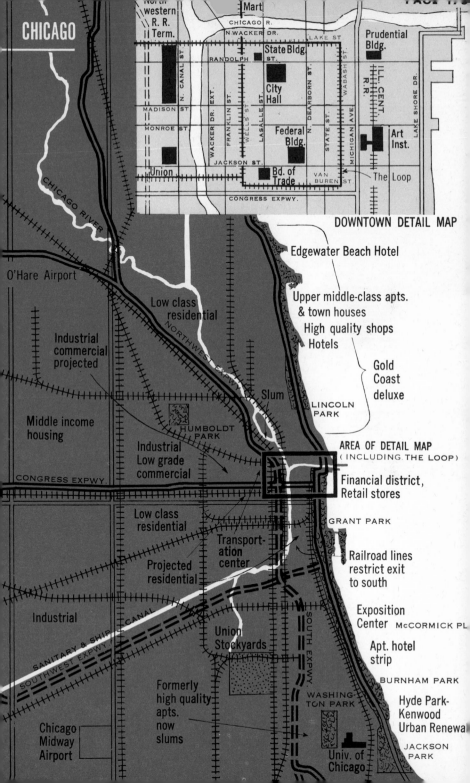

# CHICAGO

## DOWNTOWN DETAIL MAP

Mart

CHICAGO R.

N. WACKER DR.

North western R. R. Term.

LAKE ST.

Prudential Bldg.

RANDOLPH

State Bldg.
ST.

N. CANAL ST.

WACKER DR. EXT.

FRANKLIN ST.

WELLS ST.

LASALLE ST.

N. DEARBORN ST.

STATE ST.

WABASH ST.

MICHIGAN AVE.

ILL. CENT. R. R.

LAKE SHORE DR.

City Hall

MADISON ST.

MONROE ST.

Federal Bldg.

Art Inst.

Union

JACKSON ST.

Bd. of Trade

VAN BUREN ST.

The Loop

CONGRESS EXPWY.

CHICAGO RIVER

O'Hare Airport

Edgewater Beach Hotel

Upper middle-class apts.
& town houses

High quality shops

Hotels

Gold
Coast
deluxe

Low class residential

Industrial commercial projected

NORTHWEST EXPWY.

Slum

LINCOLN PARK

Middle income housing

HUMBOLDT PARK

Industrial Low grade commercial

AREA OF DETAIL MAP
(INCLUDING THE LOOP)

CONGRESS EXPWY.

Financial district,
Retail stores

Low class residential

GRANT PARK

Projected residential

Transportation center

Railroad lines restrict exit to south

Industrial

SANITARY & SHIP CANAL

SOUTHWEST EXPWY.

Union Stockyards

SOUTH EXPWY.

Exposition Center McCORMICK PL.

Apt. hotel strip

BURNHAM PARK

Chicago Midway Airport

Formerly high quality apts. now slums

WASHINGTON PARK

Hyde Park-Kenwood Urban Renewal

Univ. of Chicago

JACKSON PARK

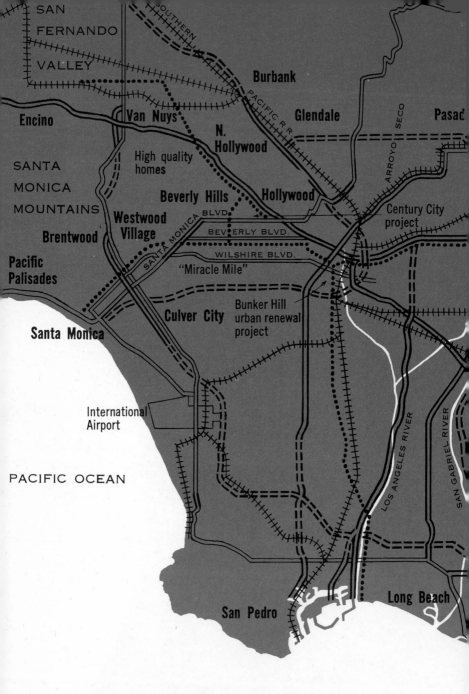

·········· Proposed Rapid Transit System (latest)

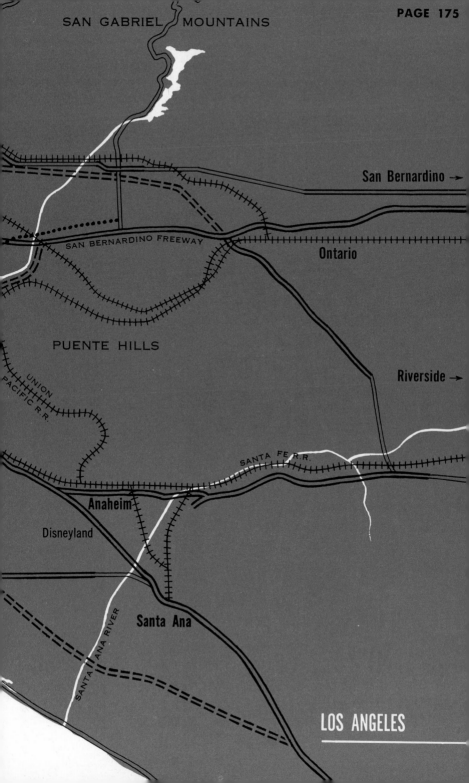

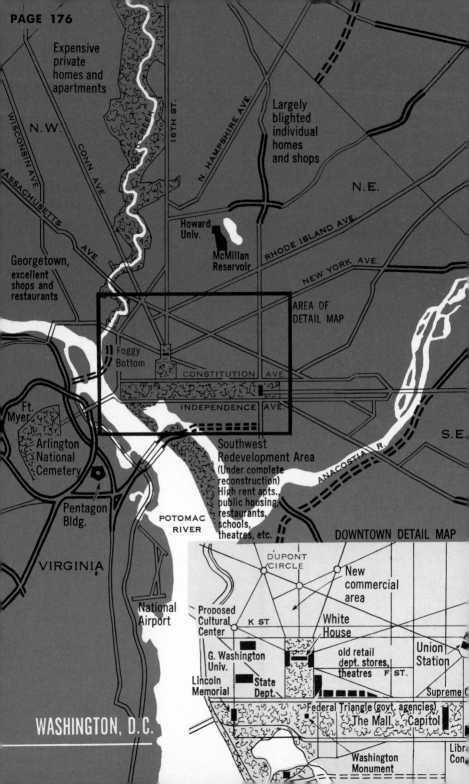

Expensive private homes and apartments

N.W.

Largely blighted individual homes and shops

N.E.

WISCONSIN AVE.

MASSACHUSETTS AVE.

CONN. AVE.

ROCK CREEK

16TH ST.

N. HAMPSHIRE AVE.

Howard Univ.

McMillan Reservoir

RHODE ISLAND AVE.

NEW YORK AVE.

Georgetown, excellent shops and restaurants

AREA OF DETAIL MAP

Foggy Bottom

CONSTITUTION AVE.

INDEPENDENCE AVE.

Ft. Myer

Arlington National Cemetery

Pentagon Bldg.

POTOMAC RIVER

Southwest Redevelopment Area (Under complete reconstruction) High rent apts., public housing, restaurants, schools, theatres, etc.

ANACOSTIA R.

S.E.

VIRGINIA

National Airport

DOWNTOWN DETAIL MAP

DUPONT CIRCLE

New commercial area

Proposed Cultural Center

K ST.

White House

G. Washington Univ.

Lincoln Memorial

State Dept.

old retail dept. stores, theatres

F ST.

Union Station

Supreme C

Federal Triangle (govt. agencies)

The Mall

Capitol

WASHINGTON, D.C.

Washington Monument

Libr Con

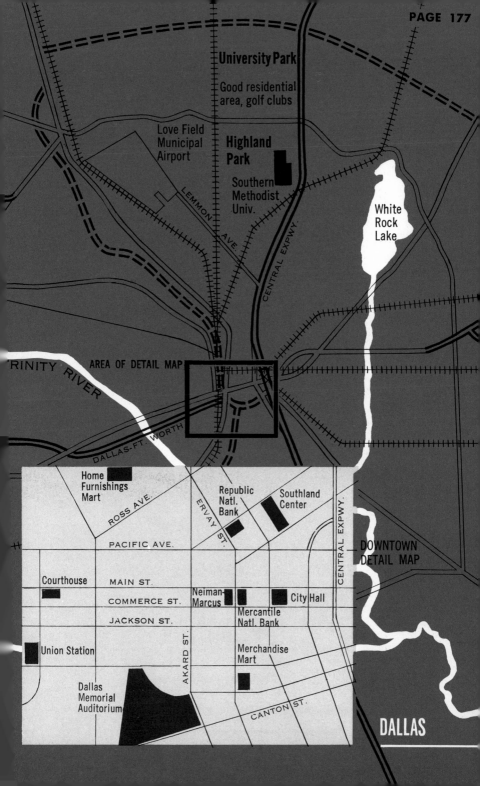

University Park

Good residential area, golf clubs

Love Field Municipal Airport

Highland Park

Southern Methodist Univ.

White Rock Lake

LEMMON AVE.

CENTRAL EXPWY.

TRINITY RIVER

AREA OF DETAIL MAP

DALLAS-FT. WORTH

Home Furnishings Mart

ROSS AVE.

ERVAY ST.

Republic Natl. Bank

Southland Center

CENTRAL EXPWY.

DOWNTOWN DETAIL MAP

PACIFIC AVE.

Courthouse

MAIN ST.

COMMERCE ST.

Neiman-Marcus

City Hall

JACKSON ST.

Mercantile Natl. Bank

AKARD ST.

Union Station

Merchandise Mart

Dallas Memorial Auditorium

CANTON ST.

DALLAS

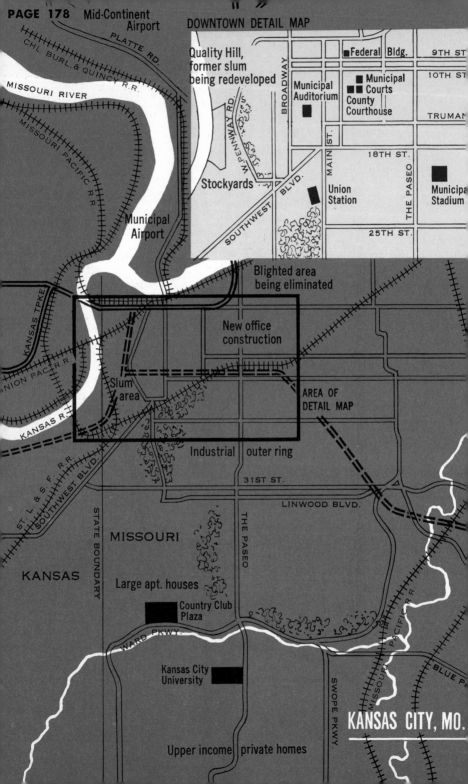

Mid-Continent
Airport

PLATTE RD.

CHI. BURL. & QUINCY R.R.

MISSOURI RIVER

MISSOURI PACIFIC R.R.

KANSAS TPKE

UNION PACIF. R.R.

KANSAS R.

ST. L. & S. F. R. R.

SOUTHWEST BLVD.

Municipal
Airport

## DOWNTOWN DETAIL MAP

Quality Hill,
former slum
being redeveloped

W. PENNWAY RD.

BROADWAY

MAIN ST.

Federal Bldg.

9TH ST

10TH ST

Municipal
Auditorium

Municipal
Courts
County
Courthouse

TRUMAN

18TH ST.

THE PASEO

Stockyards

SOUTHWEST BLVD.

Union
Station

Municipal
Stadium

25TH ST.

Blighted area
being eliminated

New office
construction

Slum
area

AREA OF
DETAIL MAP

Industrial outer ring

31ST ST.

LINWOOD BLVD.

STATE BOUNDARY

THE PASEO

MISSOURI

KANSAS

Large apt. houses

Country Club
Plaza

WARD PKWY.

MISSOURI PACIFIC R.R.

BLUE PA

Kansas City
University

SWOPE PKWY.

**KANSAS CITY, MO.**

Upper income private homes

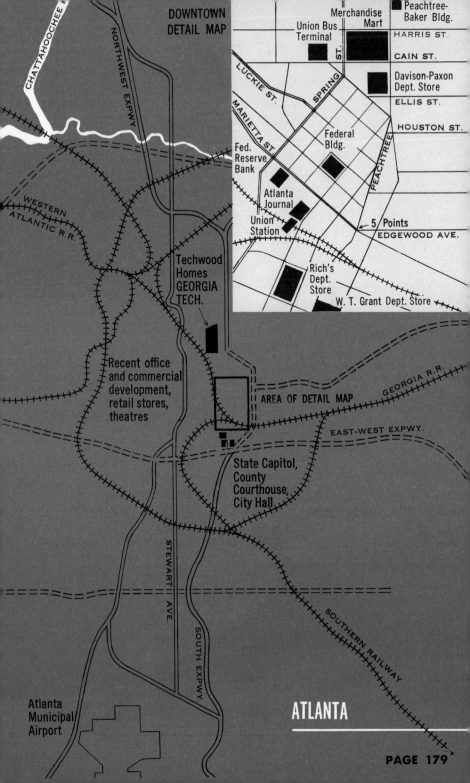

# DOWNTOWN DETAIL MAP

CHATTAHOOCHEE

NORTHWEST EXPWY

WESTERN ATLANTIC R.R.

Techwood Homes
GEORGIA TECH.

Recent office
and commercial
development,
retail stores,
theatres

AREA OF DETAIL MAP

GEORGIA R.R.

EAST-WEST EXPWY.

State Capitol,
County
Courthouse,
City Hall

STEWART AVE.

SOUTH EXPWY.

SOUTHERN RAILWAY

Atlanta
Municipal
Airport

## ATLANTA

**Detail Map Labels:**

- Merchandise Mart
- Union Bus Terminal
- Peachtree-Baker Bldg.
- HARRIS ST.
- CAIN ST.
- Davison-Paxon Dept. Store
- LUCKIE ST.
- SPRING ST.
- ELLIS ST.
- HOUSTON ST.
- MARIETTA ST.
- Fed. Reserve Bank
- Federal Bldg.
- PEACHTREE
- Atlanta Journal
- Union Station
- 5 Points
- EDGEWOOD AVE.
- Rich's Dept. Store
- W. T. Grant Dept. Store

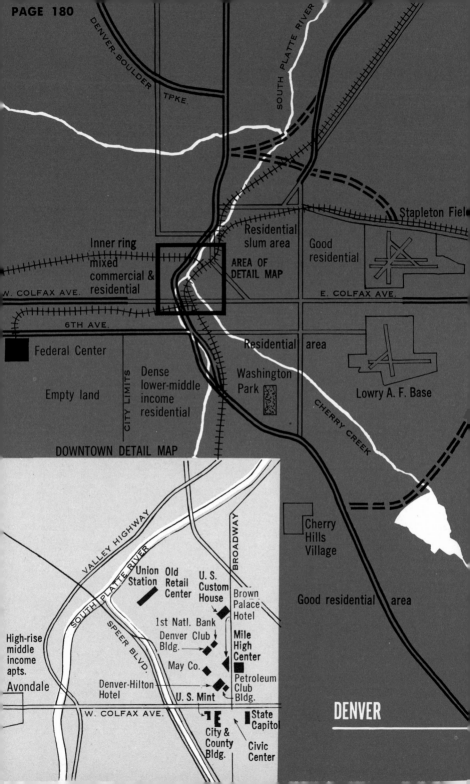

DENVER-BOULDER TPKE.

SOUTH PLATTE RIVER

Stapleton Field

Inner ring
mixed
commercial &
residential

Residential
slum area

Good
residential

AREA OF
DETAIL MAP

W. COLFAX AVE.

E. COLFAX AVE.

6TH AVE.

Federal Center

Residential    area

CITY LIMITS

Dense
lower-middle
income
residential

Washington
Park

Empty land

Lowry A. F. Base

CHERRY CREEK

DOWNTOWN DETAIL MAP

Cherry
Hills
Village

VALLEY HIGHWAY

BROADWAY

Good residential    area

SOUTH PLATTE RIVER

Union
Station

Old
Retail
Center

U. S.
Custom
House

Brown
Palace
Hotel

SPEER BLVD.

1st Natl. Bank
Denver Club
Bldg.

Mile
High
Center

High-rise
middle
income
apts.

May Co.

Petroleum
Club
Bldg.

Avondale

Denver-Hilton
Hotel

U. S. Mint

W. COLFAX AVE.

State
Capitol

City &
County
Bldg.

Civic
Center

**DENVER**

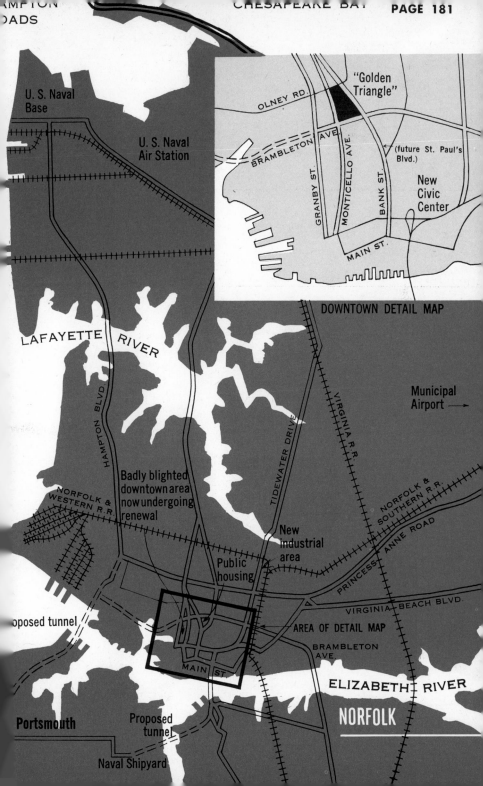

U. S. Naval
Base

U. S. Naval
Air Station

"Golden
Triangle"

OLNEY RD.

BRAMBLETON AVE.

GRANBY ST.

MONTICELLO AVE.

BANK ST.

(future St. Paul's
Blvd.)

New
Civic
Center

MAIN ST.

DOWNTOWN DETAIL MAP

LAFAYETTE RIVER

HAMPTON BLVD.

Municipal
Airport →

VIRGINIA R.R.

TIDEWATER DRIVE

Badly blighted
downtown area
now undergoing
renewal

NORFOLK &
WESTERN R.R.

New
industrial
area

NORFOLK &
SOUTHERN R.R.

Public
housing

PRINCESS ANNE ROAD

AREA OF DETAIL MAP

Proposed tunnel

VIRGINIA BEACH BLVD.

BRAMBLETON
AVE.

MAIN ST.

ELIZABETH RIVER

Portsmouth

Proposed
tunnel

NORFOLK

Naval Shipyard

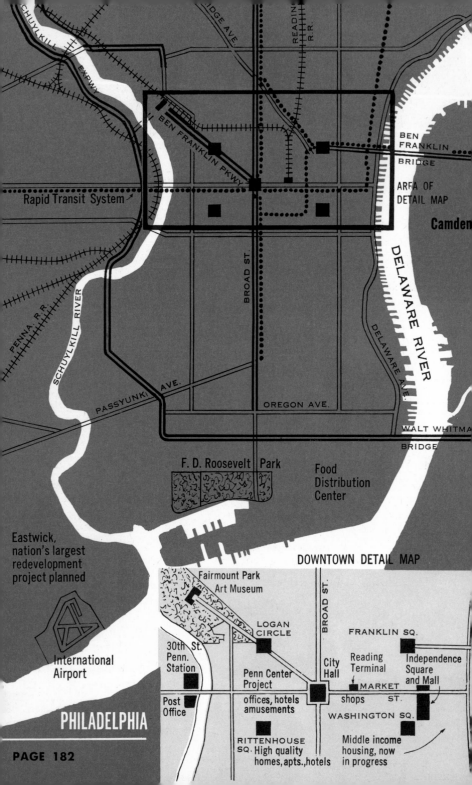

RIDGE AVE.

READING R.R.

SCHUYLKILL EXPWY

BEN FRANKLIN PKWY

BEN FRANKLIN BRIDGE

Rapid Transit System →

AREA OF DETAIL MAP

Camden

PENNA. R.R.

SCHUYLKILL RIVER

BROAD ST.

DELAWARE RIVER

DELAWARE AVE.

PASSYUNK AVE.

OREGON AVE.

WALT WHITMA BRIDGE

F. D. Roosevelt Park

Food Distribution Center

Eastwick, nation's largest redevelopment project planned

International Airport

PHILADELPHIA

**PAGE 182**

**DOWNTOWN DETAIL MAP**

Fairmount Park Art Museum

BROAD ST.

30th St. Penn. Station

LOGAN CIRCLE

FRANKLIN SQ.

City Hall

Reading Terminal

Independence Square and Mall

Penn Center Project

MARKET ST.

Post Office

offices, hotels amusements

shops

WASHINGTON SQ.

RITTENHOUSE SQ. High quality homes, apts., hotels

Middle income housing, now in progress

# CINCINNATI

Greenhills

Evendale

Montgomery

Mt. Healthy

COUNTY LINE

College Hill

Deer Park

Airy
est

Madeira

Norwood

OHIO

PENNA. R.R.

Mariemont

Newtown

MILL CREEK

MONTGOMERY RD.

AREA
OF
DETAIL
MAP

OHIO RIVER

Bellevue

Newport

Ft. Thomas

LITTLE MIAMI RIVER

Mt. Washington

Covington

LICKING RIVER

CENTRAL AVE.

CENTRAL PARKWAY

9TH ST.

7TH ST.

Inner core

DOWNTOWN
DETAIL MAP

Urban
Renewal
Area

Carew
Tower

Fountain
Sq.

Post
Office

Govt.
Sq.

4TH ST.

Distributor under
construction

Water-
front
area . . .
run down
proposed
for
renewal

OHIO RIVER

Proposed
underground
parking

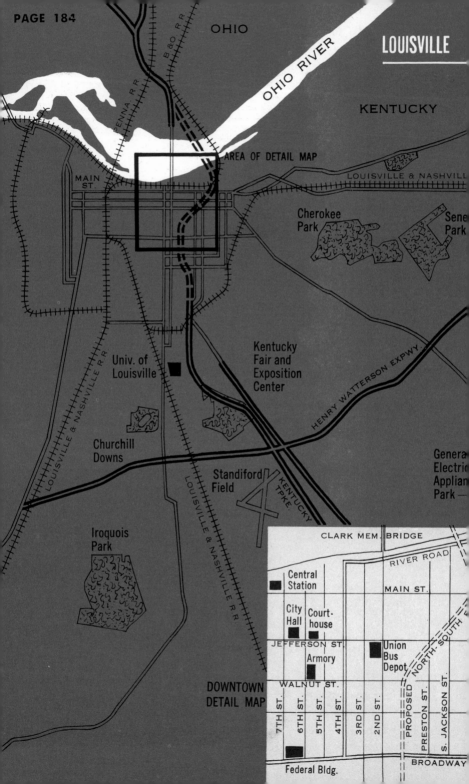

OHIO

OHIO RIVER

LOUISVILLE

KENTUCKY

B & O R.R.

PENNA. R.R.

AREA OF DETAIL MAP

MAIN ST.

LOUISVILLE & NASHVILL

Cherokee Park

Sene Park

LOUISVILLE & NASHVILLE R.R.

Univ. of Louisville

Kentucky Fair and Exposition Center

HENRY WATTERSON EXPWY.

Churchill Downs

LOUISVILLE & NASHVILLE R.R.

Standiford Field

KENTUCKY TPKE.

Genera Electri Applian Park —

Iroquois Park

DOWNTOWN DETAIL MAP

CLARK MEM. BRIDGE

RIVER ROAD

Central Station

MAIN ST.

City Hall

Court-house

JEFFERSON ST.

Union Bus Depot

Armory

NORTH-SOUTH

WALNUT ST.

PROPOSED

PRESTON ST.

S. JACKSON ST.

7TH ST.

6TH ST.

5TH ST.

4TH ST.

3RD ST.

2ND ST.

Federal Bldg.

BROADWAY

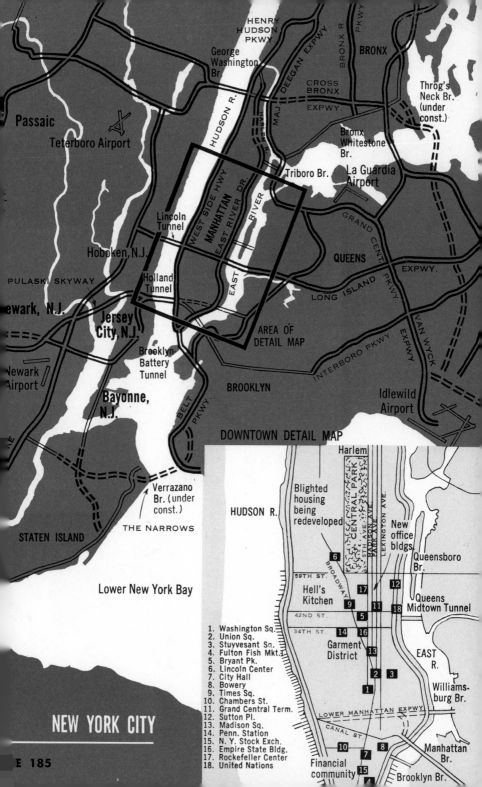

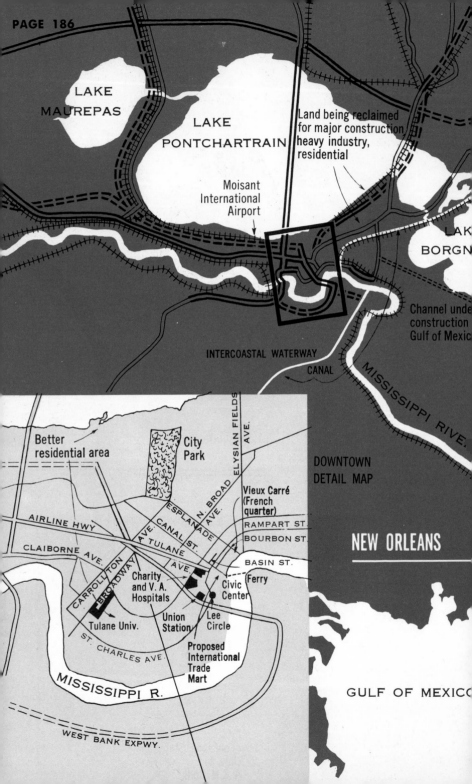

LAKE
MAUREPAS

LAKE
PONTCHARTRAIN

Land being reclaimed
for major construction
heavy industry,
residential

Moisant
International
Airport

LAKE
BORGN

Channel unde
construction
Gulf of Mexic

INTERCOASTAL WATERWAY

CANAL

MISSISSIPPI RIVE.

Better
residential area

City
Park

ELYSIAN FIELDS AVE.

Vieux Carré
(French
quarter)

ESPLANADE AVE.

N BROAD AVE.

CANAL ST.

DOWNTOWN
DETAIL MAP

RAMPART ST.

BOURBON ST.

AIRLINE HWY

TULANE AVE.

BASIN ST.

NEW ORLEANS

CLAIBORNE AVE.

CARROLLTON AVE.

BROADWAY

Charity
and V. A.
Hospitals

Civic
Center

Ferry

Tulane Univ.

Union
Station

Lee
Circle

ST. CHARLES AVE.

Proposed
International
Trade
Mart

MISSISSIPPI R.

GULF OF MEXICO

WEST BANK EXPWY.

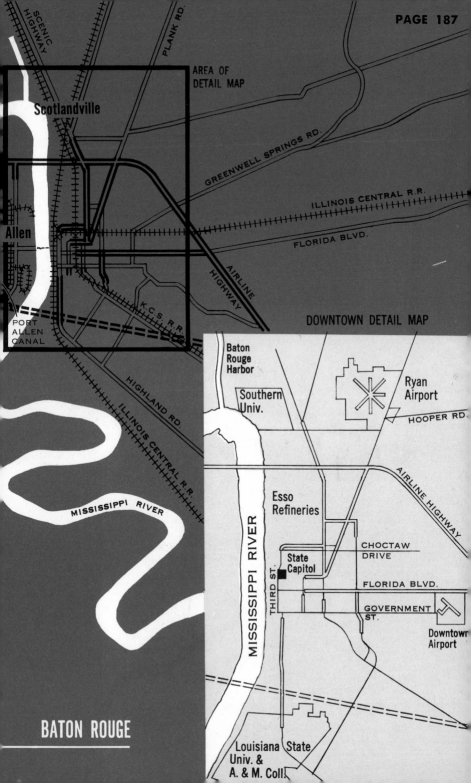

AREA OF
DETAIL MAP

SCENIC HIGHWAY

PLANK RD.

Scotlandville

GREENWELL SPRINGS RD.

ILLINOIS CENTRAL R.R.

FLORIDA BLVD.

Allen

AIRLINE HIGHWAY

K.C.S.R.R.

PORT ALLEN CANAL

HIGHLAND RD.

ILLINOIS CENTRAL R.R.

MISSISSIPPI RIVER

BATON ROUGE

DOWNTOWN DETAIL MAP

Baton Rouge Harbor

Southern Univ.

Ryan Airport

HOOPER RD.

AIRLINE HIGHWAY

MISSISSIPPI RIVER

Esso Refineries

CHOCTAW DRIVE

State Capitol

THIRD ST.

FLORIDA BLVD.

GOVERNMENT ST.

Downtown Airport

Louisiana State Univ. & A. & M. Coll.

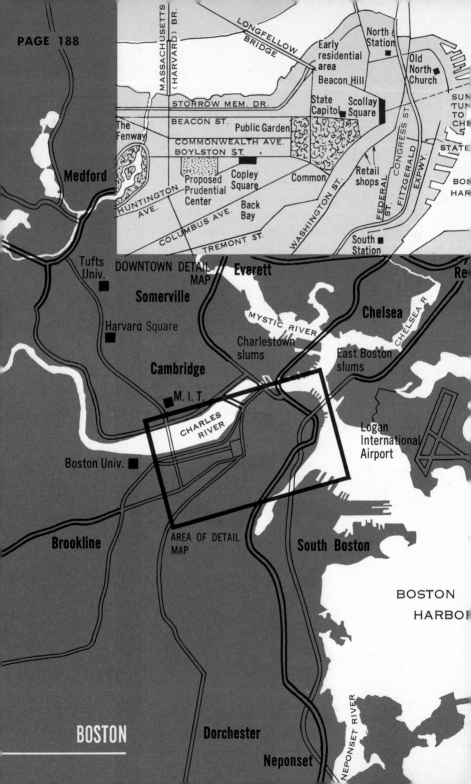

MASSACHUSETTS (HARVARD) BR.

LONGFELLOW BRIDGE

Early residential area

North Station

Old North Church

Beacon Hill

SUM TUN TO CH

STORROW MEM. DR.

State Capitol

Scollay Square

CONGRESS ST

STATE

BEACON ST.

Public Garden

The Fenway

COMMONWEALTH AVE.
BOYLSTON ST.

FEDERAL ST.

FITZGERALD EXPWY.

BOS
HAR

Medford

Common

WASHINGTON ST.

Proposed Prudential Center

Copley Square

Retail shops

HUNTINGTON AVE.

Back Bay

COLUMBUS AVE.

TREMONT ST.

South Station

DOWNTOWN DETAIL MAP

Everett

Re

Somerville

MYSTIC RIVER

Chelsea

CHELSEA R

Tufts Univ.

Harvard Square

Charlestown slums

East Boston slums

Cambridge

M.I.T.

CHARLES RIVER

Logan International Airport

Boston Univ.

Brookline

AREA OF DETAIL MAP

South Boston

BOSTON HARBOR

Dorchester

NEPONSET RIVER

BOSTON

Neponset

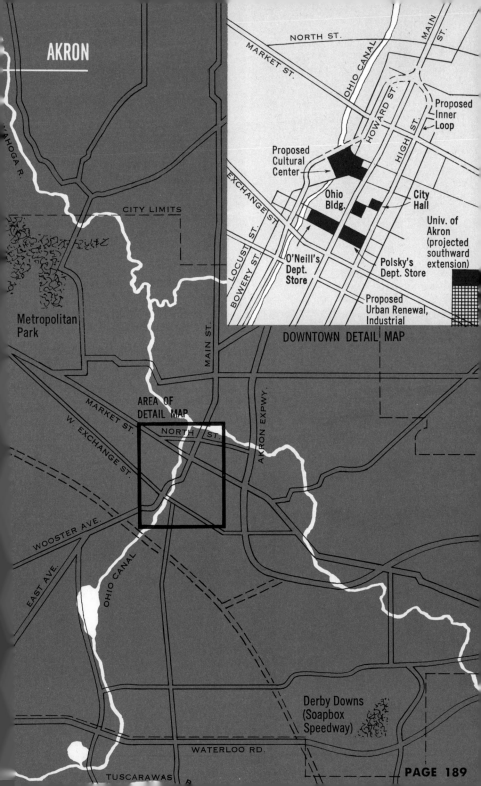

# AKRON

**Metropolitan Park**

CITY LIMITS

MARKET ST.

W. EXCHANGE ST.

MAIN ST.

AREA OF DETAIL MAP

NORTH ST.

AKRON EXPWY.

WOOSTER AVE.

EAST AVE.

OHIO CANAL

Derby Downs (Soapbox Speedway)

WATERLOO RD.

TUSCARAWAS R.

'AHOGA R.

## DOWNTOWN DETAIL MAP

NORTH ST.

MARKET ST.

OHIO CANAL

MAIN ST.

HOWARD ST.

HIGH ST.

Proposed Inner Loop

Proposed Cultural Center

Ohio Bldg.

City Hall

Univ. of Akron (projected southward extension)

EXCHANGE ST.

LOCUST ST.

BOWERY ST.

O'Neill's Dept. Store

Polsky's Dept. Store

Proposed Urban Renewal, Industrial

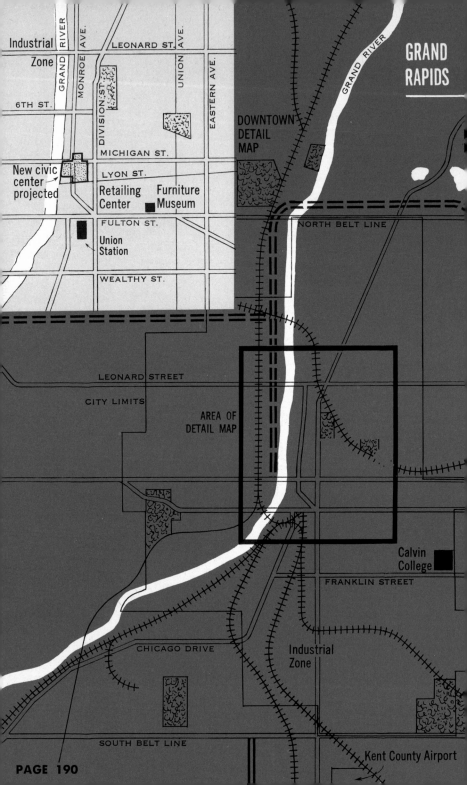

GRAND RAPIDS

Industrial Zone

LEONARD ST.

6TH ST.

GRAND RIVER

MONROE AVE.

DIVISION ST.

UNION AVE.

EASTERN AVE.

MICHIGAN ST.

New civic center projected

LYON ST.

Retailing Center

Furniture Museum

FULTON ST.

Union Station

WEALTHY ST.

DOWNTOWN DETAIL MAP

GRAND RIVER

NORTH BELT LINE

LEONARD STREET

CITY LIMITS

AREA OF DETAIL MAP

Calvin College

FRANKLIN STREET

CHICAGO DRIVE

Industrial Zone

SOUTH BELT LINE

Kent County Airport

Tulsa
North
Airport

Tulsa
Municipal
Airport

MOHAWK BLVD.

MIDLAND VALLEY R.R.

A. T. & S. F. R. R.

ST. L. & S. F. R.R.

AREA OF
DETAIL MAP

University
of Tulsa

ARKANSAS RIVER

Tulsa State
Fair Grounds

Swan Park

Woodward
Park

MO.-KANS.-TEXAS R.R.

Philbrook
Art Center

ST. L. & S. F. R.R.

ST. L. & S. F. R.R.

Oklahoma City

DOWNTOWN DETAIL MAP

Proposed
Civic
Center,
middle
income
apts.

BOULDER AVE.

BOSTON AVE.

ADMIRAL BLVD

2ND ST.

Downtown
grid

University
of Tulsa

Courthouse
Sq.

11TH ST.

Direction of
expansion

ARKANSAS RIVER

15TH ST.

**TULSA**

to Dallas

Boulder
Park

Swan Park

**PAGE 191**

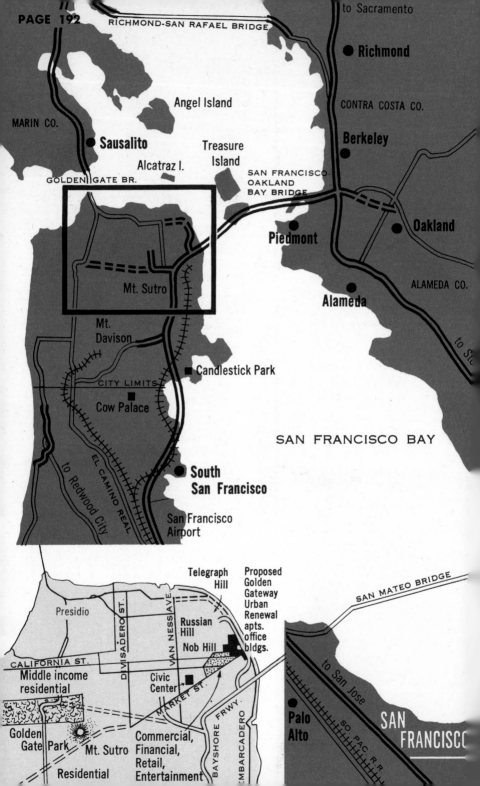

RICHMOND-SAN RAFAEL BRIDGE

to Sacramento

● Richmond

Angel Island

CONTRA COSTA CO.

MARIN CO.

● Sausalito

Alcatraz I.

Treasure Island

● Berkeley

GOLDEN GATE BR.

SAN FRANCISCO-
OAKLAND
BAY BRIDGE

● Oakland

● Piedmont

Mt. Sutro

ALAMEDA CO.

Mt. Davison

● Alameda

to Sto

CITY LIMITS

■ Candlestick Park

Cow Palace

SAN FRANCISCO BAY

EL CAMINO REAL

to Redwood City

● South
San Francisco

San Francisco
Airport

Telegraph
Hill

Proposed
Golden
Gateway
Urban
Renewal
apts.
office
bldgs.

SAN MATEO BRIDGE

Presidio

Russian
Hill

Nob Hill

CALIFORNIA ST.

Middle income
residential

Civic
Center

to San Jose

Golden
Gate Park

Mt. Sutro

Residential

Commercial,
Financial,
Retail,
Entertainment

● Palo
Alto

SAN
FRANCISCO

DIVISADERO ST.

VAN NESS AVE.

MARKET ST.

BAYSHORE FRWY.

EMBARCADERO

SO. PAC. R.R.

Area," conducted under the auspices of the Federal City Council, comments somewhat gently that "little benefit to downtown Washington will accrue from such construction at this location."

The shift of the city's center to the west has opened a broad avenue through the classic inner-ring blight. The area due north of downtown is largely Negro, but middle-class Negro, especially in the environs of Howard University and the McMillan Reservoir. The apparent permanence of a good white neighborhood in the attractive Serenity Hill region just west of Howard has given a degree of stability to the northern approaches.

Out to the west of the White House, the physically unwholesome climate of Foggy Bottom blighted the relatively small area south of Pennsylvania Avenue and the Washington Circle—and neither the State Department nor the Navy Department nor George Washington University could do much to stop the deterioration—until the general westward trend took over a few years ago. Today a new State Department office building, six luxury apartment houses and the expansion of George Washington University have made the area a center of private redevelopment and real estate activity. The projected "National Cultural Center," to be located smack in Foggy Bottom, would clinch matters.

Due northwest the winds are fair. The Connecticut Avenue-Massachusetts Avenue complex—blending from office building and the newest best shops, to the embassies and fine old residences, to the apartment houses—displays an area of upper-middle-class domination all the way out to the Western Avenue border of the district and to Chevy Chase beyond. Westward, across Rock Creek Park, the older, convenient residential section of Georgetown (the original settlement of the area and its first port) has been spectacularly refurbished in the last generation. Near the center but protected (with the Potomac to the south,

Georgetown University to the west, the Naval Observatory and Dumbarton Oaks to the north and developed Foggy Bottom between it and downtown), Georgetown seems a safe bet for prosperity even beyond the foreseeable future.

Elsewhere, the threat of increasing blight is disturbingly real, for reasons that most people choose not to discuss. Since the war, at an accelerating rate, Washington has been exchanging population with Virginia and Maryland —Negroes coming into the city, whites fleeing to the new suburbs below the river and to Maryland. Any Negro intelligent enough to hold a government job would want to get out of Virginia—and in the Washington area he can set up a new residence in an officially desegregated community without even changing his job. The typical postwar flight to suburbia has opened up large stretches of Washington to Negroes, and the typically American reluctance to live beside ethnically different Americans has put further thrust behind the movement of whites to the fringes.

Washington is or will shortly become a predominantly Negro city, the first such in our history, but perhaps not the last. The significance of the facts is still obscure, mostly because so few people have been willing to face up to them. And the situation is wretchedly complicated by the continuing failure of Congress to give the city self-government—a failure likely to persist so long as *noblesse oblige* in the Senate gives representatives of the southern states a strong voice in ordering District of Columbia affairs.

Economically, Washington is unique and uniquely safe. Industries may rise and industries may fall, but in our day and age nothing can be imagined which will make the government shrink or go bankrupt, without bankrupting the nation. The Eisenhower administration when new made a considerable effort to reduce government employment, and anyone curious about the results need merely compare the budget for 1952 (when we were actually fighting a war) with the budget for 1960. The personal frustration and agony of those RIF (Reduction In Force) days linger in the minds of Washingtonians, and as the effort brought forth no fruit except this agony it seems unlikely to be attempted again.

Government draws tourists (far and away the city's second largest industry), and nothing is going to damage Washington's tourism either. It is widely believed, especially by the many companies which package the trips, that every American schoolchild has a right to visit his nation's capital before receiving his diploma. And the very fact that everyone has three representatives working for him on Capitol Hill lures "plain folks" to the city in great numbers.

The federal government spends one-sixth of the entire national income, which means that many, many businessmen have business in Washington. Some of them come on visits; others establish permanent offices, frequently rather grand. Recently a major crop of headquarters for national eleemosynary institutions has been grown here, joining the labor unions, manufacturers' associations, farm lobbyists and the like. Decentralization of these activities, too, seems most unlikely; indeed, the trend lines predict more concentration.

Not everything about Washington's economic situation is entirely favorable. Government service, with its added security, inevitably pays something less than private enterprise, and white-collar Washington has to watch its expenditures even more carefully than its brothers elsewhere in the country. The city's gentility is necessarily a little shabby, and the chance to get rich is somewhat less than it might be elsewhere—for real estate investors as well as for other entrepreneurs. But the security *is* attractive, and in the past, when I was setting up separate "joint ventures" for each purchase, I used to balance a moderate risk elsewhere with a safe if not spectacular purchase in Washington.

The planning problems of Washington are like those of

Los Angeles. Both are "low-density" cities, which means, in less favorable terms, that the waste of prime land is gigantic. (There is an interesting comparison between the Ambassador Hotel in Los Angeles and the Sheraton Park or Shoreham in Washington, all set in the middle of grandiose parks which contribute very little to the livability of the hotel but occupy a great quantity of near central land.) Both cities became really major metropolitan areas only after the end of large-scale immigration, and both suffered from irrational zoning requirements, which established a maximum height of twelve stories in Washington, thirteen in Los Angeles, forbidding efficient downtown development. The combination of these two factors denied both cities anything resembling mass rapid transit. In both cities there is no "old loyalty" to downtown, because too much of the population is new. Finally, both sent large fractions of their population across a major topographical barrier—the mountains in Los Angeles, the Potomac in Washington—before there was adequate transportation to get people to and from their homes and jobs. More than half a million people now live in suburban Virginia, an increase of 375,000 in the last twenty years. In the tabulation of twenty-four "Standard Metropolitan Areas" which showed a population of more than one million in the 1960 Census, Washington and Los Angeles both ranked (with San Antonio, Houston and Atlanta) among the five with the greatest percentage increase over 1950 figures. But Washington war the only one of the five to show an actual decrease in the number of people living within center city itself.

Today there is a grand total of four bridges between Washington and Virginia, and one of the four, the Chain Bridge, is well out in northwest suburbia. Another is under way near midtown, and two others will connect the city's Maryland suburbs with its Virginia suburbs and carry through traffic. Fortunately, not all the traffic flows in one direction at rush hour, and rush hours are staggered. The interchange of white and Negro population, plus the development of large federal office facilities (notably the Pentagon) on the Virginia side of the river, has guaranteed a traffic jam in both directions every morning and every evening. To the north the traffic still moves, thanks to really strict and rigidly enforced no-parking laws, plus the administrative magic which makes the city's trunk routes run one way into town in the morning rush, one way out of town in the afternoon rush. As a result Washington scored only slightly under the national average on *Fortune's* scoreboard of distances covered during a half-hour's driving by car leaving the center of town at five in the afternoon. For those who live in Virginia, however—and right now the most rapidly expanding suburbs are in Virginia—the trip downtown and out is hell, which must damage downtown.

At present, no substantial public transit projects are under serious consideration, and the new zoning codes are—incredibly—even worse than the old. Bulk construction and land-utilization restrictions literally prohibit progress toward a viable downtown density. Meanwhile, the federal highway projects seem likely to benefit outlying areas more than downtown. The Washington Circumferential Highway (or Capital Beltway) will not even enter the District of Columbia, let alone provide access to downtown. There will be an inner-loop highway eventually, but nobody knows where. The new highways, though, will help to relieve downtown congestion by taking through traffic out of town (through traffic to the south now passes over the Fourteenth Street Bridge, the most central and the most crowded). But something far more drastic than what is now on the planning boards seems necessary if downtown Washington is to have the vitality the nation's capital deserves.

The job may be done. A new National Capital Downtown Committee has directed everyone's attention to the need for core redevelopment. Heavy private support is available from the department stores and the banks. The rejuvenated Redevelopment Land Agency, headed by the admirable John Searles, knows that downtown must be saved, and integrated with the Southwest and Southeast projects, if master planning is to make sense. The talent enlisted—much of it full-time—presents an impressive roster of names; but the lethargic tradition of the city's established powers makes a distressing contrast against the awakening, rootless giant in Los Angeles.

# 11. Dallas

Not everyone admires the Texas notion of doing things big
for the sake of their size, but when you have a city to build
there is something to be said for it. Few cities in America
have grown so rapidly as Dallas in the last decade—the Los
Angeles metropolitan area itself shows a lesser percentage
increase. Yet Dallas, thanks largely to its leaders' willingness to risk their money in their own city, suffers relatively
few of the horrors which boom has brought to its contemporaries.

Southland Center, on the northeast edge of the established
downtown (the best residential districts are off in the northeast direction), contains the tallest building west of the
Mississippi, a forty-two-story skyscraper housing the home
offices of the Southland Life Insurance Company. The other
major structures in the Center, connected with the office
building by a lobby, is a twenty-eight-story Sheraton hotel,
a most intelligent idea. City planners have been heard to
mention Southland in the same breath with New York's
Rockefeller Center, and this sort of tribute is hard to find.

Even without Southland, the Dallas skyline would be impressive. The city's most important single role in life is to be

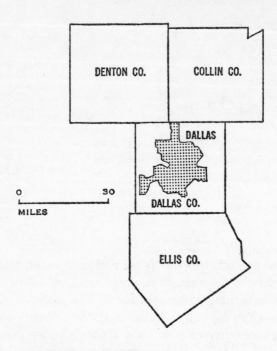

Standard Metropolitan Statistical Area.

a financial and insurance center. It is the home town of a Federal Reserve district, two extremely large and many smaller banks, and more than *two hundred* insurance companies. Financial institutions, as the entrance skyline of New York has demonstrated to European visitors for nearly fifty years, like to build big; and in Dallas they have. Los Angeles until 1957 forbade the construction of buildings more than thirteen stories high; by then, Dallas had two dozen buildings more than fifteen stories high. Indeed, Dallas in the postwar period has put up more office buildings than any American city except New York. And Dallas serves a metropolitan area with only 800,000 people in it.

Even in a city which has something more than the usual proportion of office employment, skyscraper construction can

200

produce a compact, approachable downtown. Few cities testify so plainly to the virtues of high-density commercial construction. There are traffic jams downtown—especially on Ervay Street, which leads past the main offices of the Republic and Mercantile National Banks, Neiman-Marcus and the Merchandise Mart. Getting the cars into the garages in the morning and out of them in the evening slows all motion in the Central Business District. Nevertheless, be-

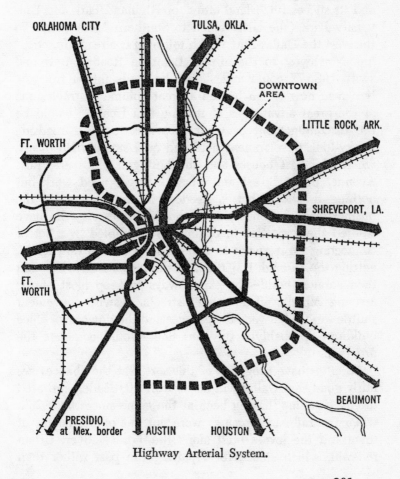

Highway Arterial System.

cause downtown is compact, access to it is relatively easy. Of the twenty-five cities *Fortune* investigated a few years ago, only Houston and Cleveland offered the motorist more mileage in his first half-hour's driving out of the heart of downtown starting at five in the afternoon.

And Dallas, still planning big for the future, expects even better access to downtown than it has today. Central Expressway, slightly improved, will be adequate to the north and its successful "island cities" of Highland Park and University Park (the latter home to Southern Methodist). To the west the Dallas-Fort Worth toll road is already functioning. Northwest to the airport Lemmon Road is new and swift. U.S. 77 could and should be made into a freeway, but even now it can handle a great volume of traffic; one of the great advantages of making it a freeway would be the discouragement of what threatens to be a roadside honky-tonk development here and on Lemmon. Northeast, where the best houses and the best golf clubs are, Ross Avenue, Bryan Street and Liveoak Street need work but nothing drastic. What is needed, in the opinion of the businessmen and Southern Methodist professors who have studied these matters in committee assembled, is a set of connecting expressways to make a loop around downtown, getting the through traffic out of the business district—and then garages beside the expressways to keep most of the arriving vehicles off downtown streets. A swift, convenient shuttle service between the garages and the downtown office buildings—probably a tiny bus line—would complete the program.

All cities have programs of this sort, but the chances are fairly good that Dallas will do its work. Its leaders are used to city planning, having been at the game since the 1920's, when the railroad crossings were got out of the center of town and the levees built along the Trinity River. Urban renewal, which smacks of repairing the past rather than boasting about the future, has been a little less attractive, and Dallas unfortunately has been too proud of its own enterprise to ask for federal money, even on a limited scale. (The city has also been a little stingy about such dull house-keeping expenses as sewer systems and water mains.) Still, the fancy new convention hall and its acres of parking space are built on what a planner would have chosen as a prime urban renewal area—just south of downtown, three blocks from the Merchandise Mart, where blighted inner-ring residences crept closest to the business district. And not the least of the reasons to root for the new loop highways is their location through what is now mostly a rotting area.

Too much of the inner ring is rotting, but even so Dallas is more fortunate than most older river cities. The floods of yesteryear kept downtown from settling on the banks of the Trinity, and left a good deal of open space between the riverbed and the Central Business District. Some of this open space was occupied by the redirected railroad lines when the city built its flood-control dams and walls in the 1920's; much of the rest of it has been built up with low-lying modern factories, unusually convenient to downtown, not handsome by any means but presenting virtually no blight problem at all. Of the residential inner ring, some at least would be suitable for park purposes, a sacrifice which Dallas can afford financially, an amenity which Dallas rather sadly lacks, and a necessity which its pride will see through.

"Big D." All right, Big D. A very strong city. A cultural center, too, with a local theater, big-time opera and a well-supported orchestra. The tribute is unsolicited, and given completely without self-interest. I don't own in Dallas, and I don't see how I can buy. In Texas, local money, some of it institutional and some from the new oil-made landed aristocracy, bids optimistically for local real estate, and prices rise to the stratosphere, carried by the lighter-than-air boom mentality. When a Dallas real estate broker offers a property, he talks in terms of very small returns.

If the city were less aggressive, its future would not seem so secure. Economically, the base has swampy spots. The city is more than a little overbuilt for its current needs. More than a quarter of all the production workers in Dallas work in an aircraft industry which makes military planes almost exclusively, and which has been painfully slow to shift into missiles. Like most of the Southwest, Dallas suffers a relative shortage of highly trained workers, and it is more difficult to import such people to Texas than to Phoenix or Los Angeles. As a manufacturing city, Dallas runs assembly lines; and missiles cannot be built on assembly lines. Synthetics represent a continuing threat to the area's cotton. There is going to be a day of reckoning in the manufacturing segment of the Dallas economy unless, as the local Federal Reserve Bank suggests, the city moves rapidly into consumer goods areas.

Manufacturing, however, accounts for only 28 per cent of the city's total employment, and the other segments are all strong. Texas state law insists that at least three-quarters of all life insurance premiums collected in the state of Texas must be invested in the state of Texas. The law drove most national life insurance companies out of the state, and started a large local insurance company business, or (in some cases) racket. Because Dallas is the banking capital of the area, the new companies located in Dallas and are still there —together with many national companies which returned, grumbling, to make money on Texas investments. (Meanwhile, some Texas companies had expanded nationally. Giant Franklin Life, for example, is controlled by Dallas' Republic National Bank.) Despite the scandals surrounding life insurance operations a few years back, this area of Dallas employment is obviously safe.

Laws also protect the primacy of the Dallas downtown banks. In Texas no bank can have branches, which means that money from all over the state tends to come into Dallas, via correspondents of the city's very large and soundly established central banks. The original role of the Dallas financial market was as capital supplier to the cotton growers and stockmen of the area from the Kansas border to the Mexican border, and the channels are all well greased. The largest spot-cotton market in America stands only a couple of blocks from Southland Center. As this area expands in production and wealth, the Dallas financial center must grow with it.

Historically, too, the city is a fashion center as well as a money center. Neiman-Marcus is one of the half-dozen style-setting department stores in America, and its presence in Dallas has stimulated an important local clothing industry. As a wholesale center, the city is somewhat less safe, because patterns of warehousing and wholesaling are changing in the American economy. But the new convention hall, the new home furnishings mart and the rehabilitation of the Merchandise Mart all indicate that Dallas will fight hard to hold what it has.

Location is Dallas' major asset, looking toward the future. For three-quarters of a century Dallas has been a transportation center. Its river, the Trinity, was never much good for this purpose, running too high or too low to carry much cargo. The river, in fact, acted originally as a boundary, protecting early settlers against Indians. (The early settlers must have been an unusual lot. No other major city in America took the name of a vice-president of the United States, as Dallas did.) But the railroads came in 1872, and during the next twenty years no fewer than seven lines fed into the city. The first two, by the way, were bribed to come —Jay Gould with a gift of $100,000 and a right-of-way down Main Street. The inhabitants of Dallas have been confident for a long time. Today the city is a prime member of the mid-continent club, and jet-size Love Field is headquarters for Braniff Airways. And even the river may help—flood-control and water-supply dams have tamed it enough to make the Army Corps of Engineers admire it as a possible barge canal.

Where is Dallas going? One answer might be, "To Fort Worth." Though the two cities are separate metropolitan areas in census definition, Fort Worth is only twenty miles from Dallas—in a state where a man may say he's going off to have a drink with his neighbor sixty miles away, it's about a forty-minute drive. Rivers separate the two cities, a fact which was more important some years ago than it is today, and the mileage between them is far less built up than one might expect. The two used to fight, and have no love for each other even now, but circumstance pulls them together. Dallas' Cotton Bowl is up northeast of downtown, in the direction opposite Fort Worth, but the new major-league baseball park will be built between the two—mostly with Dallas money. The road and rail connections between them are still improving.

Fort Worth is a more vulnerable city than Dallas and suffered an appalling depression. Today it relies even more than Dallas on aircraft production, and its second industry—the stockyards—is essentially low-wage employment and not the sort of thing one likes to fall back on. Furthermore, it depends more heavily than Dallas on the prosperity of the oil industry, and the world is moving into a period of surplus energy resources—especially oil. Fort Worth did much less than Dallas to put itself in shape in the 1920's, and thus has worse urban renewal problems today.

On the other hand, Fort Worth money commissioned what is undoubtedly the most imaginative and thoroughly considered urban redevelopment program in the country—

206

the Gruen plan. With its expressway patterns, its underground freight-delivery scheme, its shopping malls and gardens, its sure sense of the aesthetic and functional possibilities of a modern downtown layout, the Gruen plan could make Fort Worth a showplace city for the nation. Described usually as a fifteen-year project, it will in fact occupy the energies of the city for at least two generations, requiring great persistence, intelligence and political savvy on the part of its supporters. But whatever their faults, these Texans get things done.

# 12.  Kansas City

A quarter of a century ago this was the most raw, violent and corrupt of major American cities. Chicago had the reputation, but Kansas City had even more of the reality; in Chicago the hoods took their victims to garages to shoot them down in quantity, but in Kansas City they gunned away right in front of the railroad station. A meat and wheat center, which Kansas City will always be, has more than the usual call on its resources of vice: when the farmer gets away from the farm he wants to make whoopee. And in Kansas City the Pendergast machine fed on the bad habits of the city's worst citizens. It was a wide-open town; perhaps the last big city in America where crookedness flourished out in the open. Those who worry about federal urban renewal programs on the grounds that they get the national government into controlling positions on the local scene might give a moment's thought to Kansas City, because, without federal intervention in the form of criminal prosecutions, the Pendergast ring might never have been broken.

Once the weight of corruption had been lifted, Kansas City came alive. Pendergast had promised an ambitious building program, and had actually put up a palatial City

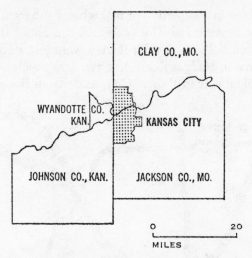

CLAY CO., MO.

WYANDOTTE CO. KAN.

KANSAS CITY

JOHNSON CO., KAN.

JACKSON CO., MO.

0          20
MILES

Standard Metropolitan Statistical Area.

Hall thirty stories high. But little things like the health of the core had been ignored, and Kansas City in the early forties was a mess. As the removal of a Republican machine later gave Philadelphia the full throttle, the removal of a Democratic machine released a powerful flow of civic energy in Kansas City. Without crediting a scoundrel too highly, it is probably true that the new leadership had few goals other than the realization of Pendergast's promises, but they meant it when they said it.

A Downtown Committee of the Chamber of Commerce was organized in 1940, the year of the Great Overthrow, and by 1943 the City Plan Commission published its master plan, "Kansas City 1980," one of the most influential such documents ever written. This was the first master plan to foresee what would happen in America after the war, and to provide for an inner loop of freeways and associated garages around the Central Business District. The major outlines of the 1943 plan are still valid, and as a result Kansas

City is closer to completion of its highway program than any other city in America. The costs will run about three hundred million dollars, all told; if they were just starting now, they'd have to budget more than twice as much.

Redevelopment in Kansas City, aside from the roads, has

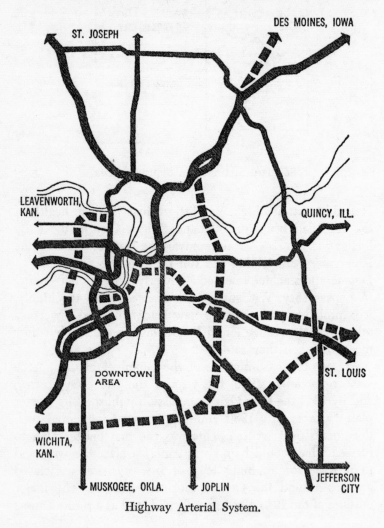

Highway Arterial System.

been in large part a private affair, local government acting as the battery to turn the engine rather than supplying the gas. The city's Downtown Redevelopment Corporation began with a capital stock subscription of $1,523,700 from downtown business interests. Unlike most such corporations elsewhere in the nation, Kansas City's Downtown Redevelopment is *not* non-profit. As long as the group desires a real estate tax break on its properties, its return after taxes may not exceed 8 per cent; and the corporation cannot begin anything without city approval of its plans, or sell anything without city consent. In all other ways, it operates as a private enterprise—in the public interest.

One of the older cities in the mid-continent belt, Kansas City was incorporated in 1850 and had built a substantial downtown well before the turn of the century. It is, of course, a river city, set east and south of the big bend of the Missouri, where the Kansas River enters. There were hills here that the floods could not touch, though the flatland between the hills and the river junction continued for years to be unsuitable for habitation. Once the rivers were more or less tamed the area grew into a prime industrial zone, railroads and barges coming in, butchered carcasses of animals and various manufactured products going out. Kansas City has long rivaled Chicago in the quantity of beef it butchers, and may now be the largest meat-packing center in the country.

The old city established itself just south of the Missouri, up the slopes rising from the river to a tableland stretching great distances to south and east. Typically, the higher you were on the hill, the better you were, and the best residential section of the early days rose in the western corner on bluffs overlooking the meeting of the rivers—a district which received the name Quality Hill and retained the name after it had become an inner-ring slum. Kansas City's most spectacular redevelopment has centered here atop Quality Hill.

The work includes a forty-acre park, an office building for cattlemen, an exclusive private club and five handsome middle-income apartment houses built by Lewis Kitchen under the city's model urban renewal law, passed three years before there was a Title I.

These first high-rise buildings were set near the edge of the bluff, which is, however, something less than half a mile from Auditorium Plaza, where the postwar convention hall is also workable as a theater. Under Auditorium Plaza is a three-level garage for twelve hundred cars, and beside it stands the Muehlebach, the city's (and maybe mid-continent's) best hotel, combining the tradition of an older building with the functionalism of a new one sharing the same lobby, connecting directly by elevator to the garage under the Plaza. Several of the high-rises on Quality Hill are now my property, and I couldn't be happier with them. Kitchen is expanding the development further, to include more apartment houses and commercial buildings, reaching in to within a couple of blocks of Auditorium Plaza. The plans for the extension are sound and attractive, and the area is a natural for development. What stands in it now, especially at the western border of the Plaza, is almost Skid Row in character and is ripe for destruction. What makes Kitchen's new plan so remarkable is the quality of the apartment house he has built—Park Avenue in Kansas City, as he calls it.

North and east of Quality Hill, where the tableland slopes to the river from the commercial center of the city, the Redevelopment Corporation and the federal highway project have been at work to eliminate an antique blight. Everything north of Ninth Street has been at least endangered by the deterioration of the area. The expressway at Sixth Street has bulldozed down some of the worst junk, while the first big project in the redevelopment scheme cleaned up the area on both sides of Main Street (legitimately named) between Ninth and Seventh. Significantly, the project, which featured new offices for the Bell System, stimulated remodeling of existing commercial buildings nearby. The area north of Ninth between Main and Grand Avenue still contains a good part of the city's banking facilities and ought to be salvageable. But most of the newer office building in Kansas City has gone up south of Tenth Street, reflecting the historic southerly shift of the city, which means that the renewal on the north slope had better move a little faster in the years ahead.

Residentially, Kansas City is the home of the nation's most remarkable one-man middle-income housing development— the Country Club Plaza well to the south, running west over to the Kansas line and beyond into Kansas City, Kansas, most of it planned and built in the 1920's by J. C. Nichols, whose organization continues to expand it. South of the Plaza great tracts of upper-income private homes sweep out on big lots. Country Club Plaza itself prospers mightily as one of the earliest and most valid of "suburban" shopping centers, and as terminus for what is a relatively good though entirely surface transit system. As though to solidify the Plaza's subcore status, large apartment houses are now going up all around it. The district is separated from downtown by an industrial outer ring, but the broad streets have prevented serious traffic jams, and a new north-south expressway (one of two, at opposite ends of town) will make access quick and easy.

The entire southern belt of Kansas City is residentially admirable, even where the homes themselves are thirty and forty years old, as they tend to be around Kansas City University. Housing deteriorates as one moves north, and parts of the northeast are bad slums, several of which are to be cleared and redeveloped with federal help. (Well to the east, matters pick up again, particularly in parts of the suburb of Independence, Harry Truman's home town.) One of the city's most deteriorated areas, just east of downtown

213

in the inner ring, has already been cleared for commercial, civic and federal office use. The new public library, which also contains the school offices (Kansas City and Indianapolis are unique in the nation in combining their school and public library facilities throughout the city), is one of the largest in the nation.

Much urban renewal remains to be done in Kansas City, but the achievements of the last decade are notable, and were accomplished without stretching the city's financial resources. Though Kansas City has raised $250,000,000 for urban renewal, its bonds are among the most highly rated in the country, and its tax rate and assessed valuation ratio are low. Kansas City has been annexing territory with great speed (it occupied only sixty square miles in 1946, and now administers more than 250 square miles), but the former city manager, L. P. Cookingham, was careful to acquire industrial as well as residential tracts. Other central cities have complained that the 1960 census cheated them somehow, but Kansas City (which has not complained) has a real reason to gripe. The census definition of its metropolitan area fails to include Platte County to the northwest, site of the city's new Mid-Continent International Airport, and actually within the city limits.

Though Kansas City has grown spectacularly since the war, there has been a refreshing degree of sobriety and solidity about the process. The new office buildings now going up are the first skyscrapers in recent years, though there was a good deal of low office building preceding them. Every industrial section of the city has moved ahead, often by means of additions to existing structures. What the visitor is most likely to notice, apart from the massive development in the corners between the rivers, is the huge Hallmark Cards plant in the middle of the Southern Industrial District, on Twenty-fifth Street not too far from Union Station. The Bell System finds economic advantages in centrality, and Western Electric has been building new facilities in this area for the last decade. TWA has both its operating and servicing headquarters here, and has sunk another $18,000,000 in jet repair facilities at the new Mid-Continent Airport. Meanwhile, the old airport, the most convenient to downtown of any in the country (it sits just across the Missouri, ten minutes by cab from any skyscraper in the city), has been refurbished and enlarged, and will continue to handle most of the passenger traffic.

Food processing is still the city's largest industry, but transportation equipment—both automotive and aeronautic —has been coming up rapidly. Ford and General Motors have large assembly plants here, and the Fisher Body division of GM fabricates chassis. The same reasons that make Kansas City a branch office center make it a distribution headquarters, and the industrial districts are full of depots, one of which—the Goodyear Building, which you think you're going to hit as you make the turn over the river to the airport—I own. I'm pleased with that one, too.

In fact, I'm pleased with Kansas City. I still consider it, despite the recent change in municipal administration, one of the best bets of all American cities. The location is next to perfect, central to both the north-south and east-west routes. (The city next door, at the other end of the state, *is* perfect in situation, but St. Louis is stodgy where Kansas City is alive, and in the years since the war has failed to capitalize on its advantages.) Mid-continent is where the great expansion of the next few decades will come, and there is nothing topographical, geographical, economic or political to keep Kansas City from receiving the biggest single share of the boom. The region's most splendid highway, the Kansas Turnpike, already feeds into the city, and others are coming. And the Corps of Engineers' work on the Missouri will help Kansas City more than any other industrial center.

Most important of all, the city's leaders know what they want to do with their good luck. By expanding the municipal boundaries, they have avoided any danger of the jurisdictional headache St. Louis suffers when it must do business with a ring of sixty-five independent, competing governments. By building their downtown slowly they have avoided the gasbag psychology which makes the inevitable downswings so costly both in human and financial terms. By and large, they have pulled new industry on their terms rather than on industry's terms, keeping the tax base sound. And their approach to urban renewal is characterized by a practicality not always easy to find. Downtown is big, but the highway loop and the railroad to the south define it neatly and the zoning pattern is excellent, everything nasty being confined within large, successful industrial districts on the river or along the railroads entering from the east.

No city which depends on agricultural markets as greatly as Kansas City can ever be depression-proof; and, like many boom cities in the Korean War period, Kansas City allowed itself to become a little overdependent on military production. But the recession of 1957–58 shook out the last weak beams in the structure—and, except for the City Hall, Kansas City never built castles in the sky anyway. With the new expressways, the new transportation center, the new skyscrapers and the new high-rise apartment houses, Kansas City seems reasonably far on its way to realizing the vision of its city planners eighteen years ago.

# 13.  *Atlanta*

Sheer weight of publicity releases made the West and Southwest seem the big boom areas of the last decade, but there is a case to be made for the argument that the great American blast-off in the years since the war has come in the deep South. And this city, whose metropolitan population just passed the one-million mark, is headquarters for the whole area south of the Tennessee Valley, east of the Mississippi and north of the Gulf of Mexico—as much the center of Dixie as Paris is of France. A center of civilization, too: at its best, a place where the old stuff about southern gentility can bear examination. Its hinterland is still coming up economically. Barring racial warfare, which Atlanta is more likely to avoid than any other city of the Deep South, the next decade seems sure to hear an even louder noise from the Peachtree.

Atlanta is a classic case of a city built by transportation; in this example, by man-made transportation. There is no river worth mentioning. The city sits on high ground (of all the major metropolitan areas in the United States, only Denver boasts a greater altitude), with the coastal plains

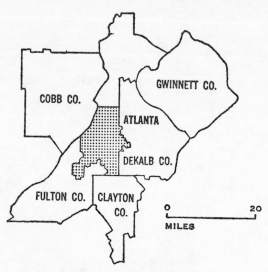

Standard Metropolitan Statistical Area.

sloping off in two directions. Peachtree Street runs along the crest of the ridge which forms the divide between the Atlantic and the Gulf watersheds. Atlanta is where it is apparently because a railroad surveyor of the 1830's thought this particular patch of farmland would make a good terminus. He was right; by the turn of the century seven major railroad lines were passing the site of that spike, near the present Five Points, still the heart of the city's downtown and, according to the local Chamber of Commerce, "one of the five most valuable corners in the world."

Transportation to and from Atlanta has never stopped improving, and the next decade will see even greater advance. Three major segments of the federal highway program will hub in Atlanta. Their juncture, at a site just south of the state capitol, will require a grade interchange, recently started, covering no less than *125 acres*, the biggest to date. The airport, with its brand-new terminal and runways big enough for the Delta DC-8 jets serving the line's national headquarters, is still expanding, with direct flights to Europe to start this year, realizing the old Confederate dream of access to England without tribute to the North. On a per

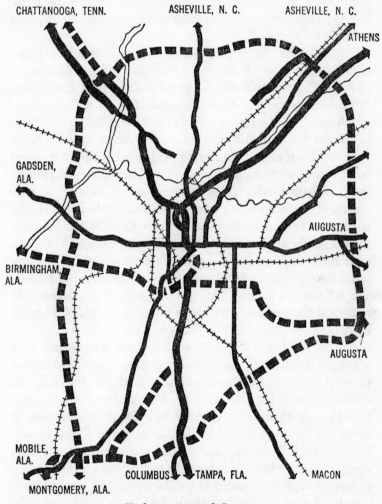

Highway Arterial System.

capita basis, Atlanta already has the greatest volume of rail and truck freight shipment of any city in the world. The airport already ranks fourth in the nation in number of plane departures per day. Communication facilities match the transportation advantages; though it is twenty-second in population in the country, Atlanta ranks third in number of telephone and telegraph messages passing over its wires.

Primarily the city is a trade and financial center, the home of a Federal Reserve district, containing offices of substantially all the nation's fifty largest life insurance companies. It leads both the South and Southwest in its dollar volume of wholesale trade, and is second only to Dallas in the South in annual bank clearings. Much of its recent growth, however, has been in manufacturing, which is logical for a cheap labor transportation and trade center. Coca-Cola is no longer the dominant product; the city's expanding industry is now anchored by automobile assembly plants which serve the entire southern market, part of some three thousand companies newly arrived in Atlanta since the war. And if trade or manufacturing should by any chance go sour, the city has a strong base in government employment; among them, the federal, state and city governments pay salaries into sixty-odd thousand of the area's fewer than 300,000 households.

Atlanta's secret may be that it has no orientation: it is a center point, with the surrounding countryside oriented to *it*. Atlanta is indubitably a southeastern city, but the Atlantic Coast cuts west as it runs south, and the city, though less than two hundred miles from the ocean, is almost as far west as Louisville and closer to Chicago than to New York. It stands astride the main routes from both the Midwest and the Northeast to expanding Florida. When this advantage in situation is combined with relatively open country for expansion, relatively low wage rates and relatively enlightened city government, the issue is scarcely in doubt.

An aerial photograph of Atlanta shows running through the heart of downtown something that looks very much like a river. It is, at any rate, where the river would be in most American cities. In Atlanta, however, the broad belt without buildings is the railroad right-of-way, and the town has grown up around it the way other cities have grown up around waterways. For a brief four-block stretch the air rights have been built over; then the black line of the railroad trackage moves majestically on again.

Oddly enough, the tracks—seemingly a more certain divider than any but the widest rivers—have not greatly influenced the direction of motion in downtown. The state capitol and its associated office buildings, the County Court House and City Hall all sit just south of the railroad tracks and their clinging warehouses. West of them, still south of the tracks, is one of downtown's two retail centers, dominated by Rich's, the largest department store under one roof south of New York and the prime guarantor of the general cleanliness and sanitation of its district, most of which it owns.

Five Points itself is just north of the tracks, formed by the splitting of wide Marietta Street into Edgewood Avenue and Decatur Street, at the point where Whitehall Street becomes the trunk of Peachtree, a street that branches northeast and northwest as East Peachtree and West. Most of the city's recent commercial development has been in the tiny grid due north of Five Points, one of very few squared-off sections in a city of bending streets. The new office construction is heavily concentrated in this area (led by the new Fulton National Bank Building, which dominates the skyline), with skyscrapers rising also in the area farther north, just east of the big new expressway. Just above the little grid, where the trunk of Peachtree straightens out to run due north at another, less celebrated but almost as important five-point intersection, stands the movie theater center and the city's other retail section, led by Davison-Paxon, a ponderable rival to Rich's.

It is a relatively easy downtown to get to (especially now that the north-south expressway is in), and well supplied with parking space and garages. Unfortunately, it is not very attractive, being deficient in greenery, proportion and design; big but more than a little shabby. A city as rich as Atlanta is entitled to something more elegant. At present everyone seems to be relying on the natural forward drive of the region and the considerable commercial construction boom to pretty up the center without help from private committees or public funds—let alone a master plan. Recent suburban shopping center competition has begun with a bang, however—Lenox Square, seven miles north of Five Points, may do as much as sixty million dollars of retail business a year, much of it taken from downtown. Not long after it opened the head of Rich's complained at the absence of "any cohesive group effort by public and private interests" to improve downtown. Mayor Hartsfield has said that: "Putting up new buildings is not the answer by itself, but it helps; it sure helps." Downtown Atlanta will have to decide fairly soon whether putting up new buildings is really enough. I, for one, have yet to see it as an answer to long-range functionalism.

From downtown the city jumped residentially to the north, industrially to the south and west. What was left behind in the inner ring varied from poor to ghastly, but the city, despite its unconcern about downtown itself, has not been backward about securing federal funds for inner-ring renewal. The first public housing project in America, Techwood Homes, went up as part of the effort to save the environment of Georgia Tech. Some $150 million of urban renewal projects (including the east-west expressway, which will cut through the blight south of the capitol) may open the way for sounder development of the inner ring. Negroes, comprising a third of the city's population, live predominantly in this ring in substandard (to say the least) housing. But Atlanta also has a thriving Negro middle class—the proportion of Negro to white doctors, for example, is higher than the proportion of Negro to white population—and by no means all the Negro areas are slums. There are no fewer than ten Negro institutions of higher education in Atlanta, headed by Atlanta University, a "Reconstruction" project dating back to 1867 and the first such institution in the nation. Its president sits on the city's Board of Education, and there is probably less public pressure against school integration in Atlanta than in any other major southern city.

Industrial development in the west is continuing, and may burst into bloom if plans become realities in the project to improve navigability on the Chattahoochee River, the city's western boundary. What really dazzles the eye right now, however, is the development in the airport section, a development great enough to dwarf the twenty-million-dollar work being done on the airport itself. Both factories and distribution centers are involved in the new southern industrial area (most of which, unfortunately, is outside the city limits and will not help the tax base unless annexed), and there is more than a chance that a substantial commercial development will accompany them. International Office Park beside the airport will be a reality, and the 310-room Hilton Hotel is already operating. In fact, I'm building a hotel down there myself—inside the city limits, that is to say on the airport itself, an annexed island smack in the middle of the industrial boom, where I have obtained an exclusive franchise.

Atlanta's worst problems in the next few years will probably be governmental. Despite all the efforts to bring industry to the state, Georgia as a whole is still pretty much a backwoods proposition, with a long if not noble tradition of hatred for the city slicker. Yankee city slickers are of course the worst (though Atlanta's Mayor Hartsfield once pointed out that "the Fourteenth Amendment guarantees northern money equal treatment"), but the local city folk are not much better—especially that Ralph McGill, editor of the city's great paper, the Atlanta *Constitution,* always a big force here. (A statue to editor Henry Grady stands in the middle of Marietta Street in front of the new Fulton Bank Building and just off Five Points.) The state constitution is the nation's most archaic, guaranteeing control not only of the state legislature but of the governor's office as well to the red-neck farmers of the hill country. At this writing there still hangs over the city the threat that the state may compel it to close its schools rather than integrate them— and, as Little Rock discovered, nothing stalls an industrial development campaign more abruptly than closed schools.

In most other areas, however, Atlanta does not greatly need help or even goodwill from the state government. General Motors and Ford are still expanding their Atlanta plants; such companies as DuPont, General Electric and Owens-Illinois are new in the area; the federal payroll is almost certain to grow. The new Merchandise Mart, which will be the largest of its sort outside Chicago, will solidify the city's wholesale position. Like all the boom cities, Atlanta has a big aircraft plant—Lockheed, the largest employer in the state. As branch offices grow everywhere across the country, Atlanta, with its mid-continent counterparts, the most inevitable of all branch office cities, must grow with them.

Like its transportation net, Atlanta's boom radiates in all directions. And in all directions the coast is clear. It probably won't be so cheap to live in Atlanta as it is today, but other-wise the conditions that promoted the city's expansion in the fifties will persist for years to come. This will be a much bigger city in 1975 than it is now; let's hope it will look better, too.

## 14. Denver

A boom and bust city, historically, with many relatively brief booms and relatively long busts. Built originally on rumors of gold, and fattened in the mining rushes, forced to maintain itself between times as a processing and distribution center for a poor farming area. The land west of the Missouri, wrote Major Stephen Long in 1820, "is throughout uninhabitable by people depending upon agriculture for their subsistence." He was wrong, of course, but not so far wrong as the early twentieth-century farmers thought. This is drought country. Sugar beets and sheep have given Denver agricultural functions—a quarter of the manufacturing labor force is employed in food processing, and the city is the largest sheep butcher in the world—but not enough to maintain the standards to which American cities are accustomed.

The new boom may or may not be different. Since 1940 the metropolitan area has more than doubled in population, and is now pushing a million. For once, the big drive is not based on mining and the servicing of miners; but what it *is* based on is hard to see. The city's advantages are all well

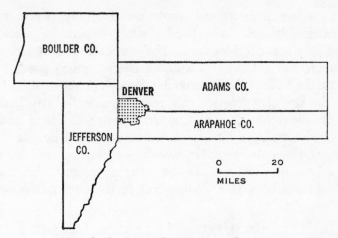

Standard Metropolitan Statistical Area.

known. The climate is notoriously healthful, and some of Denver's income still comes from its hospitals: it was in Fitzsimmons General Hospital here that President Eisenhower recovered from his heart attack. The recreational possibilities are almost unrivaled (the tourists bring in more money than the miners ever did). Transportation is excellent and improving, with jet flights daily to both coasts, and Denver's Stapleton Field is operating headquarters for United Air Lines. But there is still relatively little non-agricultural industry in the Denver area (the only big plants are a Martin Missiles factory, Samsonite luggage and a rubber producer). Empty land, quality transportation and a growing regional market should draw manufacturers over a period of time, but they haven't done so yet. East and west of Denver are economically barren territories, and to be metropolis of the north-south chain from Pueblo to Cheyenne is not really a very important function.

Up to now what has made Denver more than a sheep and tourist town (assuming a difference between sheep and tourists) is the federal government. After Washington,

227

Denver has more federal employees than any city in the country (Atlanta ranks third); every department except State maintains offices here. The concentration of federal workers has not done downtown Denver much good, because the bulk of the government space is in a special center on the site of a former army camp outside the city limits to the west in Jefferson County. Twenty thousand office workers take up a lot of space, however, and, despite the size of the federal center, which occupies an area about equal to all downtown Denver, the government has had to rent nearly 200,000 square feet in the city. A big new

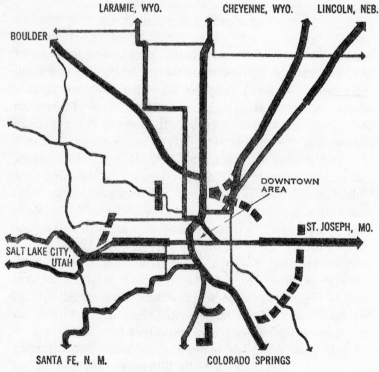

Highway Arterial System.

government office building will be located in downtown itself; Washington has learned that even in the West in the age of the automobile you cannot get a large enough choice of staff when you move ten miles out of town.

Governmentally, Denver is much more than a federal branch office. It is also a state capital, a county seat and a big city in its own right; and the lesser governments employ half again as many people as collect from Uncle Sam. The location of so many governments in Denver has not been an unmixed blessing; they don't get along together very well. The state makes a disgracefully small contribution to the city and its school system, which would be in trouble without the federal per capita grant to the schools for the children of federal employees, given on the grounds that any other employer would be paying school taxes on his property. The county government is completely superfluous, city and county boundaries being identical, and serves mostly as a drain on inadequate tax revenues. City government itself, though now modernized, once worked to block the expansion of the area; led by a cabal known locally as the three B's, from the first initials of their names, the municipality as late as the forties actively discouraged industry from settling in Denver.

Governmental problems are still Denver's worst immediate liability, because the city is virtually broke. In recent years it has followed an expansionist policy, absorbing considerable tracts of new land and perforce paying out for new water mains, sewer pipes, streets and so forth with only the inadequate additional tax revenue offered by lower middle-income houses. It has also had heavy expenses incident to its big water project, which will tunnel water from the other side of the Continental Divide down to the capital. At present the city's streets are in shocking condition and its capital improvements budget is insufficient to prevent further deterioration, let alone provide real "improvements."

Most city political leaders believe a sales tax is the only answer; but nobody wants to impose a sales tax on Denver alone, while the surrounding countryside which lives off Denver builds tax-haven shopping centers. Hamstrung by the difficulties of paying current bills, the city can do little to plan for the future. A downtown committee seeks a master plan, which cannot be prepared for much less than $150,000; the city, groaning mightily, allows that it might find $17,000 for this purpose, provided the committee finds the rest. At present urban renewal in Denver is at dead center and must remain so until one of the usual boring appeals against the law gets its comeuppance in a high court. But in the present state of the city's finances nobody can be sure Denver will be ready to move when the courts clear the way.

And Denver needs urban renewal as badly as any but the oldest American cities. Despite its Far West location, it is by no means a new city; its population crossed the 100,000 mark before 1890. The city had been planted originally in the corner just northeast of Cherry Creek's right-angle entrance into the South Platte River, and the original grid ran parallel to the two rivers. Cutting the grid at an angle were the two main streets into and out of town—Broadway running due north-south; Colfax, due east-west. The railroads came in along the Platte, and Union Station, a surviving piece of nineteenth-century Americana, rose beside the river. The original downtown clustered nearby in the northwest corner of the little grid.

At the opposite end of the grid, where Broadway and Colfax crossed beside a little hill, the state capitol was built, its dome flaked with Colorado gold. In the 1920's the park running down from the capitol to Broadway was extended, and Denver built a Civic Center consisting of a few monuments, greenery, a museum, and the very large City and County Building, kept low to preserve the capitol's view of the mountains, spreading out along an adequate if not

230

very graceful curving façade. Behind the City and County Building stands the U. S. Mint, source of most of the nation's coins, a tribute to the silver and copper once in the hills. The major postwar addition to the Civic Center is a handsome, open public library across the greensward from Colfax Avenue.

Little was done to change Denver's pattern in the early postwar years—indeed, little of anything was built except houses and schools. Many of the overhead wires, a distinguishing feature of the city as late as the 1940's, were put underground. But deterioration accelerated in the old retailing and commercial downtown, rather shoddily built to begin with (Denver had suffered badly in the panics of 1893 and 1907, and the twenties, it will be recalled, were a period of poverty in agriculture). A rapidly expanding city needed new stores and office buildings, and money came to Denver from the outside to build what was necessary and take away the profits. The old downtown, though deteriorated, was still too expensive to lure private redevelopment, and no public help was available. The city's street layout, however, virtually forced redevelopment within the old grid, because the rest of the city had grown up on streets parallel to Broadway and Colfax, and the diagonals of the original grid were still the most convenient from all directions. The moneyed outsiders seized on the area near the civic center, run down as such areas usually are, but preserved from blight at the Broadway anchor by the Brown Palace, one of the nation's first great hotels.

In this area, in the late 1950's, Denver rebuilt spectacularly. Across Broadway from the Brown rose the Denver-U. S. National Center, known to publicity as the "Mile-High Center," an office complex built around pools and fountains and open space, surely one of the most beautiful structures of the postwar period. Two blocks northwest of the Brown the Texas investors built the Denver Club Building and the

First National Bank Building (at twenty-eight stories the city's highest). The Brown itself added a picturesque annex, a little tower on stilts, brown in color of course, with curved corners. A block southwest of the Brown rose the city's triumph—the twenty-two-story Denver-Hilton, complete with three stories of underground parking, its lavish second-floor lobby attached via a vista-dome bridge to a striking new May Company department store. The development also includes a charming little outdoor skating rink, à la Rockefeller Center. Between the Hilton and the civic center on one side stands the University of Denver's postwar business school (preposterously located, in current terms, and probably to move), and on another side the new Petroleum Club building, symbol of the Texas oil money which has built most of the new skyscrapers and occupied their space.

But much of what went into the new buildings came out of the old ones, and the vacancy rate is worse than the figures show, because the owners of the new skyscrapers are paying off the tag end of the leases on the space their tenants used to occupy. There is a dangerously abandoned look about the old downtown. None of the new buildings is closer than half a mile to the old 100 per cent location at the corner of Sixteenth and Larimer, from whence the May D & F store has now departed, leaving behind its dilapidated tower, once the tallest structure in Denver and a state landmark. And the new development beside the Civic Center has already straggled across Broadway up the hill by the state capitol, moving farther and farther from the old core.

North of this collapsed downtown are the railroad tracks and the river (more often, in this region, the riverbed). West of it, across the Platte, is inner-ring mixed commercial and residential, much though not all of it bad, site of the city's largest single urban renewal project, a set of high-rise middle-income apartments at Avondale, to be joined with old downtown by a brief, quick "connector" expressway, also serving the big new north-south six-lane Valley Highway. Northeast of downtown is the city's disaster—headquarters of an antiquated distribution industry now moving out to a string of new red brick angular warehouses along Route 72, north and west of the airport and equally convenient to the railroad tracks. This is the worst of old Denver, a residential slum which for sheer lack of amenities has few rivals in America, tending to blight everything it approaches —including the old downtown.

Residentially, the city after the war exploded to an outer ring. East of downtown and across the Platte in the near West Side, once decent residential areas declined rapidly. The blight crept out as far as City Park, well east of Capitol Hill. Formerly middle-class residential areas, especially those in the near south, down as far as Washington Park, began to slide. West, east and south Denver today present a picture of good residences and pleasant neighborhoods with an air of uncertainty about them—still easily conserved, but ready to collapse if community action is not forthcoming. The few "low-rise" apartment houses near the capitol are no substitute for city-inspired neighborhood action.

Fortunately, the drive to the suburbs went out in all directions. Wealthy families built in unincorporated places due west in Jefferson County (there are twenty miles between downtown Denver and the first steep bluffs of the Rockies); in Cherry Hill to the south; and east, inside the city, not far from the airport along Monaco Boulevard. Lower-middle-class developments went up mostly within the city limits, to take advantage of city utilities and protection, and rose on pitifully small lots. From the look of the southwest, Denver residential zoning seems to provide only that the house may not be larger than the lot.

The spread of housing tracts in all directions, however, kept Denver from the worst traffic jams of car-borne commuters. Streets are broad in the west. What with the north-south Valley Highway, the Sixth Avenue speedway to the west, and Speer Boulevard running southeast on Cherry Creek, it is probably true that even in rush hour one can get anywhere within a dozen miles of the Civic Center in thirty minutes. And cars can safely come into downtown; at present, according to Perry Anderson of the Downtown Denver Improvement Association, there are five parking places for every four cars.

Denver still has an enormous amount to do. Both Broadway and Colfax are shocking examples of strip development in the worst American manner, genuinely hideous from any angle. Downtown must be revitalized, blight rooted out of the northeast, good nearby neighborhoods conserved, city finances improved. A master plan is a necessity, and the planning commission must be given some power to guide development. If the new commercial building should ever jump the barrier of the Civic Center and move south, the old downtown could become a running sore.

The doubts will not down. As Robert Fischer of the First National Bank of Minneapolis told a Denver urban renewal meeting: "You've had a lot of very dramatic development in the last few years. Don't let that fool you. We've had that kind, too. That's our first sixty million dollars. This is a little bit like selling automobiles in 1947—it was no trick at all. You didn't have an office building in Denver for just about as long as we didn't have an office building. This was pretty easy. The next step is going to be a lot harder. All you've really done is fill up the empty garages that were there from the long period of time when you did nothing."

There were only two points in Fischer's presentation with which one could quarrel. The first is the figure, sixty million dollars—Denver has seen major building worth much more than that in the last few years. The second was the use of "you." The citizens of Denver have played no great part in

what renewal has been done to date; Texas money, some of
it channeled through New York, has built nearly all of it.
Before an outsider can have any great faith in Denver's ability to solve its problems, its own citizens, who know the
problems better than anybody else, must be prepared to
ante up at least part of the price of their own salvation.

Their reluctance to do so may reflect intelligence as much
as conservatism. The Texas money is spent; the city is only
slowly digesting the new space the money built. Mile-High
Center provides an aura of prosperity, but you can't rebuild
a city in one new district. What odds against another bust
before the next boom?

# 15. Norfolk

World War II ended, and presently so did the celebrations marking the victory. Most American cities looked around them, noted with distaste the deterioration worked by fifteen years of depression and war, and worried about the prospect of further decay in their physical facilities. Norfolk did not have this worry. Its physical plant was so wretched, its downtown so run-down and inaccessible, that further decay was virtually impossible. The organism fights for survival, be it an animal or a city. Wars, fires, earthquakes bring bursts of energy to re-create, to restore, to make something better than what has been destroyed. In Norfolk, decay—simple decay—became the generating force.

This is an old city, the farthest east and therefore most accessible of the Virginia Tidewater ports. Sections of the waterfront area as it now stands were built directly after the end of an earlier war, the Revolutionary War, to replace structures which the British Navy, standing idly in the Elizabeth River, had gunned down to teach the rebels a lesson. It was in Hampton Roads, between Norfolk and Newport News, that the *Monitor* and the *Merrimac* proved how

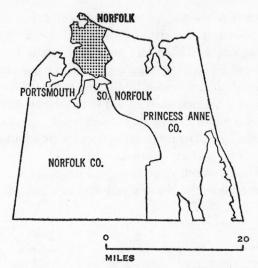

Standard Metropolitan Statistical Area.

difficult it would be for ironclad warships to do each other any damage. A major naval base from the days when Virginia was a colony, Norfolk and adjacent Portsmouth today contain the world's largest collection of permanent naval installations as well as an air force and army base. The naval shipyard—on the wholly protected, virtually inland south branch of the Elizabeth—is the biggest drydock facility the Navy has, and a scenic attraction of the first order. Other cities may have mountains or skyscrapers, but nowhere else can one see from downtown an aircraft carrier moving through a narrow river channel, dwarfing the buildings in the background, on its way to or from the repair shop.

The same safe harbor that attracted the Navy made Norfolk a major Atlantic port. For most commercial purposes, it is the southern terminus of the inland waterway, and the nine railroad lines that service the city drained the produce of an area reaching from South Carolina to West Virginia, to feed the docks. In recent years the Hampton Roads ports

237

have handled a greater volume of export cargo than any other port area in America, including New York. As an *entrepôt* the city has been less successful, partly because its railroads serve a relatively poor section of the country which exports high-bulk low-value items and cannot afford many imports, partly because road access to the docks was terrible from anywhere. Until very recently Norfolk was a city you reached only by rail or by ferryboat, unless you happened to be coming from eastern North Carolina.

Now all the transportation is improving at once. The city's major railroad line, the Norfolk and Western, has been active

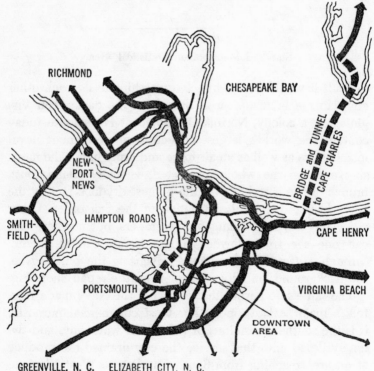

Highway Arterial System.

in the merger market with an obvious eye to North Central States traffic, especially from Ohio. Since 1952 a bridge-tunnel combination has linked Norfolk with Portsmouth, across the Elizabeth. Since 1957 another bridge-tunnel has connected Norfolk with Newport News, providing access by car to the west bank of Chesapeake Bay. And presently yet another bridge-tunnel will cross the eighteen miles separating Norfolk from Cape Charles on the eastern shore of Chesapeake Bay. When this two-hundred-million-dollar project is completed, conceivably as early as the end of 1963, Norfolk will sit astride the major north-south roadway system from New England to Florida, enjoying all the advantages of its magnificent waterways and none of the disadvantages (in the nature of limited access by land) which magnificent waterways usually imply.

Economically, the city rests on too narrow a base. Government payrolls directly support nearly a third of the labor force, and probably account indirectly for more than half the area's employment. Because so many people work for the government (which always pays less well than private enterprise), and so many others are engaged in the manual labor of a port city, per capita income in Norfolk is unusually low. Retail sales in the metropolitan area run way below the national or even the southern urban average—largely because so many people can buy at the PX in the naval base. But industry is coming in, drawn by the improved transportation picture and the low wage scale itself, lured by the new Tidewater Virginia Development Council. And the government payroll is at least secure; we are always going to need a military, and the Navy especially is always going to need Norfolk. Indeed, the Navy and Air Force are still expanding in the Norfolk-Portsmouth area, and a new $17,500,000 naval hospital dominates the view across the river from Norfolk's downtown.

As an ordinary matter, the advantages of location which

Norfolk enjoys would guarantee a city's future. Norfolk is one of the few cities which could have dissipated its advantages through decay. When the war ended the city's downtown was so disreputable and so hard to reach by car—a tangle of narrow streets and alleys inherited from Colonial days—that strangulation was more than a possibility. Despite the great prospects of the site, Norfolk lost in the early 1950's some of its major commercial tenants—including the Seaboard Airline Railroad, which shifted its headquarters to Richmond, a smaller city and in many ways less central to the line's operations, simply because Norfolk was so unpleasant.

There is much to be said, however, for the proposition that a badly blighted city is a better bet than a mildly blighted one. Nobody could ignore Norfolk's condition. And the federal government seemed to feel almost guilty about the damages wrought to Norfolk by its minions, both directly (in the person of sailors on wartime shore leave not seeking culture) and indirectly (in matters like the railroad loop tightened about central Norfolk, with grade crossings on all but one of the radial streets). As a matter of national policy, it was laid down that highway improvement and urban renewal aid should be given first to "federally impacted areas," of which Norfolk was probably number one.

The city was lucky in its leadership. Lawrence Cox, now executive director of the city's Urban Renewal and Redevelopment Authority, had come to Norfolk in 1940, and the city fathers had enough sense to keep him there. Local government pledged Norfolk's rebirth and harnessed the immense energies of Charles Kaufman, general counsel for Norfolk and Western, the local newspapers and the National Bank of Commerce among others; occasional lecturer on tax problems at universities as far afield as New York; and chairman of the Authority which Cox directs. Kaufman is among the most admirable civic leaders in America, a sort of Albert

Schweitzer whose religion is urban civilization. Between the two of them, with help from government and business, they have seen that Norfolk's planning stays on target and produces results.

In Norfolk first things had to come first. There had to be a good road east to the growing suburbs between the city and Virginia Beach; and there had to be a north-south road which would permit people to get to and from the coming Portsmouth and Hampton Roads tunnels. Virginia Beach and Princess Anne boulevards were to provide the first, Tidewater Drive and Military Highway the second. Temporary wartime housing for workers at the naval base was a disgrace to the city and had to go; so did the worst of the slums. Housing projects went up on the northern and western inner ring, just west of Tidewater Drive and south of Virginia Beach. The strip between Tidewater Drive and the Norfolk and Western tracks, site of one of the wartime shack projects, was rezoned for industrial use and became a considerable contributor to the city's tax rolls.

Redevelopment's necessary second phase, now nearing completion, centered on additional highway development. One of the new roads is a limited-access expressway along the route of Brambleton Avenue, leading up from south Norfolk, bending west to form the top of the inner loop over downtown—then over through the now isolated Atlantic City area across a creek from downtown, and north again on Hampton Boulevard to the naval air station. A second tunnel under the Elizabeth to Portsmouth will connect with Brambleton in Atlantic City. Meanwhile, old Church Street near the harbor will be given the more specific name of St. Paul's Boulevard, will take a broadened path and slice through existing deteriorated blocks to run north, crossing Brambleton. Via an extension tying into Monticello and other major northbound roads, the new St. Paul's will provide far easier entrance and exit for downtown. Associated with the high-

241

ways here are the municipal auditorium, a light-industry development, a major medical center in Atlantic City—and a persuasive effort to induce private money to invest in Norfolk's core.

The push has already created substantial building. On Monticello Avenue beside the heart of downtown, private capital has raised a three-in-one building two blocks long—providing new office space in the Rennert tower, new parking space in the Rennert ramp garage, and the East Coast's largest new J. C. Penney department store. And where Brambleton, Monticello and the Bank Street extension of St. Paul's create a large and wonderfully convenient five-acre triangle, my associates and I are engaged in our largest building project. The end product will be Norfolk's "Golden Triangle," a combination hotel, office building, motel and convention headquarters, which, in the words of a local newspaper, "has put a gilt edge on one of the major urban renewal programs in the country."

Redevelopment's third phase, which has already begun, will see the cleanup and rebuilding of virtually the whole eastern section of downtown. Much of it has already been knocked down and swept away. Seventeen acres of the area between Monticello and Tidewater will be given over to a new Civic Center, a fifteen-million-dollar job at current estimates, including a municipal office building, a courthouse and a school administration center. Most of the rest is earmarked for private development, the widening of streets, and the completion of the highway loop via a Waterfront Drive to ride over the ruins of the old sailor's shantytown by the harbor. There is very little in the area that anyone would miss.

The days of disreputability are over; Norfolk is already a must-see on the list of everyone connected with municipal planning anywhere in America. Once public money has finished the decontamination of the core, private money in quantity will be ready to provide showplaces. Princeton's Charles Agle, who came down to Norfolk to make a first survey in 1949, has put the matter plainly. "As soon as the [Chesapeake] tunnel is in," he told *Newsweek* recently, "Norfolk will be the Manhattan of the South."

It will be something more than that. In a period when most cities are just beginning to reverse the decentralization of the fifties, the new Norfolk stands as an inspiring example of what *can* be done once the leaders of a city realize that blight at the core is less a disaster than an opportunity, an opportunity not greatly different from that presented to Chicago by its fire, San Francisco by its earthquake. The lesson of Norfolk is simple and relevant: a brand-new city is not some visionary nonsense hatched by dreamers from theoretical eggs. It is practical business and practical politics—much more practical, in fact, than letting a self-polluting urban civilization take its course.

# 16. Philadelphia

"Philadelphia," said an editorial in the Denver *Post* admiringly in the fall of 1958, "is far ahead of the other major cities in redevelopment. In fact, half the redevelopment projects in the United States are located in Philadelphia." The second part of the statement is no longer true; other cities have been catching on to the federal towline, and Philadelphia can no longer claim an actual majority of projects-in-being. Too much credit can be given; Philadelphia most needed this much work. Nonetheless, it is true to say that Philadelphia has *done* what other cities have merely talked about, that both in conception and execution it leads the march of our major metropolitan areas toward urban renewal.

The Philadelphia story begins in the early fifties with a political revolution which threw out the country's most stand-pat, corrupt, landed aristocracy municipal government, and substituted charter reform and a rare combination of remarkably tough-minded reformers in Joseph Clark and Richardson Dilworth. Philadelphia had been a kind of banana republic in the heart of America, for seventy years controlled

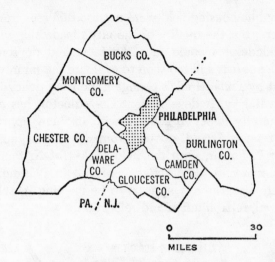

Standard Metropolitan Statistical Area.

dictatorially by the same political machine, which used the inertia of the citizenry to benefit a few economic giants. The Democratic victory was like a successful banana republic revolution, and liberated the enormous energies of a previously oppressed and ignorant peasantry.

Money poured in and out—in via the federal and state governments and well-drawn bond issues. It developed that Philadelphia, despite the decay and the grumbling, was still a rich city, with private capital to be tapped provided profitable opportunities were opened. "In Boston," Mark Twain once wrote, "they ask, How much does he know? In New York, How much is he worth? In Philadelphia, Who were his parents?" Suddenly, Philadelphia no longer cared who his parents were.

The city began its renewal work with more or less conventional slum-clearance low-income housing projects, which failed to solve the problems they were planned to eliminate. (See Chapter 7.) Philadelphia's hopes and disappointments in the public housing field were not too different from those elsewhere; but the quality of the city's leadership was such that Philadelphia could face the facts and do something about them. It is still too soon to evaluate the improvements wrought by Philadelphia's change in housing policy in 1957. William Rafsky, Redevelopment Co-ordinator, has outlined what the city hopes to achieve with its "new approach to urban renewal," and quotes from his report appear in Chapter 7. So far, with the help of ACTION, founded in Philadelphia and more active here and in Baltimore than anywhere else, the city appears to be meeting its schedules in renewal, rehabilitation and relocation.

Highway Arterial System.

Meanwhile, the renewal program has begun to remake the face of downtown and to develop outlying areas of the city which had never achieved settled or prosperous existence. The best known of the downtown projects, now largely completed, was a private venture—Penn Center, running from City Hall at Penn Square West along Market Street, where once the famous "Chinese Wall" stood. The Wall carried the Pennsylvania tracks along sixteen blocks of inner-ring honky-tonk and slum from the Schuylkill River to the heart of town. Penn Center comes complete with large office buildings, shopping mall, skating rink, transportation center, parking and a big hotel (this last a most courageous but successful gamble on the part of the Sheraton chain, because most of Philadelphia's hotels are seriously underoccupied). I once got blasted in the local press for saying that Penn Center was not part of downtown and wouldn't help downtown. Well, the heart of downtown is south of Penn Square and Penn Center is just northwest, essentially an inner-ring project when it was built, hard to see as part of a downtown master plan. Now that the buildings are up and selling, however, I must admit that the project has made its site a major part of center city, even if it never was before.

Penn Square was one of five open spaces which William Penn gave the city he founded in the narrow alley between the Delaware and the Schuylkill rivers. The two squares to the west—Logan and Rittenhouse—have never deteriorated. Logan became a grassy traffic circle on the great boulevard linking nearby Fairmount Park and the Art Museum to the center of the city, one of the triumphs of the City Beautiful movement in the early years of this century. Rittenhouse has remained continuously, from the time the city moved far enough west to populate the neighborhood, a stretch of elegant residences, apartments and residence hotels. The squares to the east, however, once the center of the city's life, have been going downhill for more than a century. Renovation of the area around one of them—Washington Square—is a matter of national pride, because this is the hallowed ground of American history. Renewal of the other—Franklin Square—has become a question of public sanitation, because the Poplar district just north of Franklin grew into one of the nation's most gruesome slums. Federal money has been available for both these redevelopments, and the government will pick up the entire seventeen-million-dollar tab for turning the area just northeast of Washington Square, including Independence Hall, into Independence National Historical Park.

Perhaps the most interesting of all the downtown projects is the one which will work over the areas east and west of Washington Square, quite near the heart of the city. Philadelphia's original commercial downtown lay largely between Washington Square and the Delaware River. Part of the financial district (especially the insurance companies, with their interest in maritime matters) has remained to this day; indeed, the Penn Mutual Life Insurance Company has its headquarters directly east of the Square. But the area is very unevenly developed, and much of it, especially around Dock Street, is a peculiar combination of distributive and residential slum. There is real colonial housing around here, and not all of it has indoor plumbing. But some of the buildings have both aesthetic and historic value (no area in America contains so many eighteenth-century churches), and should be retained.

The redevelopment of Washington Square East, now proceeding, is a model of what such projects should be. Rather than tear up block after block, the municipal authority has hunted out individuals and organizations which could be persuaded to restore or rehabilitate everything of historical interest. The food distribution activities of the area have been rehoused in a great new center well to the south—built at a point of convenience to the new Walt Whitman

Bridge and the projected Delaware expressway; and built, most important, *before* anybody's business got torn down by the bulldozers of Washington Square East. The Distribution Center site is enormous, covering 375 acres, and the job is being done without a penny of federal or state aid, via a municipal investment of about $1,750,000 and private investments which may reach a total of a hundred million dollars. (This is by no means a money-losing proposition for the city; taxes on the 375 acres ran eleven thousand dollars a year before work began on the Food Distribution Center, and the Authority estimates a tax income of $680,000 a year from the land when the center is completed.)

Basically, Washington Square East is to become an upper-middle-income residential neighborhood, though there will be plenty of facilities for the tourists who wish to visit the cleaned-up Old City. (If all goes as planned, the tourists may come to visit Washington Square East, taking in the historic monuments as a side attraction.) High-rise apartments will alternate with "town houses," as the planners call the modernized version of the old Philadelphia row house, a name no longer in favor. The biggest of the apartment houses will rise thirty stories, giving upper-floor tenants an unrivaled view of the Delaware River and New Jersey—from a sufficient height to mask the fact that the area overlooked is not really very attractive.

To the north, Washington Square East will be protected by the giant Independence Historical Park and Independence Mall projects, which have cleared or will clear out Philadelphia's Skid Row and the city's oldest assortment of commercial and loft buildings. These facilities were never really congenial neighbors to the Georgian complex of Independence Hall, where the political leaders of eighteenth-century Philadelphia created the nation's first "Civic Center." Astride the new Independence Mall the Authority envisions an area "ideal for redevelopment of office and commercial buildings including administrative headquarters for large corporations, wholesalers and other users desiring space near the heart of the city, but not in the most expensive locations close to City Hall." A few good buildings are in the district already, most notably the headquarters of Curtis Publishing, on Independence Square. North of the Mall, in the Franklin Square area, the Authority hopes for a belt of light industry to take advantage of transportation facilities and insulate the good commercial and residential districts of Independence and Washington squares from the excellent but very-low-income housing projects springing on both sides of Poplar Street. One of these projects, a series of low apartment houses in Georgian-like architecture, was the first to be completed under the Federal Housing Act of 1949, and the group as a whole has not been so successful as the Authority hoped. In fact, the failure of East Poplar to clean up the adjacent area was one of the reasons for the city's change of renewal policy in 1957. But nobody has quit, and as the projects march out from the center of the old slum it begins to appear more likely that a decent neighborhood will eventually emerge—at, admittedly, a very high price.

There is a degree of bossism about the Philadelphia urban renewal program and about the reform government as a whole. It took courage for a Democratic city administration —and a relatively left-wing Democratic administration, at that—to sell off the newly completed subway system to private owners who hoped to make a profit running it. Even greater courage was required to subsidize the suburban railroad lines to keep up the quality and frequency of their service, as part of the effort to prevent heavy flow of new automobile traffic into the center. The slum areas that are being cleared east of Washington Square and near Independence Hall will not be offered to low-income residents; these sections are being deliberately upgraded, which means an upgraded tenancy. The Authority has worked to avoid wreaking hardships on the dispossessed, and its Relocation Bureau processes more than twenty-five hundred cases a year—a very large load. About the only touch of sentimentality to be seen is in the name of one proposed housing project well north of the city center, to be called "Nicetown."

While work continues on the inner ring, Philadelphia has mapped and planned an enormous, half-occupied swamp on the southern edge of the city—Eastwick, which will be in point of area and perhaps of expenditure the nation's largest redevelopment project. Most of the area's 2,140 acres lies below grade, without storm sewers or public sanitation, and the estimated cost of filling the land, all by itself, runs ten million dollars. The total investment, public and private, in buildings and improvements, will approach five hundred million dollars. And the result, if the plans are carried out, will be a community of eleven thousand or so houses, almost all of them new, many of them cheap enough to be feasible for the evicted occupants of the inner-ring slums—ten-thousand-dollar homes, offered by the Authority on no-down payment forty-year mortgages. They will supply twenty thousand workers to new industrial and commercial buildings flanking the city's new airport and the naval installations on the Delaware where the Schuylkill flows in.

Because Philadelphia is so near New York on one side and Washington on the other, few people realize how important a center the city is in its own right. Its industry is incredibly variegated. Philadelphia is the nation's number-one producer of textiles and largest oil-refinery center. Its docks form the world's largest fresh-water port, and the second biggest port in the United States (Philadelphia's import tonnage, in fact, is greater than New York's). Its mills make it the nation's third largest steel producer, and its output includes a giant slice of heavy industry, especially electrical machinery and locomotives.

The Delaware Valley, particularly to the north of Philadelphia, has been one of the industrial frontiers of the last decade, and few areas are undergoing more intensive development today than the stretch between Philadelphia and Trenton. Levittown, built to service the enormous Fairless Works of U. S. Steel, will presently become the fourth largest city in the state, trailing only Philadelphia itself, Pittsburgh and Harrisburg. At present the northern development has given Philadelphia little more than fringe benefits, but Levittown will not have any great downtown of its own, and, once the Delaware Expressway is in, central Philadelphia should reap the greatest rewards from the Delaware Valley expansion.

New roads have already helped Philadelphia, once one of the nation's most difficult cities to enter or escape. The Schuylkill Expressway has made central city convenient to cars coming from the west on the Pennsylvania Turnpike, and the southern part of the Expressway, with the Walt Whitman Bridge, has made downtown easily accessible to customers coming north on the New Jersey Turnpike and to the burgeoning South Jersey area. The roads to be built in the 1960's, when the money from the federal highway program really begins rolling in, will give the city yet another boost.

And yet, despite all the favorable signs, it is hard to be too optimistic about Philadelphia. Washington and New York *are* close, and Philadelphia, despite tremendous Convention Hall, can offer major corporations few inducements to place their headquarters here rather than in one of the neighboring cities. The historical trend works against Philadelphia: first in the nation at the Revolution; then second to New York; third to Chicago—now fourth to Los Angeles.

252

Philadelphia's economic solidity is essentially industrial. About two-fifths of its labor force works at manufacturing jobs, as compared with less than a third in Los Angeles, less than a quarter in New York. It is wonderful to have industry (where would we be without it?), but factories do not add much to the *quality* of city life. Like Chicago, Philadelphia suffers the drabness of the blue-collar city. Even when all the redevelopment projects are completed, very large parts of the city will be only habitable rather than joyously livable.

And the success of projects like Independence Mall is jeopardized by the city's existing surplus of commercial space. The vacancy rate in Philadelphia's office buildings is something like 12 per cent, which means that the city's commercial structures in sum are paying their mortgages and salaries, but not returning much profit, if any, to their owners. Since the end of the Korean War, the federal government has pulled out of its rented space in Philadelphia, and soon both state and city offices will be moving into their own buildings. I had something of a trauma in Philadelphia myself, when our building on the corner of Broad and Locust, four blocks south of City Hall, lost its three biggest tenants in bing-bing-bing fashion, leaving me dependent on the corner drugstore. We have cured that problem, thanks to an extensive modernization program which attracted major new tenants. Several of the other older prewar prime buildings in downtown are also installing air conditioning and high-speed elevators—among them the Fidelity-Philadelphia Building on Broad and Walnut, the Suburban Station Building and the First National Bank Building, three of the largest in town. But suburban competition continues, and the city's many older and poorer buildings drag down the market.

Since the war Philadelphia might be compared to the spectacle of a rather inexperienced, overdignified man walking the high wire. Everything is a little risky—the industrial prosperity of a high-wage region, the expansion of the port in the face of increasingly severe competition to be expected from Norfolk to the south and the St. Lawrence Seaway-Great Lakes ports to the northwest; the maintenance of energy and office by an effective administration of the sort which, historically, has been rather short-lived in the United States. The new charter is of the strong mayor variety. It needs a strong mayor if it is to mean anything. To compare Philadelphia with the newer cities of mid-continent and the West Coast is a rather discouraging exercise; Dallas, for example, which has done virtually nothing in the line of urban renewal and has openly denounced federal aid, is in far better condition than Philadelphia after a decade's massive effort.

Philadelphia has not fallen off the tightrope, however, and in these matters the first ten years are the hardest. Among the city's assets is a sympathetic state government that knows about and appreciates urban renewal, and can give the wire a tug if it looks like it's getting too slack. There is an urgent national reason to root for Philadelphia's success; if this city can be saved, no city is doomed. I think a man might well risk his own money on the ability and dedication of Philadelphia's city planners. But when it comes to other people's money—well, anyone who is subject to the Prudent Man rule wants to be safely prudent. . . .

# 17. Cincinnati and Louisville

Cincinnati and Louisville are in a sense twin cities—though they are ninety miles apart as the airplane flies, and history has often pushed them in different directions, geographically, culturally and economically.

Both are pre-eminently Ohio River ports, though shipping means more these days to Cincinnati than to Louisville. Cincinnati's original eminence as a port came from its convenience to the tributaries which drained the southern Ohio and eastern Kentucky valleys—the Miamis and the Licking. Louisville was a transshipment point, set down where the Great Falls of the Ohio made the river impassable. The first canal to carry barges around the falls dates back to 1825, and the present locks were finished as late as 1929. Both cities are great railroad centers, especially strong in north-south routes, though Cincinnati's influence veers heavily to the east. Both cities will benefit from the Corps of Engineers' big effort on the Ohio; indeed, much of their growth in the fifties was due to technological improvements in the realm of barges.

Both were frontier cities of the Revolutionary War period,

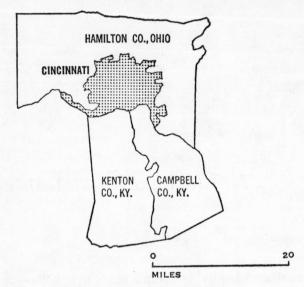

HAMILTON CO., OHIO

CINCINNATI

KENTON
CO., KY.

CAMPBELL
CO., KY.

0                    20
MILES

Standard Metropolitan Statistical Area.

and metropolitan centers of the *real* Old West, in the early
days of the nineteenth century. Before the Mississippi and
Missouri valleys became the nation's granary, they were
agricultural processing centers. Cincinnati processed corn
through pigs, and the number of its packing plants gave it
the vulgar name "Porkopolis." Food and kindred products
still account for one-eighth the city's manufacturing employment, but the great heritage from those days is probably soap, originally (not now) an animal-fats by-product.
Proctor & Gamble is here, home office and all. In Louisville
grain processing continues to play a major economic role,
but here the grain is processed through distilleries; this is
the heartland of Bourbon whiskey.

Both grew rapidly in the nineteenth century—Cincinnati
was once the third largest city in the United States—and
developed cultural traditions of some distinction. Thanks in
part to its very large German population (the Fountain in

Fountain Square was cast in Munich), Cincinnati was one of the first cities in the country to support a symphony orchestra, and its civilization gave it a reputation as a major metropolis which its size does not now warrant. Buffalo and San Antonio, for example, are bigger cities than Cincinnati, but few Americans would believe it without seeing the figures first. Boston, which people tend to regard as rather quaint, has a metropolitan area almost three times as populous as Cincinnati's million, more than four times as large as Louisville's 700,000. In Louisville, until the war, cultural development tended to move along English lines, with great stress on the masculine pleasures of drink, tobacco and horseflesh; the Kentucky Derby is still, deservedly, the city's biggest annual event. There is no other city in America where the major social and business club is named after a

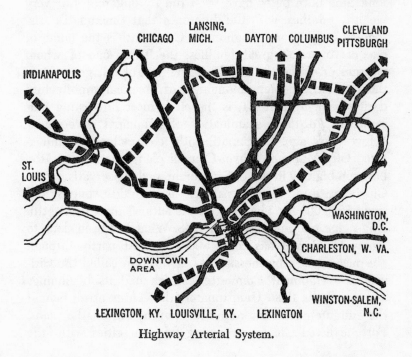

Highway Arterial System.

257

character in Thackeray. The *Courier-Journal* has about the same standing in Louisville as *The Times* in London, and the city's outer loop expressway is named after Henry Watterson, who edited the paper for three decades around the turn of the century. Guided by Charles Farnsley—an astonishingly art-and-culture-conscious mayor now returned to private politicking in an attempt to promote an urban renewal project around the University of Louisville—the city in the forties and early fifties developed into a center of American musical and plastic arts. Though Cincinnati still has the reputation, Louisville is a much more lively place to be.

Neither has ever been a "democratic" city in the traditional American sense, despite Mrs. Trollope's disapproval of the familiarity of people in Cincinnati in the 1830's. For a long time both cities have been run by oligarchies of very wealthy families, with the difference that Cincinnati's aristocracy is far more enlightened. Cincinnati is the home of one of America's great families, the Tafts, one of whom was mayor of the city for the better part of this generation; their ancestral home, a monument of American architecture dating back to 1819–21, is the city's most interesting museum. In *Fortune's* examination of municipal government a few years ago, Cincinnati, with its excellently administered City Manager/Mayor-Council plan, was labeled "the best-run big city in the U. S." Enlightened conservatism gave Cincinnati a master plan as early as the mid-twenties, and spent $250,000 for what may be the nation's most thoughtful long-range plan, published in 1948. What has been done to renew Cincinnati has come about at least partly through the pushing of a businessmen's organization called the Citizens' Development Committee, which had its beginnings as long ago as 1943. Unfortunately the conservatism behind the enlightenment has refrained from acting on the plans. *Fortune* listed Cincinnati among the four cities with "the most professional planning departments," and among the five cities that "use the planners most effectively." Elsewhere in its ratings, the magazine noted that Cincinnati was one of three cities rated triple-A on their bonds, and pointed out that "all three have spent comparatively little for urban renewal." Great solicitude about relocating poor displaced families notwithstanding, there is a limit to the length of time that a city can maintain a reputation for "using planners effectively" without spending real money on the large-scale plans.

In Louisville the oligarchy tends to occupy suburban areas in Jefferson County and, as proper gentry will, to ignore the county seat whenever possible. Everyone likes to talk urban renewal, and the real estate editor of the *Courier-Journal,* Grady Clay, is a man of such energy and talent that everybody of importance in the city reads his stuff—so that anyone who wants to look like a leader in Louisville must at least talk up the physical future of the city, whether or not he intends to do anything about it. Most of the time he doesn't. The city has a certain manic-depressive tendency, excited as all get-out one day about what is going to happen now that everyone agrees it should, devastated the next by the realization that the agreement makers have also agreed to forget about it. There is a consistency here—conservatism juxtaposed to the free-for-all Kentucky Derby, Bourbon and Happy Chandler. Accentuating the problem is the fact that Louisville is, except in the liquor and tobacco business, a branch office town, with many of its leading "citizens" on temporary assignment rather than permanent residence. On the other hand, it must be said that many of the city's genuine triumphs (the Orchestra's commissions of new music, for example) have been financed by funds from the outside, and that Zeckendorf's ambitious plans for downtown came to nothing partly because he couldn't find any local money to co-venture with him. As an example of Grady Clay's ability to make what is usually a dry subject good reading for people who couldn't care less about real estate promoters, his column heralding Zeckendorf's visit was all about "Big Zeck." Some writers have had to live down their drum-beating for a Paul Bunyan, but Clay may very well win through—though not downtown, as he thought.

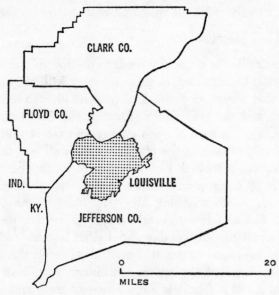

Standard Metropolitan Statistical Area.

Like most nineteenth-century American cities, Louisville and Cincinnati started at the river and spread back (north, for Cincinnati; south, for Louisville) in a series of leapfrogs. The river was too big a barrier to be crossed in force, though Cincinnati threw a suspension bridge across the Ohio as early as 1873. Louisville still has only one all-vehicular bridge over the river (there is also a combined railroad and auto bridge at the northwest corner of town), though another will be coming as part of the federal highway project —and about time, too, considering the way the inadequate Clark Memorial Bridge backs up traffic on Second Street. In both areas the leapfrog is continuing: in Cincinnati, with a rush of suburban light industry and the nation's worst glut of shopping centers; in Louisville, with one of the biggest single industrial leapfrogs of the postwar period, General Electric's Appliance Park, which has done wonders for the tax rate of suburban Buechel while the city itself abandons its public kindergartens and debates what other services can be eliminated. Meanwhile, Louisville's residences spread in broad, boring progression out along the southern flatlands.

Between the jumps, the leapfrog leaves blight, which tends to be more concentrated in Cincinnati, less appalling because less dense in Louisville. In Cincinnati a ravine to

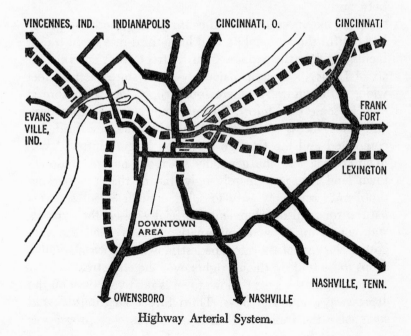

Highway Arterial System.

the east and Mill Creek to the west made barricades against preautomobile sprawl; indeed, the topography of the city is sufficiently rough to have restrained the grid pattern to downtown. Louisville's tableland permitted movement in three directions. Cincinnati has tackled part of its slum-clearance problem, both through public housing and the redevelopment of marginal sections into attractive indus-trial areas; Louisville to date has refused even to protect the area around its fine university, the oldest municipal school of higher education in the country. Both cities have run-down waterfronts, where successful distribution enter-prises did not dare build anything too expensive lest the river rise and wash it away—the 1937 flood, among others, completely inundated the riverfront areas of both cities. Today the river is tamer, though old-timers will never trust it, and its natural attractiveness could certainly be put to better use.

Again, like most nineteenth-century cities, both are poorly laid out for the automobile, and have third-rate rapid-transit facilities, all on the surface. Fourth Street, front entrance for six of Louisville's eight major dry-goods stores, is fifty feet wide, with sidewalks where four people can walk abreast only in some discomfort. The new north-south expressway will make access easier, especially when the new bridge is completed and the through trucks no longer clutter down-town streets; and the generally sawtooth nature of down-town land use, now merely ugly, means that the parking problem is relatively easy to solve. Fourth Street seems a natural for mall development, especially when the express-way comes in; or, as an alternative, Grady Clay has sug-gested the use of elevated pedestrianways, with attractive shops to be built in the air rights over the city streets.

In Cincinnati access to downtown is relatively easy on the expressways, and the new "Third Street Distributor" will soon solve the traffic snarl. But inside the core progress is slow, and improvements in parking facilities have been remarkably scarce for a city where three-quarters of all the people who enter downtown come by car. For some years it has been certain that there will be underground garages beneath Fountain Square and adjacent Government Square (both of them names for wide places on Fifth Street, a major east-west street feeding the viaduct over the east ravine). But these garages are not yet built. The compact core—bounded by Race and Main, Fourth and Seventh, with extreme concentration on Vine and Walnut, Fifth and Sixth—could be a great asset for the city, provided the commercial ring around it was wisely rehabilitated. Density has been used intelligently, notably in the combination of department store and hotel at the first big postwar hotel, the Terrace-Hilton; and in the combining of Cincinnati's tallest office building, Carew Tower, with her finest hostelry, the Netherlands-Hilton. But the city's great buildup of shopping centers indicates that something is seriously wrong in convenience factors at the core.

Concern over the Central Business District is relatively recent in Cincinnati, but has already produced a breathtaking (and expensive) plan—written up, incidentally, in an unusually literate manner. What is envisioned is a series of pedestrian conveyor belts one flight up from street level, a combination of malls and pedestrianless through streets, mosaic-tile pavements for decoration, and safety signals, artificial trees and fountains in the malls, as well as substantial refurbishing of the older commercial structures. One's admiration for the plan is enormous, though one does wish they would get at least the Fountain Square Garage finished before they looked so deeply into the blue skies of the future. Ownership records indicate that the exercise of eminent domain may be necessary to awaken a few old and fattened estates to the needs and realities of a modern metropolis.

In Louisville there is no plan for the Central Business

District—or, indeed, for the city as a whole, though able men are presently to publish something of the sort. For some years the city has had an authorized bond issue to pay for its share of urban renewal, and has done nothing about it. The project which has received the most talk—high-rise apartment houses with garages and an expressway along the river-front—will be killed cold as a stone if a private developer goes through with his announced plans to put up a twenty-eight-story apartment house just south of the Broadway boundary of commercial downtown, in the public library-churches area of the city. This structure, which required and received a special change in the zoning laws, would be the largest building in town, and would almost certainly take care of all the available local demand for middle-income and higher apartments. Meanwhile, former Mayor Farnsley has managed to secure majority but not the necessary two-thirds referendum approval for his university neighborhood idea. Downtown itself has been cleaned up, new lighting installed, alleys swept and so forth. But this city needs a great deal more than housekeeping.

Louisville is one of the few cities where I have sold what I bought, though I still own the mortgage on one of the properties. Cincinnati is one of the cities I added to my portfolio only recently. The buildings I own in Cincinnati are 1) out in the northeast section of the grid, between Main and Sycamore on East Eighth Street; and 2) a block west of Race Street on Fourth Street, just above the new "Third Street Distributor," a necessary renewal area for the expansion of the core and a site that would be greatly helped by the construction of the Planning Commission's pedestrian conveyor belts. I bought in Cincinnati largely because I think the plans eventually will come through, in one form or another; the government of this city is simply too intelligent to allow further deterioration of the center. I sold in Louisville largely because I was disappointed by the city's failure to use either its money or its brains for self-improvement.

Yet Louisville has a great future, once it stops feuding with the state government and its leaders manage to control their distaste for each other. The postwar expansion of the city was based on its remarkable situation, as a Midwest metropolis with southern labor, and that asset persists. Ohio River traffic will grow heavier with the years, and that part of it destined for the area south of Louisville—one of the growth areas of the future—will increase in even greater proportion. Today, as a hangover from the days of the falls and the transshipments, Louisville is the nation's only inland port of entry, with full customs service. This facility is not likely to be more important in the future than it is today; but the city's location at the major lock in the nation's lowest-priced transportation system, the Ohio-Mississippi complex, gives it a permanent attractiveness for heavy industry. And the neat south edge of downtown, the barrier created to the east by the new Medical Center and the expressway, to the west by slum clearance, make the city's future easy to envision and thus attractive to money.

Once the third largest city in America, Cincinnati will presently become the third largest city in Ohio: Cleveland is already well ahead of it, and Columbus is catching up rapidly. (In part this phenomenon reflects the expansionist tendencies of the state capital, which has been absorbing its suburbs into central city while Cincinnati is ringed with independent municipalities. The Cincinnati metropolitan area will continue much larger than Columbus.) Nevertheless, the city is solid, as one of its newspapers is always pointing out. Already a major industrial center with a highly diversified output, its convenience to both raw materials and markets makes it more interesting than most North Central cities to new industry seeking a home. It will maintain its dominance as the world's largest coal port. It gains even more than Louisville from improvements in the Ohio River channel, and the coming redevelopment of its waterfront areas will make it more efficient as a distribution center. The outer-ring slum-clearance program is vast and in being, and the execution of the master plan has been held up as much by a creditable humanitarian concern for relocation as by any other factor.

In the years right after the war, it seemed likely that Louisville would replace Cincinnati as the dominant Ohio River city. But during the fifties Louisville grew only slightly more rapidly than its sister, and currently Cincinnati is outstripping it. If you left out the human factor, Louisville would seem the better bet, certainly for the short run. But you can't ignore humanity. Because leadership is so important a natural asset of a city, Cincinnati will remain the Queen.

# 18. New York

Tokyo has a larger population (much larger, if you include adjacent Yokohama); and London, too, may be home to greater numbers of people. But everywhere in the world people know that the prototypal modern city is New York. With its skyscraper colonies and endless strings of apartment houses, its insistence on plane geometry in three dimensions, its quick and crowded subways, its central role in the economic life of the modern world—New York represents the *idea* of a great city. Now as always in the history of this country, most of the worrying about our cities is merely a shadow of the great worry about New York, which presents in macrocosm all the problems except rapid transit.

For twenty years now, it has been the almost universal opinion of the experts that New York is dying. Sociologists and philosophers can see for the future of New York only senescence and decay, a diminution of population and economic activity, a spreading of slums both commercial and residential. These gloomy conclusions are what the headline writers draw from the most thorough, intelligent and literate study ever done on any city—the series of books by Ray-

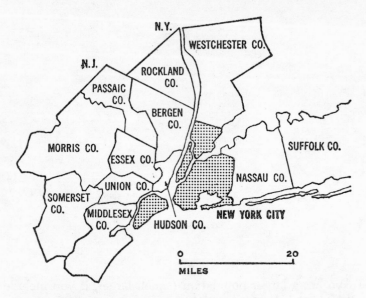

New York-Northeastern New Jersey Standard Consolidated Area.

mond Vernon and his associates at Harvard's Graduate School of Public Administration, prepared for New York's Regional Plan Association and published in 1959–60. Actually, Vernon and Company are too thorough and too intelligent to be as pessimistic as the summary writers believe, but even theirs is at bottom a gloomy view.

And yet, the city's great vitality continues undiminished. "New York, the nation's thyroid gland," wrote Christopher Morley some years ago, and the comment holds. The years of gloomy prophecy have been the greatest years New York has ever known, have seen the city established as political headquarters of the world and corporate headquarters of the world's economy. Since the end of World War II, more new office space has been built in New York than *exists* in any other city in the world. And in recent years, though the population of the region is not growing rapidly, New York

268

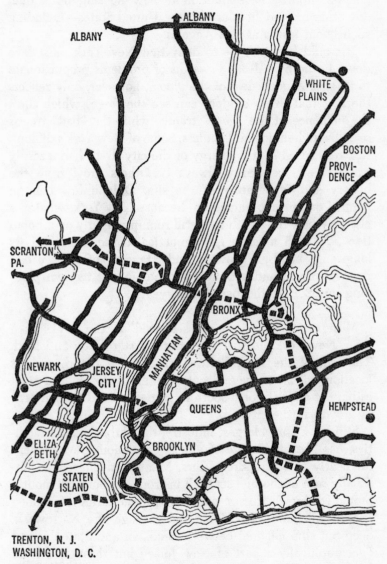

Highway Arterial System.

and its suburbs have built more new housing units than any other metropolitan area in the United States—including such boom towns as Los Angeles.

It would be nonsense to deny that New York must face down in the next decade swarms of problems proportionate to its size. A good deal of the gloom, however, only reflects the fact that every student can see the forces which limit the influence of the "good" trends, while the "bad" trends seem overwhelming and endless. Some of New York's difficulties are caused by the energy of the city itself, haphazardly transformed, as energy always is. Others grow from the history and topography of the site. Only a few can be blamed on current stagnation, because New York, whatever else may be wrong with it, is still running rapidly on a boom tide . . . with a fairly good practical consciousness of its long-range needs, a growing understanding of what urban renewal means and a thorough contempt for its own planning mistakes in the past fifteen years.

Most major American cities started on the banks of a river. New York did that, and more; it started on an island. The fact of the long, narrow, rocky, hilly island, and its location within a magnificent natural harbor in the tidal estuary of a great north-south river, determined the patterns of growth in the city.

Still New York's largest industry, the harbor and its facilities, has been in a state of almost continuous development for nearly three hundred years. Manhattan offered an unusually safe anchorage set well in from the harbor's mouth, protected by fortresses and the promontories of Coney Island and Sandy Hook, entered through the Narrows, a deep but slim channel between Brooklyn and Staten Island (geographically a part of New Jersey but through a legal freak part of New York State and then New York City). The large inner bay split at the point of the Battery, where

a major fort became a theater and later the nation's immigration center. One branch of the harbor fed up the "East
River," actually an arm of the sea, connecting New York
port with Long Island Sound; the other branch led to the
Hudson River, navigable even by the larger boats of the
mid-nineteenth century for 150 miles of its length. Pough-
keepsie, eighty miles up the river, was once a ponderable
rival to New York, as its decaying mansions demonstrate;
and Benedict Arnold's treason was an offer to sell the British
the boom which hung at West Point and closed the upper
Hudson to warships. Probably the greatest single stimulus
to the early growth of New York as a port was De Witt
Clinton's Erie Canal, which permitted barges to travel from
Manhattan up the Hudson, around the bend and west on
the canal to the Great Lakes.

Throughout the nineteenth century the harbor was improved. The "Harlem River," basically a canal connecting
the East River and the Hudson across the northeastern and
northern ends of the island, was dredged and made safe for
traffic. At the Hudson end engineers tamed the whirlpool
of Spuyten Duyvil; at the East River end they blasted over
and over again to remove rocks and do *something* about
Hellgate, even today the world's most dangerous heavily
traveled waterways, where ships must be guided through
by trained pilots.

Cornelius Vanderbilt started toward his millions in the
barge business, and the railroads were relatively slow to
influence New York's economic life. Railroad bridges could
not be thrown across the wide Hudson (even now, there
is only one bridge over the Hudson at New York). The first
bridge over the East River—the wonderful, famous Brooklyn
Bridge—was not completed until 1884, and its successors,
the Queensboro and Manhattan bridges, opened in 1909.
All three are engineering marvels, very heavily traveled;
but none is strong enough to carry railroad trains. Freight

cars had to be ferried across a river, an expensive and lengthy procedure. Heavy distribution and industry inevitably looked toward the Jersey shore of the Hudson, where the harbor met the railheads, and the subcores of Jersey City, Bayonne, Hoboken, Elizabeth and Newark grew up to serve the new transportation and the new industry. The most recent great improvement of the port has been the deepening and widening of channels leading around Staten Island to Port Newark beside the Newark airfield, a major shipping center for the region.

Industry oriented toward the west naturally grew in Jersey; industry oriented to the city itself and markets on that side of the Hudson, and therefore to the upstate and New England markets, naturally grew in the Bronx, north of Manhattan. The clipper ships continued to land along the East River at the foot of the island; and across the narrow tip on the Hudson shore, the provision ships came in by North Street to service the produce markets. But there was a limit to the number of good docking places on the two sides of the island, and soon the focus of cargo shipping moved across to the other side of the East River and the Brooklyn docks. To expand the shipping resources of this area, the Gowanus Canal was dredged, creating New York's most valuable industrial complex, across the river from what is now the United Nations.

By the time the railroad tunnels were dug under the rivers, the area's pattern of development was solidly established. Manhattan Island could not be an industrial center, except for those few industries (most notably clothing) which produced items bearing a high price per pound. But in all other respects it was the center of the area—financial, commercial, residential. Fourteen miles long and only two miles wide at its widest point, the island offered little scope for east-west expansion; the city had to drive north from its point. So the hills were flattened, or at least smoothed off

272

on top, and the growing city leapfrogged up the island between the rivers.

At first trade and fashionable residence concentrated in the tip of the island, south of the City Hall; north of Chambers Street, the workshops and the slums straggled to Canal Street and above. The great fire of 1835 and rumors of cholera drove the better element of residence up to Washington Square and Stuyvesant Square, and the Bowery carried the traffic downtown to the crowded commercial streets near the harbor, which the financial and shipping interests have never left. The first hotels were west of City Hall, convenient to the ferries which ran to the New Jersey railheads. Then the railroad came into Madison Square, creating a new hotel and business district (of which several major monuments remain, most prominently the Flatiron Building, the city's first skyscraper). Later the railroad terminal moved to Forty-second Street; its site became Stanford White's Madison Square Garden—an auditorium which, retaining the name, leapfrogged to the Times Square district and will presently jump again somewhere up the West Side. When the Garden left, the site was given over to the home office building of the New York Life Insurance Company. The Metropolitan Life Building was next door, Guarantee Life nearby. Equitable Life went from Wall Street to Penn Station at Thirty-fourth, and just the other day moved up to join the expanding Rockefeller Center complex in the Fifties. In the hotel leapfrog, the Astor went from City Hall Park to Madison Square to Times Square, and now would move again if the name Astor had retained its old power.

By the turn of the century Manhattan had fixed its zones in a pattern which was to see only minor changes over the next fifty years. The big department stores, which had started just north of City Hall in the mid-nineteenth century, moved up to Union Square (near Washington and

Stuyvesant Squares, and only a few blocks south of Madison Square), then north to Thirty-fourth Street, convenient both to Pennsylvania Station and Grand Central; and finally, in the 1920's, up Fifth Avenue toward the new hotels rising at the southeastern tip of Central Park. The great private homes, showplaces for Ward McAllister's "400," stood on Fifth and Madison north of Grand Central. The upper middle class was lining the edges of Central Park, a great green oasis two and a half miles long, which William Cullen Bryant and Frederick Law Olmstead had wrested from the city's ordained grid pattern in the middle of the century. The great apartment houses were going up on the high hill above the Hudson well to the north of downtown, near the area where Columbia University had relocated; establishments slightly less grand lined what was obviously the most desirable end of Central Park, at the southern edge of the old Dutch Haarlem, facing south over the greenery to downtown. On the East Side, where the breweries did nothing for the atmosphere, Effingham Sutton saw the residential possibilities of the Place which now bears his name. . . .

Meanwhile, Brooklyn Bridge had been thrown across the East River in an epic construction job, and a new borough had been absorbed in "Greater New York." The city's magnificent transit system was functioning profitably, subway and el and trolley; there were elevated lines in those days up First and Second and Third and Sixth and Ninth and Tenth avenues—more than a third of all the north-south streets on the island—supplemented presently by subways under Lexington and Broadway and (later) Eighth, and, of course, by the railroad which ran over, then under, Park Avenue. Riding the transit systems, the working population spread out to Brooklyn, which developed a commercial subcore almost as large as Newark; to the East River borders of Queens; to the lower Bronx. Two of the city's most miserable slums, which are only beginning to be cleaned up, were already rooted: the lower East Side, which had been an unwholesome neighborhood (it started as a lake and adjacent swamp, the Collect, and before there was any large-scale immigration it was home to Five Points, the city's first Skid Row); and the west forties and fifties, already known as Hell's Kitchen, and partly Negro in those days. To these the coming years were to add the east forties (which the Dead End Kids called home), and Harlem itself. It is worth mentioning that one of these slums has been completely eradicated—that of the east forties, wiped out by the extension of lavish housing, the growing demands of downtown, the early walk-to-work housing at Tudor City and the construction of the United Nations. Other slums have spread in the meantime (particularly in Brooklyn); but New York has demonstrated that a slum area need not be a slum forever.

The constriction of the island forced high densities, and the rock of the island made possible the economical construction of skyscrapers. Two of the city's tallest buildings were in place before 1910 (Mr. Woolworth's monument to Woolworth, across City Hall Park with a view of the Brooklyn Bridge; and Mr. Clark's monument to his company—Singer Sewing Machines—a few blocks farther down Broadway). The great expansion of finance and shipping due to the crises and then the wars in Europe produced enormous demands for downtown office space, and the Wall Street skyline took on that famous appearance which scarcely changed between 1928 and 1957 (it is now changing rapidly, like everything else in New York). And in midtown, in the area focusing on Grand Central Station, the office structures shot skyward. By an extraordinary fluke, the largest of them all went up south of what was rapidly becoming central midtown. On Thirty-fourth Street and Fifth Avenue, the site of the famous old Waldorf-Astoria, New York's premier hotel from 1897 to the late 1920's, a syndicate erected a 102-story tower and called it the Empire State Building. They suffered horribly through the depression, and never managed to rent out all their space for cash money until the wartime expansion of city and country rented all New York office space. Ill-timed as a commercial venture, the mistake helped the city, saving the hotels which had been built to service the railroad terminal when it was on Madison Square; drawing some of the tourist traffic away from already overcrowded downtown; and enabling the heaviest concentration of the city's retail trade (the Macy's-Saks 34th-Gimbel's complex on Herald Square, Altman's, Franklin-Simon and Lord & Taylor on Fifth Avenue) to remain south of the major new office development.

As the 1920's drew to a close, the city planners—especially those bemused by the "Garden City" concept—were dreadfully concerned about New York. But how optimistic everyone else must have been! The city's underground transit system was still expanding, and the unsightly els were coming down. Both "downtowns"—the financial and shipping center near the Battery, and the commercial-retail-tourist center around Grand Central—were new, handsome according to the taste of the time and extraordinarily impressive. Quality residences lined Central Park and Park Avenue, where the tracks had been sunk and covered over; and the chain of apartment houses above the Hudson had been completed, two blocks deep, on the two-mile stretch between Seventy-second Street and Columbia University. Out in the boroughs, the Bronx, still heavily industrial, was shabby; and where Queens and Brooklyn approached Manhattan an inner-ring blight was plainly visible. But the speculative builders had populated the larger stretches of Brooklyn and built more elaborately in selected garden spots in Queens. The lower East Side and Hell's Kitchen were both thinning out, and there was a promise (fulfilled) that the railroad tracks would

276

be removed from the Hell's Kitchen streets. Harlem had already begun its descent to slum, but the area was blessed with the city's widest avenues and largest collection of small parks.

Between the lines of optimism an observer could see large patches of rot. From Canal Street to Washington Square, the leapfrog had left inferior buildings to stand and decay; from Union Square to Thirty-fourth Street on the West Side the garment industry lofts could not stand too close an examination; between the Riverside Drive development and the Central Park apartment houses a degrading Irish slum endangered the West Side; Harlem was deteriorating rapidly. Fifteen years of depression and war, lack of will, the ignorance of the migratory inhabitants, and then lack of materials for conservation and rehabilitation, could ruin most of the land area of Manhattan. And did.

It can be argued that what was done in New York in the 1930's saved the city from catastrophe when the flight to the suburbs began after the war. Robert Moses built the great highways along both riverfronts and out of the city in three directions, the fourth subway system was completed on the West Side and out to Queens, relief projects rehabilitated much of the city's public plant (schools, post offices, hospitals and so forth). Parks were added to both the east and west riverfronts, and out in Queens the bay was filled for an airport and a World's Fair. But in its residential and commercial cores the city suffered a decay still not entirely arrested. All cities—indeed, all places, cities or not—are uncomfortable for the poor. Deterioration through depression and war made New York uncomfortable for the middle class.

Nowhere in America was the exodus from central city more violent than it was in New York in the late forties and early fifties. Some stayed within the city limits—out in the "garden apartments" of Queens or the seaside edge of Brooklyn—but most fled to the surrounding counties. Nassau County, out on Long Island beyond Brooklyn and Queens, doubled in population during the 1950's, rising to more than 1,250,000 inhabitants. Southern Negroes and Puerto Ricans arrived almost as fast as the previous tenants departed, keeping the city's population relatively stable. Meanwhile, by the aging process well described in Vernon and Hoover's *Anatomy of a Metropolis*, the worst of the old slums were thinning out—which means that many of the older middle-class neighborhoods became crowded with slum dwellers and new arrivals from the bottom-income brackets.

The deterioration of middle-class neighborhoods was hastened by New York's preposterous rent-control law, adopted federally in 1943 as part of emergency wartime regulations, and still on the books of the state legislature today though somewhat improved by successive modifications starting in the early 1950's. Basically, the law drove professional management and ownership out of middle-class residential real estate, substituting a remarkable new breed of cheap-jacks who made their fortunes by eliminating services, reducing maintenance and often cutting individual generous middle-class apartments into numbers of mean slum flats. Western Brooklyn, southwest Bronx and a good piece of West Side Manhattan fell apart under the hammers of the slumlords—and those who predict the future by projecting trends can see the same horrors overtaking those few neighborhoods which retained their middle-class characteristics.

In many parts of New York, however, decay has already been arrested and the trends are reversing. The West Side of Manhattan from Fifty-ninth Street north to Columbia (a distance of three miles), though it seemed doomed only five years ago, now seems certain of rescue. Lincoln Center—an enormous redevelopment project including a concert hall, an opera house, a university, a conservatory, several little theaters and galleries, plus apartment houses and garages—is currently going up on an area about half a mile long by a quarter of a mile wide at the southern edge of the district. It seems likely that future generations will point to Lincoln Center as one of the most abominable examples of bad site planning in the history of architecture, but as *city* planning the project has its advantages. On the northern edge, Columbia University and other neighboring institutions are sinking something like a hundred million dollars into the preservation of their neighborhood. Midway between Columbia and Lincoln Center, Yeshiva University has undertaken the rehabilitation or reconstruction of several blocks running between Central Park and the river; and up nearer the Columbia end of the zone, one of the city's largest middle-income housing projects has replaced one of the district's nastiest patches of slum. The most encouraging aspect of the West Side resurgence is the fact that both Negro and Puerto Rican communities are already entrenched in many of the areas to be rehabilitated, and nobody plans to dislodge them. Like South Side Chicago, West Side New York presents as a possibility the pleasing prospect of a successful, prosperous, integrated neighborhood.

In west Brooklyn, too, a major urban renewal project—a civic center with apartment houses, built about the exit roads from the Brooklyn Bridge—offers hope for the revival of both retailing and residence on what is probably the most convenient site outside Manhattan itself. With wealthy Brooklyn Heights to one side of the project and middle-class Clinton Heights to the other, the Civic Center looks like an unusually good bet. Meanwhile, in Harlem, south Bronx and the inner sections of Brooklyn slum, the nation's most massive low-cost housing project continues to tear down dumbbell tenements and replace them with high-rise apartment projects. No doubt the tenants in these projects hate them; no doubt vandalism and violence reflect the rootlessness of the new communities shoved into the housing projects by a soulless and sometimes brainless bureaucracy. Nevertheless, experience is that projects become more stable as they get older, and only a lunatic would prefer what was on the site before the apartment houses went up. The human dimension may have been compromised, but the previous high density demanded a spacious verticality.

There are patches of slum on upper Manhattan, in outer Brooklyn, north Bronx, Queens and Richmond; indeed, there is scarcely an area in the city that would not be better off with a neighborhood watchdog committee à la ACTION. And much of the city, despite the housing projects, is little less than shocking in the quality of the life its inhabitants must lead. But the notion that New York is turning into one big slum residentially bears no relation to the facts.

Industrially, the situation is probably as gloomy as the forecasters claim. There is scarcely a factory within the city limits which can hope to expand substantially in its present site, which means that successful manufacturers must tend to move at least their increased production to out-of-town locations. Processing and distribution centers now should be in the inner ring, whence they can ship a good part of their goods without going into downtown traffic, rather than in the city's center. A few manufacturing industries, notably clothing, cosmetics, toys, notions and printing, require central locations—partly because of the famous need for face-to-face communication, partly because any seasonal business must set itself down where there is a floating labor supply.

Commercially and culturally, of course, the city's situation is superb. As national headquarters for finance, advertising and communications, New York is in position to demand the attendance of major offices for every major corporation. Shortly after the war it was believed that many companies would transfer their main offices to the greensward around the city, and a few did move. A mobile office force is now available in the suburbs. But, despite all grumbles about the subways and the commuter service, the fact seems to be that most white-collar workers do not much like the isolated country office—and neither, what is more important, do the executives.

Both the city's "downtowns" have participated in the building boom, though the Wall Street area got there only during the last few years. The placement of the new office structures in midtown, however, is not entirely pleasing. Only a handful of the new office buildings have gone up south of Fortieth Street or west of Fifth Avenue, except as additions to Rockefeller Center and the garment center. (Renting agents find that the same space in the same building will rent for as much as 20 per cent more if the address is just east of Fifth rather than just west of Fifth.) In the beginning the boom was concentrated on Madison Avenue, where a few of the town houses still survived from the Gilded Age; then it moved a block east to Park, where demolition and new construction—the only effective battler against rent control—destroyed some of the city's grandest apartment houses in the rush to create luxury office suites. The next stop, obviously, was a block farther east, on Lexington; and then to refurbished Third Avenue, wide and handsome now with the el out of the way. East of Third, however, tends to be inconvenient to public transportation (including the commuter railroads); and as the lofts come down the likely replacements are UN-oriented offices and new luxury housing.

The northern borders, too, are hard to pierce. Traditionally, Fifty-ninth Street has marked the edge of the Central Business District, and, though a few of the new office buildings have pushed up to Sixtieth or Sixty-first on Lexington and Madison, zoning laws backed by the self-interest of the city's highest priced residential neighborhood prevent any further expanson in that direction. Lexington in the fifties has been turned into a residential street to house the people evicted from their Park Avenue apartments by the new office buildings, and Third also seems likely to develop residentially in the fifties. What remains is actually a very small area to hold so many very big buildings, and, though there are not so many more people in midtown as appearances would indicate (in corporate headquarters, each worker gets a higher allotment of floor space for the mechanical equipment which grows annually more elaborate), on some blocks density threatens to become too high even for a high-density man like myself.

In the last year or two the powers that be have apparently decided that they can live outside the most popular area (*just* outside). Time, Inc., and Equitable have raised enormous central offices on the west side of Sixth Avenue in the lower fifties as integrated extensions of Rockefeller Center, and three more major structures are already in the hole-in-the-ground stage. One of these will be a hotel, and the other two will be offices, including headquarters suites and showrooms for the men's clothing industry, which will leapfrog a mile and a half from the area just west of Madison Square to arrive at Rockefeller Center. This north extension of Sixth Avenue probably portends luxury apartment construction just south of Central Park, where the Avenue is now bordered by abandoned and condemned upper-floor tenements erected when this street was still the route of an elevated transit line. To the south, Sixth Avenue will rise on the northwest surge of the ladies' garment industry, which has already erected some large monuments to itself across from Bryant Park, forming a new backdrop to the Public Library.

Southeast, the stretch between Madison and Third presents increasing office development, though the advance is blocked by the luxury apartment boom on Murray Hill. On Forty-second Street itself companies are building home offices as far east as Second Avenue, separated from the United Nations only by the plateau upon which rests the high-rise Tudor City apartments.

Whatever gain might be anticipated from this slight spreading out, however, will be nullified by the construction of the Pan Am building, originally Grand Central City, 58 stories high and in point of floor area (2,400,000 square feet) the largest office building in the world, which may easily create pedestrian traffic jams on the midtown East Side. The crowding will be aggravated by a towering office building to replace the unwieldy converted old Manhattan Hotel at Madison and Forty-second. A few smaller building projects on the way could be the ultimate straws on the camel's back, assuming that the monsters haven't already crushed it.

Only one solution seems possible for this disastrous overcrowding of the Grand Central area: a pedestrian mallway running the length of East Forty-second Street, from the UN to the Public Library, and perhaps to Times Square.

There is also danger that the eastward movement of the garment district will threaten the below Forty-second Street department stores, but otherwise the retailing picture is rosy. Inevitably downtown's share of retail volume has dropped over the last decade—one is amazed at the calamity-howling that occurs when a store opens a suburban branch and then reports that the downtown store which once handled all the business now handles only four-fifths of it. No damage has been done. The office employees in the new buildings may not be very well paid, but often they think they are—and, in the general luxuriousness of corporate headquarters, they often have a lot of time for shopping. The unrivaled concentration of customers also assures the perpetuation of the world's most spectacular collection of specialty shops, especially on Fifth and Madison and Lexington in the fifties.

Like all big American cities, New York has mass rapid transportation problems. There are probably enough subway lines to carry the burden without intense discomfort, but their placement was dictated by the residential patterns of the period 1900–1935, and it is not wholly relevant to the New York of the 1960's. The two areas within the city limits which have seen the greatest population increase since the war (central Queens and East Side Manhattan) are serviced by one subway line each, while the thinning slums of Brooklyn and Washington Heights are interwoven with transportation. The situation in Queens is especially serious, because expansion still continues all along the Jamaica line of the subway, which is already badly overburdened and, while land scarcity and the new zoning code's bulk and height restrictions will limit any substantial expansion from Forest Hills west, the eastward trend is already quite visible. On the whole, the infant Transit Authority has been a success; many of the older cars have been retired, the stations and platforms are relatively clean, and resistance-proof doors and longer trains have improved rush-hour service, though midday service has been somewhat curtailed.

For the metropolitan area as a whole, the commuter railroads are the new rapid transit, and here the story is longer (too long to tell) and sadder. Whether or not the New Haven and the New York Central actually lose as much money as they claim to lose on commuter service, they are behaving as though they do. Both track and car maintenance are down and prices are up, encouraging more and more suburbanites to come to town by car—a disastrous trend. On the other side, the Long Island Railroad has picked itself up by the seat of its own pants since it came under state control after bankruptcy reorganization, and now offers Nassau County an efficient, not-too-unpleasant entry to New York, mostly via the Jamaica (Queens) and Brooklyn sub-cores.

The CBD's greatest failure, despite elaborate planning suggestions, has been in the area of the automobile—a problem so clearly insoluble in New York terms that the city fathers have scarcely dared think about it. A great deal of work has been done or is being done to bring traffic *to* *Manhattan* and route through traffic *around it*. The New York and New England thruways, the Long Island Expressway, the third tubes for the Lincoln Tunnel and Queens Midtown Tunnel serve the first purpose. The second is met by the extra deck on the George Washington Bridge, the Throg's Neck Bridge from Long Island to the Bronx and the Verrazzano Bridge over the Narrows for easy communication between New Jersey and Long Island. But Manhattan itself, except at access points, has been virtually forbidden territory to the road builders. North-south traffic still moves on the expressways along the rivers, and on the now one-way avenues running the length of the island. But even north-south motion is slowing down, and the east-west situation is intolerable, despite the creation of no-turn limited-exit streets in midtown. The city desperately needs crosstown expressways just above Wall Street, in the Canal Street area, from the Queens-Midtown to the Lincoln Tunnel in the Thirty-fourth Street area, and probably somewhere else just below Central Park. Otherwise all the improved access roads, tubes, bridges and interchanges must become terminals rather than pathways.

From the long-range planning point of view, the most encouraging developments in New York are the growing downtown residential districts, which seem likely to create the best imaginable sort of "inner ring." High-rise apartment houses feature the plans for redevelopment of the East River frontage north of Wall Street, and to the south there are now final plans for a World Trade Center with apartments nearby (though someone will have to get rid of the Fulton Fish Market before any plans can be consummated). The area south of Washington Square, leapfrogged more than a century ago, seems to be redeveloping naturally, with a little help from state and federal legislation rather than municipal subsidy, into middle-class housing. If Klein's can be got out of Union Square, much the same would be probable around that little park, too, connecting the Metropolitan Life developments along the East River to the upper-class and middle-class housing of Greenwich Village. Chelsea, in the west twenties, is the beneficiary of several of the city's best low-income housing projects, and has recently shown remarkable signs of regeneration, with remodeling projects on almost every street. Up in the east fifties and just below Central Park the executives maintain their *pieds-à-terre*. (If Carnegie Hall had been torn down, which fortunately it wasn't, the likely candidate for the site would have been a luxury apartment house; Louis Glickman's original project for an office building on the Carnegie site could not be built because wiser heads thought offices were the wrong use for the land.) There are even indications that the influence of Lincoln Center and the hideous Coliseum, plus the continued success of Otto Kahn's big Parc Vendôme apartments, will produce a decent residential neighborhood in the now loathsome west fifties and even forties, completing the ring as the west thirties are rebuilt up to the Pennsy tracks.

Indeed, the real source of worry about New York should be what will happen to the *outer* ring and the suburbs in the years to come. With the best will in the world, it is simply impossible for private funds to build four-room apartments to rent for less than $150 a month even in those parts of Manhattan where land values are lowest and even under the provisions of New York State's almost revolutionary incentive legislation, the Mitchell-Lama Act, which calls for forty-year mortgages at four per cent interest to cover ninety per cent of the cost of building new middle-income apartments. As more and more of Manhattan is refurbished, more and more working-class inhabitants will be driven off the island to settle elsewhere in the area. Meanwhile, a growing number of smaller manufacturing shops or offices will be eliminated by the new housing or the new skyscrapers. Descending upon the older suburbs, they can produce fairly rapid deterioration in what is now a moderately successful subcore.

A city as large as New York needs subcores, and has them—from Elizabeth in the southwest to White Plains in the north to Hempstead in the east. While concentrating their efforts on the city itself, the planners might give more than an occasional thought to the mounting problems of the subcores, already graphically demonstrated in the collapse of Yonkers (my home town, and for years distinguished by one of the worst and most provincial city administrations in America). Perhaps the greatest threat to the future of New York lies in the area's failure to develop even metropolitan-area political co-operation—let alone a metropolitan government.

But tristate regional planning must some day produce a united metropolitan-area government. This millennium will dawn when the petty political overlords of the suburbs find that the self-interests they represent have learned their survival does not lie in taxing their lifelines, the railroads, into decay, delay and exorbitant commuting costs. Even the *Wall Street Journal*, which in 1959 editorialized so prettily about its desire to keep under local control the little villages where its subscribers lived, has come to see the need for government aid, planning, zoning, tax-supported rehabilitation of the commuter railroads, tax-sheltered middle-class housing, government-supported commercial and warehousing development.

Ultimately, leadership is the critical shortage. We wait impatiently for a third Moses, who will lead New York to the often-promised land.

# 19. New Orleans and Baton Rouge

Old Man River's city, of course; but almost everything in it is man-made. The French settled here originally because a "ridge" two feet high provided a dry portage between the Mississippi and Lake Pontchartrain; most of the site had to be bailed out. Were it not for the levees, Old Man River would be rolling through the streets most of the time—and even so, New Orleans is saved from periodic inundation only by the artificial spillway which sends any rise in the water level over to the lake, north of the city. Dig down five or ten feet almost anywhere in New Orleans, and you are likely to find water; there are sections of the city, including very good sections, where even private residences must be built on piles driven deep into the ground. Though New Orleans appears to be a good distance from the Gulf of Mexico in all directions, its mean elevation is about five feet. The city rests on silt brought by every river from the "Big Muddy" to the Red, named for the soil they carry. What has made much of it habitable is a vast system of drainage pumps capable of removing sixteen and a half billion gallons of water a day. The high ground here is by the river rather than away from

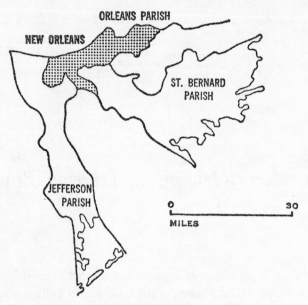

Standard Metropolitan Statistical Area.

it, because the banks of the river received the most silt in the river's periodic overflows. An artificial city with all the magic charm of artificiality—and the great possibilities for expansion which come with practiced artifice.

Today the city's experienced land reclamation teams are at work on enormous tracts northeast, served by the lake and the Gulf Intercoastal Waterway, the Southern Railroad and the Louisville and Nashville Railroad, U.S. Routes 90 and 11 and a new Federal Highway project superroad to the eastern Gulf cities and industrial Birmingham. Here, fifty square miles of land—an area larger than all San Francisco, twice the size of Manhattan Island—is being cleared and propped up to hold everything from heavy industry to residential subdivisions. This is not an "urban renewal" project; there is nothing urban here to renew. It is straight pioneering-for-profit, and despite its overweening ambition it can hardly miss.

Rapid expansion is evident now, even greater expansion inevitable later, in the entire area from New Orleans up to Baton Rouge, where a bridge over the river marks the maximum penetration of ocean-going vessels up the Mississippi. This is an area with all the economic advantages of barge transportation along waterways through the swamps from Texas to Florida; with the natural river-port activity of the Mississippi terminus; with the great in-an-out harbor trade of the ocean port most convenient to the Caribbean area, northern South America and Central America, all expanding markets and expanding producers. New Orleans alone has

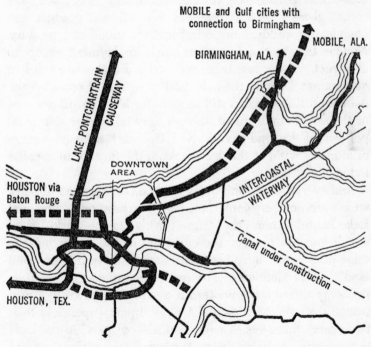

Highway Arterial System.

twenty miles of dock facilities, and a free port to service international trade destined for places other than the United States. No port except New York and Chicago does so much of the necessary and profitable work of transshipment.

And the area is more than a service point; it is rich in the minerals of modern society, especially oil, natural gas and sulphur. Louisiana ranks second only to Texas as a producer of crude oil, and in Baton Rouge stands the world's largest refinery, property of New Jersey Standard Oil. Perhaps most important of all, the area has an unlimited supply of that oft-neglected necessity in manufacturing—water.

Here local and South American oil become gasoline, petrochemicals and plastics; local gypsum becomes wallboard; South American bauxite becomes aluminum; Caribbean nickel and cobalt pass through processing; local sand becomes glass; local salt becomes salt. Mineral product and chemical by-product are mingled to produce end product. None of this, by the way, gives much employment, except to construction workers; these industries are the vanguard of automation. Despite the industrial expansion of recent years, manufacturing workers still account for less than 18 per cent of the area's employment, though they take home nearly 30 per cent of the total payroll. New Orleans has the advantage of industry without the drawbacks in the form of blue-collar living conditions.

And everything is improving at once (except the railroads, which are not very important here). A new road runs over Lake Pontchartrain (the "longest bridge in the world," from which one can observe the curvature of the earth; but the same piles would have been necessary to drive it over "solid land" in this alluvium). The road then connects via an expressway through the western fringe of downtown to a new bridge over the Mississippi. A new airport (open less than two years) takes jets. A new channel—or "pass" in the local terminology—is being driven through between the river and

292

the Gulf to cut fifty miles from the 125-mile trip up the previous man-made Delta channel. The most important of the existing passes, incidentally, was dug by the river itself back in 1879, when a clever engineer saw that the force of the water could scour a channel clean, provided the flow was contained in a fairly narrow passage and the strength of the current increased by blocking the other branches.

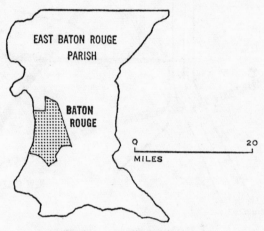

Standard Metropolitan Statistical Area.

Despite the high concentration of petroleum and related activities, New Orleans is decently diversified. Like all major ports, it has a sizable shipbuilding industry, and its transshipment business makes it one of the nation's great wholesale trade centers. As the only major city between Georgia and Texas, it has financial functions to perform, though generally it looks to Atlanta or to Dallas for leadership. Tourist trade is by no means a minor part of the city's income, and the business has been carefully nourished with good food and new accommodations, sporting spectacles, Mardi Gras festivities and the like.

At the other end of the line Baton Rouge has been the

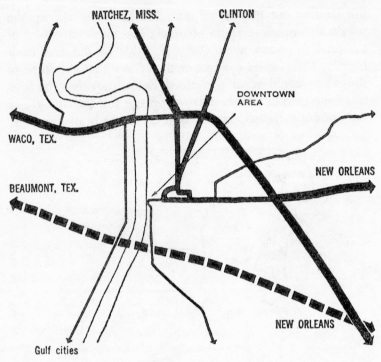

NATCHEZ, MISS.

CLINTON

DOWNTOWN
AREA

WACO, TEX.

NEW ORLEANS

BEAUMONT, TEX.

NEW ORLEANS

Gulf cities

Highway Arterial System.

South's fastest-growing city, rising from a 1940 population of 35,000 people, mostly working for the state government and mostly named Long, to a 1960 population of 175,000. The local Chamber of Commerce likes to claim diversification, but in fact a painfully large proportion of the Baton Rouge economy can be traced directly to petro-chemicals. The port may now be among the nation's top ten, but if you take Esso and Ethyl out of the picture it dwindles to insignificance. As a transshipment point, Baton Rouge can hardly hope to compete with New Orleans in the long run, especially now that the senior city has awakened to its need for improved port facilities. It is cheaper to send barges a longer

294

distance and ocean-going ships a shorter distance. At present, wholesale and retail trade account for less than 17 per cent of the area's work force, as against 30 per cent in New Orleans. What guarantees Baton Rouge is the size of the state capital operation and the swollen but still swelling dimensions of the state university. And, of course, if there is any one industry other than electronics to which a city can safely tie its kite in the year 1961, that industry is petro-chemicals, the raw material for a constantly increasing variety of plastics.

New Orleans is the Crescent City, standing mostly inside a sweeping curve which widens the isthmus between the river and the salty lake. Originally a French settlement, of course, ceded to Spain, regained by Napoleon via a secret treaty with a conquered nation, then sold to Jefferson with the rest of the Louisiana Purchase. The plantation slave economy goes back farther here than anywhere else in the South, and was hardest to break in this region. The city was the site of the most unnecessary battle in American history, the French fighting willingly with their barbaric American overlords against the British, three days after a treaty had been signed ending the War of 1812—a famous battle, partly because it was the only one we won. For years thereafter, a French city; still the only Catholic city in the South, though recent immigration has given all Protestant sects together a slight majority. But a southern city to such an extent that some local leaders seemed willing to risk excommunication by their Church rather than acquiesce in integration of the parochial schools. Nowhere in urban America have ethnic lines been more rigidly drawn.

A slum but not an indecent one (and now becoming the site of quality private housing), the Vieux Carré, the French Quarter of the city, has been carefully perserved as an American historical monument. Nothing that might be inconsistent with the old French architecture can now be built in the district, which directly adjoins the modern downtown of the city across the boundary of Canal Street, the main street and an ethnic barrier between French and Americans. Business did penetrate, however, before the historical sites commissions came alive: the city's largest department stores, the Maison Blanche and D. H. Holmes, stand on the French side of Canal. The French Quarter was, and perhaps still is, the home of jazz; places like Basin Street, Rampart Street and Bourbon Street have been immortalized in song and story. French names are all over the city, including a Champs-Elysées, anglicized to Elysian Fields, running to an amusement park on the shores of the lake.

The modern city grew up west of the French Quarter, dipping crescent-like to follow the line of the river. The distribution center by the docks, served by a grade-level railroad, is about as unappetizing as such places usually are. It will be jolted to improvement if the city follows through as contemplated on its plans to build a huge International Trade Mart and Venetian-style open plaza at the foot of Canal Street, where the ferry still carries tourists across the river. Commercial downtown begins a few blocks north of the river, and runs north roughly to South Rampart, with a scattering of commercial buildings of varying quality straggling up as far as Claiborne. Canal Street does not precisely mark the eastern edge of downtown, but it will, what with the zoning restrictions of the French Quarter; and the western boundary comes half a mile from Canal around Lee Circle, a center of the city when the Union Station just north of it was at the height of its influence. The new expressway, running from the new Pontchartrain causeway across the city to the new bridge over the river, passes central New Orleans just west of Lee Circle, and will doubtless form a relatively permanent boundary to the westward expansion of downtown.

Inner-ring problems north of downtown have been with New Orleans for a long time; Basin Street, you will recall, was the place where the white and the dark folks meet. Back before there was "urban renewal," in the days of "slum clearance," New Orleans built housing projects above the French Quarter. A few blocks north of the commercial center stands an imposing medical development, including the medical schools of Tulane and Louisiana State, a big Veterans Administration Hospital, and Charity Hospital, the largest in the South. The area due east of Union Station, between Central Business District and the hospitals, was shabby enough but has now been glorified with a twenty-million-dollar Civic Center, including not only the usual City Hall and office buildings, but also one of the nation's most handsome public libraries.

Otherwise downtown is relatively safe; the Garden District west of the commercial center, despite its early settlement, has never seriously deteriorated. Houses had to be built on the invisible "ridges" above the swamp, and land on the ridges was too expensive to abandon. Not until the 1920's did the drainage pumps make the basins of swamp between the "ridges" habitable for white folks. The traditional American leapfrog was a topographical impossibility in New Orleans.

The combination of barriers created by the French Quarter, the Civic Center, the new expressway and the river should hold downtown within its present limits, and force higher density development in the core. As this is written construction is nearing completion on a twenty-eight-story building on Baronne Street, two blocks south of Rampart and two blocks east of Canal; with 421,000 square feet of rentable space, it will be the largest commercial structure in the city. On Rampart Street, near the the Civic Center, the Oil and Gas Building, complete to landscaped plaza, is now finished and rented. On Lee Circle, at the western fringe, the

John Hancock Life Insurance Company is building its own branch headquarters, again using only part of the lot.

Access to downtown by car is good in New Orleans, especially from the better residential sections stretching up to the lake in the northwest section (one lakeside development there is locally believed to carry the highest land prices in America). The only serious traffic block comes, ominously enough, at a big shopping center on Carrollton Avenue, not far from the intersection of the radial streets from the crescent riverbank. At that focal point, where Tulane meets Carrollton and once there was a baseball park, tourists will be served by the nation's biggest motel—453 rooms eventually, with two hundred and the ballroom already working. The growth of shopping centers (another large one will shortly open by the lake) indicates that all is not well with traffic and parking inside downtown itself, though the figures look all right. Improved rapid transit would obviously be a good idea.

In any event, similar shopping center developments in Baton Rouge have demonstrated to the city fathers there that something must be done soon to improve the attractiveness of downtown. Though the city is built beside the river, there are no port facilities at the core. Front Street lies below the levee, atop which runs the Illinois Central tracks. Though a part of the city was laid out with some science by General Beauregard, Baton Rouge is now something of a hodgepodge, especially in contrast to the planned state capitol area directly north, the equally planned university area directly south. Third Street, the city's north-south main street, is so narrow that four cars abreast would scrape fenders; Florida Boulevard, the main route in from the east, is much easier to navigate but also serves the big shopping centers and acts as the main access to downtown from the north-south expressway on the eastern edge. At present the city fathers are still thinking small about their downtown, as befits the leaders of a community which *was* small until very recently. Repair of sidewalks and improvements in lighting will not be enough to keep business at the core. But everyone feels the pinch of suburban development, and when the squeeze hurts enough more decisive measures will be taken. Baton Rouge has the money to pay for radical solutions, and the newer elements in this industrializing community should be enough force to spark the drive, as they are in New Orleans.

## 20.  *Boston*

They call their city "the Hub," and out at Logan International Airport a legend beneath a map of the earth reads: "Boston—the Hub of the Universe." But it isn't anything of the sort. Indeed, though the place is a state capital and possesses one of the world's great natural harbors, though its concentration of money and culture cannot be rivaled by any city its size, Boston barely maintains itself as hub of its own metropolitan area. There is an old popular song expressing a willingness to

> . . . . . . . . . . . . sit all alone
> Like a King on a throne,
> And let the rest of the world go by.

At about the time that song was written, Boston opted to follow its advice. As a result, no downtown in America needs quite so much work as Boston—or seems quite so unlikely to get it.

Four rivers of various sizes—the Chelsea, the Mystic, the Charles and the Neponset—feed into the large mouth of Boston harbor. Gloucester to the north and Cape Cod to the south protect Massachusetts Bay, and the harbor itself is guarded by a series of islands, of which the most important

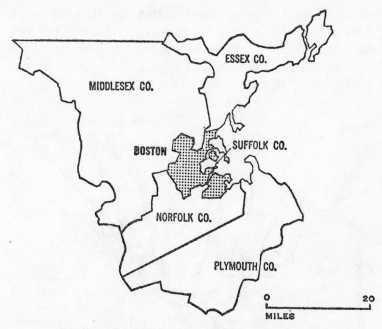

Standard Metropolitan Statistical Area.

are Deer and Long. For a sailing ship, Boston offered an even better harbor than New York, and until steam power replaced wind power for cargo ships, the city was the center of American mercantilism. Federal Street, Boston's Wall Street, a respectable collection of skyscrapers between the harbor and the patriotic monuments around Boston Common, is a still-functioning monument to the enterprise of the eighteenth- and nineteenth-century merchants.

But the greatest monument to nineteenth-century Boston enterprise is the land area of the city itself. More than two-thirds of central Boston rests on land reclaimed from the harbor or the tidal basin of the Charles between 1803 and 1901. The Boston of the Colonial period was virtually an island; South Bay and the Charles almost met at about the

301

point Tremont crosses Massachusetts today. The North Station area and Back Bay, the dock areas of south and east Boston, the wharves on the Mystic and the great flat of the airport—all these rest on filled land, and except for the airport all were completed before the turn of the century.

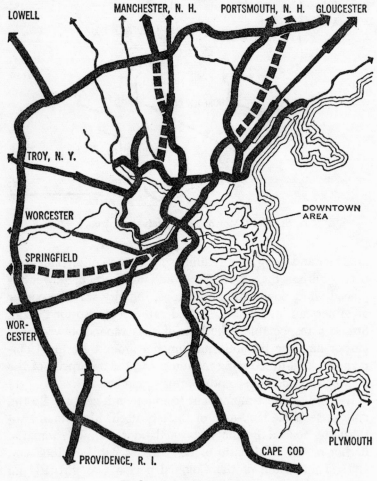

Highway Arterial System.

Heavy industry grew up naturally on the northern side of the harbor, partly because the inner harbor swung north and the Mystic was navigable where the Charles was not, partly because the Charles itself, swinging south and then east, presented so many barriers to the efficient movement of goods to and from the port. (The American Army in Italy half-believed that every river was called the Arno, because a course due north crossed that stream so often; an army fighting west from Boston would have the same feelings on a lesser scale about the Charles.) To service that industry, slums grew in Charlestown and East Boston, and by and large are still there. South Boston above Dorchester Heights was separated from central city in the early days by a broad, shallow arm of the harbor, and did not come into its own, industrially or as a slum, until the second half of the nineteenth century.

Meanwhile, central city was spreading out from Beacon Hill. The slope southwest from the State House had been reserved for the Common and the Botanical Gardens, probably the largest downtown open space in America. (Not entirely a blessing, by the way. The natural southward movement of downtown had to leap over the park, and that running broad jump seems to have taken all the energy out of the old Central Business District.) North and west of the State House, at the top of the hill and down the slopes, were government buildings and a residential district of a certain charm, early decayed, now gradually coming back, an almost inevitable renewal area for upper-middle-class apartment dwellings, if Boston ever gets around to working seriously on these matters. To the east Tremont Street bordered the Common as a natural site for commercial development, and behind it, between the financial district and the Common, ran narrow Washington Street, which became the city's retail headquarters. Both disappeared to the north into the market area and Scollay Square, which became the city's

Skid Row, and is now to be redeveloped (maybe) by federal and state office buildings, adding nothing to the tax rolls of the city.

The great nineteenth-century residential expansion of the city came in the filled land of Back Bay, behind a dam which kept the ocean out of the Charles. Beacon Street ran down the hill at the border of the Common and then out through the newly created land beside the river. A block farther back from the river ran the great width of Commonwealth Avenue, its traffic lanes divided by a park, itself wider than a good-sized street. In this area, Silas Lapham and his contemporaries built their fine brick homes, which still make an impressive show today—though a disturbing proportion of them are now rooming houses, college fraternity houses, or second-rank office space. To mark the end of the planned development, the Fenway was built around a tributary of the Charles—first of a great chain of parks which would arc south, at varying widths, ten miles to the city's borders.

Eastward, too, across the widened neck of the old isthmus, the planners and developers were busy. Nothing so lavish as the Back Bay area was attempted, but even across the New Haven tracks residences of middle-class quality extended the livable area of the city. With the deterioration of this area, better housing leapfrogged out to the line of parks at Jamaicaway—and then beyond, into the nearby suburb of Brookline.

From the nineteenth century, Boston was surrounded by suburbs which maintained an independent—often antagonistic—municipal status. The harbor area (including Bunker Hill in the Charlestown section) was fairly rapidly surrounded by the city of Boston. Just north of the harbor, however, Chelsea and Revere and Winthrop maintained their independent condition. And Cambridge, right across the Charles—more convenient to downtown than most of Boston itself, once the bridges were built—continued to resist absorption. Independent Brookline separated downtown Boston from the city's own Brighton and Allston districts, which extend along the Charles well beyond Cambridge itself, out to Watertown. North of Cambridge, Somerville, Medford, Malden and Everett, all within ten miles of Beacon Hill, remained ferociously separate from the city which gave them their excuse for being.

Nowhere in America was the battle between the ins and outs more hard-fought than it was in Boston in the latter nineteenth and early twentieth centuries. The heavy Irish and Italian immigrations found no acceptance from the established "Brahmins" and their poor whites. Weight of population in the Boston slums, well organized by the local Democratic machine, finally pushed over the older moneyed interests, and they fled to their established enclaves, the independent municipalities all around the cities. Indeed, the organization of the area was such that they were able to escape even Suffolk County, for the Boston area was cut into half a dozen counties.

There is a sense in which Boston was the first city to develop extensive middle-class suburbs. (Parts of them have gone pretty far downhill by now, simply through the aging process.) But the Bostonians who were moving into Brookline and Newton and Belmont stayed physically closer to the heart of their city than the New Yorkers in Brooklyn and Queens. Cambridge around M.I.T. is much closer to the center of Boston than any part of Brooklyn to Grand Central Station; but when New York was absorbing Brooklyn, in the late 1890's, Cambridge was asserting once and for all its independence of Boston.

The city is plagued, therefore, by governmental problems. Because so many independent municipalities cluster about its core, mass transit cannot be run by any one of them, and in this single area the state government has stepped in to form an intercity Transit Authority. Otherwise, the schools, police departments, fire departments, traffic courts and such are separately established, and in each petty principality a prince asserts his unique position and power. Worst of all, the tax base has been appallingly diluted. Boston has seen its real estate decline severely in assessed valuation over the last generation—down half a billion dollars since 1932. One result is a tax rate of $10.70 per $100, far and away the highest of any city in the country. Meanwhile, the suburbs grow, industry builds along the semicircle of Route 128, twenty miles from Park Place, and workers move out to be nearer their jobs. The city of Boston lost one sixth of its population between 1950 and 1960, despite a growth, for the metropolitan area as a whole, to a grand total of 2,600,000.

Boston's middle class feels an almost aggressive lack of interest in what happens to downtown. The manager of the Urban Redevelopment Department of the Greater Boston Chamber of Commerce writes that "each year since 1955, the chamber has filed or supported legislation to create a Boston area regional planning agency. Each year, the bill has been defeated . . . but suburban support is mounting." Behind the politesse, what he is saying is that the communities other than Boston which would have to be involved in a regional plan are having none of it, but the Chamber of Commerce hopes things will change. That is what a Chamber of Commerce is for essentially—to hope.

Complicating downtown's problems still further is Boston's European reluctance to tear down anything which can even remotely be defended, or to alter street patterns. Washington Street is shockingly inadequate as a retail center, but nobody has suggested ways to widen it, or drawn any plans for a new downtown with Washington as a salvageable pedestrian mall. (Though there is a proposal for an eentsy-weentsy mall on one of the side streets.) Except for the garage now under construction beneath the Common, the big new projects are to the north of downtown, around

306

Scollay Square, and well to the south, at the edges of Back Bay, where Prudential is putting up a group of large commercial buildings on the air rights over the main Boston and Albany Railroad yards. Neither is quite contiguous with downtown by any juggling, and the Prudential project is out beyond the current Copley Square border of the "new downtown" which has been draining the vitality from the old urban core. Even Boston's dreamboat, the Atlantic Avenue waterfront project over the little-used old docks, would be separated from the office area by a dangerous belt of blight. None of it seems likely to happen anyway—even the Prudential project, which would cost the city nothing, was almost lost by political stupidity, accepting the commercial stupidity of vested interests who feared for their own property values.

The universities attract people and business, and there are lots of them—Harvard, M.I.T., Tufts, Brandeis, Boston University, Boston College. (Of course, they don't pay real estate taxes.) Economically, the future is not nearly so bleak as some pundits have had it. Finance is still strong, electronics is booming, the machine shops are doing well, the leather industry is looking up, most of the textile losses have been replaced. Real wages have risen faster of late in the Boston area than they have in most parts of the country. The city itself is still attractive near its center, because the old merchants built well and the old planners planned well. The new inner-ring highway is excellent, though traffic is dreadful when you get off it. Some day they may even bring the Massachusetts Turnpike into the city, instead of allowing it to feed nothing but Route 128. This extension would appear to be a sure thing, but I have seen too many routes drawn for it to be confident. Nothing is sure in Boston until it happens.

Yet despite the charm of the place I know no more hopeless downtown than Boston's. Let it be a lesson. Innate conservatism is dangerous enough to a city, though self-interest can overcome it, as Cincinnati and Indianapolis demonstrate. Add a political pigheadedness based on ethnic prejudice, however, and no amount of culture or money can save your city.

# 21. *Akron*

If you remembered your Greek, you'd know it was a hill town, like the city of temples that towered above Athens. Our pioneer forebears may have been, in the judgment of Europeans, little better than barbarians; but they knew their Greek and Latin. They settled Akron around 1825, and a few years later the canal came through at the foot of the hill, making the settlement a city. Farming country with good clay; along the banks of the canal the factories made cereals and pottery, and shipped their production up the canal to the Great Lakes—or down a short-lived second canal to Pennsylvania.

How and why the city became the Rubber Capital seems to be something of a mystery. It was not, of course, near the raw material; but only the then-underpopulated Pacific and Gulf Coasts were near raw material, and they were too far from the market. The Akron Chamber of Commerce likes to say that the city is in the "market center of America—100,000,000 people within 500 miles, with 75 per cent of the nation's buying power." But virtually every city in the north-central region can make the same claim, when you talk in terms of "500 miles."

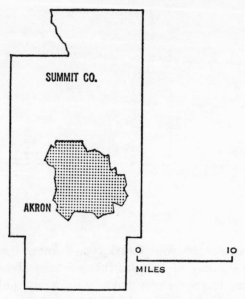

SUMMIT CO.

AKRON

0            10

MILES

Standard Metropolitan Statistical Area.

In the early days of the automobile, when Detroit and Indianapolis were the capitals of a new industry, Akron was almost equally convenient to both, which may have helped. (Today Akron is not, really, very convenient to Indianapolis; because I own property in both, I once had to get from one to the other rather quickly—and wound up chartering a private plane.) Essentially, the secret seems to be that, here in Akron, Benjamin Goodrich was able to raise the twenty thousand dollars he needed to start a plant to make fire hose—and it was in Akron, as a result, that the Goodrich Company made the first pneumatic tire, shortly before the turn of the century. Every successful business draws flies, and before the lure of rubber profits had diminished, Goodyear, Firestone, General, Mohawk and Sieberling Rubber all had their home offices and major plants in Akron.

Geographically, Akron's situation has improved greatly in

310

the last decade. The Ohio Canal is still in existence but no longer in service (unfortunately, through planning failures, it doesn't even serve recreational functions). Akron was a rail city, industrially, with the typically excellent rail connections of the north-central area. Now it is a major truck city, too, the Ohio Turnpike cutting through its outer edge

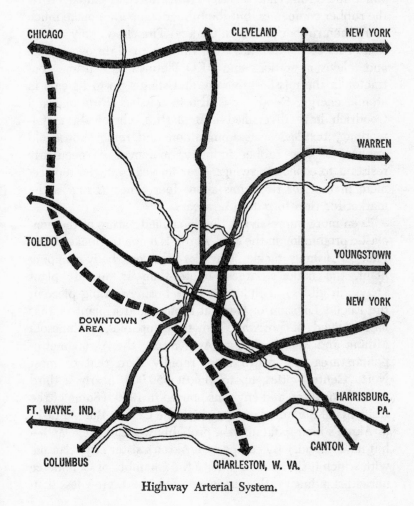

Highway Arterial System.

and the new north-south Ohio Freeway crossing the Turnpike not far away. Only thirty-five miles from Cleveland
(the suburbs of the two cities touch), Akron will benefit in
some degree from whatever the St. Lawrence Seaway brings
to the Lake Erie ports.

Economically, too, the postwar years have seen rapid advance in Akron. Half the city's work force is employed by
the rubber companies, but the rubber companies make much
more than rubber products. General Tire shows only a fraction of its corporate sales from rubber: the firm owns radio
and television stations and RKO Pictures, is a prime con-
tractor in the missile program, and stands up to its ears in
atomic energy. Goodyear is also in missiles, Firestone and
Goodrich have diversified into plastics, chemicals, metalworking, textiles, even ammunition and minor household
appliances. The rubber industry, moreover, is peculiarly
resistant to economic swings. Year in, year out, the replace-
ment market for tires runs about four times as big as the
market for tires to put on new cars.

Even more impressive is the diversified nature of the non-
elastic production in the area. Akron is home to Quaker Oats,
Pflueger fishing tackle, Chrysler's largest body-stamping
plant, the nation's largest lighter-than-air aircraft plant
(navy dirigibles), a children's book business, a big piece of
the Euclid Division of General Motors and a plant of that
longest-lived of postwar "growth companies," Minnesota
Mining and Manufacturing. As a result, the Akron metropolitan area has grown more rapidly than that of most
North Central cities, up to almost 550,000, nearly a third
more than Akron and environs housed in 1950. (Some of the
residents of Summit County, which the Census Bureau takes
as Akron's metropolitan area, probably work in Cleveland—
but never mind.) By comparison Akron's sister city, Canton,
with which it shares a large but (the Chamber of Commerce
notwithstanding) rather inconvenient airport, grew less than

one-fifth in the fifties, because it was overdependent on metals, metals fabricating and heavy machinery.

Downtown Akron has been lucky. The city was laid out originally with broad north-south streets which can carry more than the usual volume of traffic. (Main Street is as wide as it is because the canal to Pennsylvania ran down its middle; the water now passes through a conduit under the pavement.) East-west, unfortunately, there are only two through streets cutting across downtown—Market to the north, Exchange to the south, each cutting the center of one of the two original settlements which joined to form Akron—and the existing traffic pattern is pretty dreadful. But what is wrong with downtown traffic could be cured much more cheaply in Akron than in most cities.

Despite the nearness of the Ohio Turnpike, industry has not been moving out from Akron itself to the strip of concrete in the countryside, and does not seem likely to do so. The inner ring around downtown is blighted, like all inner rings, but not severely; despite the unfavorable evidence of strings of used-car lots, hasheries, bowling alleys, gas stations and the like just outside downtown, these descendants of German immigrants are good housekeepers. Though the city is spread out residentially, with few apartment houses anywhere and nearly three-quarters of the community living in homes they own, shopping centers are hard to find. The two downtown department stores, O'Neill's (a May Company subsidiary) and Polsky's (one of the Allied chain), have done so superb a job of merchandising that in recent years they have been killing off the dime-store and specialty-shop business along Main Street. The healthiest of these enterprises have been drawn gravitationally south toward the giants, and the less healthy have died. Whichever occurred, gaping vacancies were left in the storefronts.

In Akron, as in many middle-sized cities, it is downtown

itself which needs the work. By which is meant *work*, not talk. Despite the prosperity and growth of the metropolitan area during the last decade, relatively little of substance has been built downtown. Actually, matters are not so bad as the bald statement indicates, because many of the older downtown buildings have been substantially refurbished. The Sheraton chain is not putting up a new hotel, but it *is* spending upward of a million dollars to modernize the hotel it has. My own Ohio Building, though little changed on the outside, is a much sounder piece of property today than it was ten years ago. In the Second National and Akron Savings and Loan Buildings, many of the office suites are decorated in a style which would do credit to corporate headquarters anywhere. If an integral part of urban renewal is preventive maintenance and conservation, Akron cannot be flunked from the course.

Nevertheless, downtown is deteriorating, because the traffic pattern is so awkward and because even the best conservation efforts cannot entirely substitute for new construction. Some of Akron's downtown structures date back more than a hundred years, and many are nearing their fiftieth birthday; one of them, on the older northern edge of downtown, fell into one of the city's central streets only a few years ago. The jailhouse is still adjacent to City Hall, representing probably the best definition of the "lowest and worst" use of valuable downtown land. There is a severe shortage of greenery, and despite the Soapbox Derby the town is somewhat short of entertainment facilities. There is no convention hall worth mentioning.

Nobody is going to build in downtown Akron unless the city does something about bringing expressway traffic to downtown and garaging it on arrival. And to date about the only muscles moved in that direction have been those involved in writing and printing plans, and talking. There is a fairly thorough plan for downtown redevelopment, involving an inner loop of one-way limited-access highways, a pedestrian mall for Main Street, quick access to the east-west expressway, an additional eight thousand parking places in downtown and an elaborate "cultural center" (convention hall plus theater plus art gallery plus parking plus trees). Nobody seems to have put a total cost figure on the plan, and I am not entirely happy with it as a matter of personal judgment. Neither, apparently, are the citizens of Akron, who voted it down decisively; the popular mayor who had campaigned for it was saved only by a recount. Certainly the inner-loop program ought not to have been tied to the cultural center. Akron needs the inner loop whatever else is done; otherwise it will receive little value from an outer-belt expressway situation—a gift from the federal government—for which most cities would mortgage their virtue, civic or private. The location of the proposed cultural center is highly debatable. The plan places it where the old Quaker Oats factory now stands, backing against the canal and a bluff. Myself, I think there ought to be high-rise apartment houses on the site, and I would be willing to co-venture with local money and build them if the city made the land available.

Whatever the arguments pro or con the specific master plan, however, Akron would doubtless be better off today if it had begun acting on most of the recommendations, especially the roads, when the plan was first published some years ago. Deterioration has not slackened in the interim, and today the city is short of funds—or so it says.

As matters stand, I have been unable even to proceed with plans to build a twenty-story office building and a four-deck parking garage up the hill from the Ohio Building. (And "up the hill" is the phrase, too. The slope is so steep that one and a half of the parking decks would be "underground" from the High Street entrance to the building, but plainly out in the open air on the other side.) The only progress

has been the construction of a four-way bridge over
Church Street linking my building, the Second National,
City Hall and my garage on the site of the projected office
building.

There is no use mincing words about why so little has
been done in Akron, despite the evident need. The reason
is the failure of the six rubber companies to take a serious
interest in the redevelopment of downtown. There was not
a single representative of the rubber companies on the
Downtown Committee of the Chamber of Commerce, which
organized the master plan. It would doubtless be too much
to say that the rubber companies are opposed to the revitali-
zation of Akron; so long as their property taxes did not rise
as the result of an urban renewal program (and Akron taxes,
at $3.87, are relatively low), the rubber barons would
probably just as soon live in a city with a healthy downtown.
They are themselves, of course, located at the edge of the
inner ring; and their new research laboratories are even
farther out. Each of them is like a feudal baron looking at
the market place where his subjects indirectly service him
by servicing those who directly service him. Each takes a
distant, benevolent interest in what his servants do, provided nothing costs him any money. And each watches his
fellow barons, naturally—to the extent that if one company
took steps to help the city's redevelopment, the others would
probably join in. That goes for the labor unions, too.

The city has artificial assets to set against this artificial
liability. One is Akron University, educationally outstanding
and institutionally a force for civic progress. Its campus, in
the inner ring, will soon be extended southward, demolish-
ing much deteriorated property—with the help of federal
money. Perhaps an even more potent force is the Akron
*Beacon Journal*, which may be John Knight's best newspaper. Its editor Ben Maidenburg has roasted me over specially heated coals, but he can't burn out my admiration for

his intelligence, his alertness and his deep desire to help his city.

Not that I think that, on this occasion, Maidenburg had the right target. His main concern should be, and usually is, to find out what it is that stagnates a city with such historical vitality. Misdirected conservatism is what Maidenburg and the city administration must hit together. If Akron's forces for progress could work together—with the pressure of the city's great natural advantages behind them—they could bulldoze their opposition in a day.

# 22.  Grand Rapids

A river city, where the river brought the raw materials to the factories. But not a port. Because the raw material was wood, and required no barges for its transportation, and the factories made furniture. That was some time ago, and what happened thereafter was for years less interesting and less pleasant. This has been one of the cities that had to come from behind, helped by the industrial vitality which makes such miracles possible.

The Grand is the only river of any substance draining the Michigan peninsula. It flows west through a pleasant valley of its own devising, and ends in Lake Michigan. Open to the west, Grand Rapids forms part of the complex directed toward Chicago rather than that directed toward Detroit. It is an old city, with an old industry. By rights, it should have disintegrated when the furniture business went south; it was saved partly by the quality of the local product (which kept some factories in the neighborhood despite higher wage rates and older plants), partly by diversification into metalworking, now the largest industry of the area. The city is also a little metropolis (population, 200,000) for

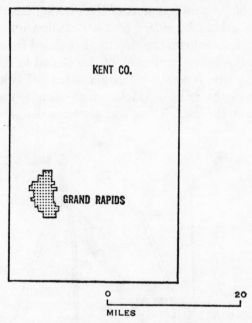

Standard Metropolitan Statistical Area.

a fertile valley with successful farms. And the quality of its railroad connections, built originally to service the furniture industry and including both the New York Central and Pennsylvania systems, has made it the wholesale distribution center of western Michigan.

Few cities the size of Grand Rapids have such massive office buildings; not because the city leaders planned big as a commercial center, but because the old furniture factories were suitable for conversion to offices after the furniture makers moved on. Downtown is square, lying on the eastern bank of the river but offering no fewer than three bridges to the western bank (in addition to a railroad trestle) on its seven east-west streets. Later, when the north-south expressway is complete, a fourth bridge will angle across just south of the southernmost of the existing crossings, and form the southern boundary of the new downtown. North and south of downtown the riverfront is zoned for industrial uses, as is the entire west bank of the Grand in its passage through the city. A somewhat larger industrial belt runs on both sides of the railroad tracks which parallel the river a few blocks to the west. There was always a danger of floods

Highway Arterial System.

in Grand Rapids, and even today not every inch of the river-bank is recommended for settlement.

Industrially the base is sound. Despite all the old jokes, "Grand Rapids quality" still means something in the furniture business, and the local woodworking industry is all the more firmly established since the cheap-jacks went South. Today, both General Motors and American Motors have plants here, GM making diesel equipment and automobile bodies, American Motors running a large household appliance factory. The city is also home to the Bissel Carpet Sweeper, which dominates its tiny industry, and to Allen Business Machines, as well as a number of heavy-industry plants, including Keeler Brass and Lear. Neither Kalamazoo nor Muskegon is in a position to challenge Grand Rapids as the retail and wholesale center of the area. Depressions will always hit harder in a city like Grand Rapids than they will elsewhere, because so large a percentage of the population (nearly half the work force) is engaged in actual manufacturing; but at least there is a wide variety of industries, not likely to be hit all at once.

What makes Grand Rapids particularly appealing as an investment, oddly enough, is its age and general dilapidation. This does not usually recommend a city, but Grand Rapids, like many of the old industrial centers, is well-to-do and can afford something better. The city is underbuilt; it needs a variety of new or rehabilitated structures, new civic buildings, new entertainment and cultural facilities. It also needs industrial redevelopment, to end the leakage of factories out to the suburbs; in recent years most of the city's industrial growth has come south of its borders, in sites convenient to both the railroads and the U. S. 131 expressway.

Much of downtown is visibly obsolete; much of the inner ring, on both sides of the river, is clearly ready for destruction. The city needs access highways and an inner loop, parking, new residential districts convenient to downtown, a Civic Center and cultural facilities. Restoration of the muscle power of the heart can best be achieved when a new circulatory and respiratory system replaces the old. Urban renewal is a natural, and a must. When I bought, I bought a good property, sound in itself and sure to benefit when the city did something for civic betterment. I thought at the time that urban renewal would come quickly, and I was wrong; the city has been dragging its heels. There is something about these older cities with population under half a million which seems to prevent quick, effective action, until the death rattle replaces the noises of vitality. Too few people have the power, and they are too old; they would as soon keep their home town as it was until they die, or it does, and figuratively the two amount to the same thing.

Still the need is there, and needs get met. There is a city planning commission, with ardent spirits working for it, and federal highway money is just around the corner, and there are now two million dollars of federal and one million of local urban renewal money available for the north-west segment of downtown.

The projected expressways will form two parts of a loop for downtown: north-south running just west of the river and cutting east across the Grand below downtown; and the Chicago road crossing just north of Michigan Avenue, forming the northern border of the Central Business District, and meeting the Muskegon-Detroit expressway east of the city. The natural closure for the loop is Fulton Street, leading to what is now the southernmost of the bridges over the Grand (the expressway will cross south of it), and the right of way along Division and Ransom streets, seven blocks east of the river, meeting Fulton at the projected cultural center.

Key street in the Grand Rapids Central Business District is Monroe Avenue (demonstrating the age of the city; in the later nineteenth century, who would have named Main

Street after James Monroe?). Monroe runs north-south a block from the river, then bends east to run four relatively short blocks at a diagonal into Fulton. Virtually the entire four-block area is devoted to retailing, and the diagonal stretch of Monroe is the 100 per cent location of the city. According to the city's planning commission, four of the seven blockfronts on Monroe are deteriorating structures. Above the bend, where the rest of the major retailing is done and a few old hotels stand at the northern end near the Michigan Avenue intersection, Monroe is either substandard or deteriorating—further damaged by several factories still operating between the river and the avenue, though the district was zoned against industry thirty-seven years ago. Where the factories stand, and in the deteriorating blocks across Monroe, the renewal plan calls for a new Civic Center.

Parking facilities would be included in the Civic Center, and would be built south of the Monroe diagonal, on Louis Street, which is *really* deteriorating, and out on the eastern edge of the district. Finally, the cultural center would be completed on the southeastern corner, some of the area between the Monroe bend and Michigan to the north would be turned over to pedestrian malls, trees would be planted, a few small parks blocked off—and so forth and so on.

All very pretty. But *when* is it going to be done? Enough money was raised to bring in one of the nation's better-established consulting firms—Ebasco—to draw maps, make legal forms, suggest relocations of streets and sewers and utility lines. Under Michigan law, Grand Rapids can buy up as much of the Central Business District as seems necessary to its plans; and federal money could doubtless be found. The local newspapers have mentioned that *private* money, including mine, would be available to make the plan a reality once the city put it in motion. But talk is not motion. And the conflicts of interest in the southern section of downtown give too many people a stake in stopping any rational plan.

Sometimes one has the suspicion that Grand Rapids is waiting for a depression to idle a big piece of its labor force and justify redevelopment under the name of public works. But the private money might not be available at that time, and, as Philadelphia has demonstrated, it is private money, flowing under the stimulus of public action, which can make urban renewal a reality. When do we start? I guess when the landed industrial aristocracy joins hands and works together with the nouveaux like myself. Survival again becomes the dominating and generating force.

# 23. *Tulsa*

Plenty of American cities like to think of themselves as "new," but most of them can show at least a hundred years of history. Tulsa is *really* new. There were no white settlers here until 1882, and not much chance for them to multiply until the Oklahoma Territory opened to homesteading in 1889. The Arkansas, beside which Tulsa stands, is not by any means a navigable river. It rises in the Rockies at a height of 11,300 feet, cuts the Royal Gorge in its descent and is still flowing fairly swiftly and not a little dangerously when it passes Tulsa. (And its banks are not as watertight as one might wish them to be; every so often one has to pump water out of the basement of Tulsa office buildings.) Though the city was something of a railroad center from an early point in the game, its rail traffic was never in the same league with, say, Wichita. But in 1905 Glen Pool began spewing oil over the countryside, and Tulsa was given its *raison d'être*.

Yet the city has a history, too. It was on the banks of the Arkansas that the three Indian nations met—the Osage, the Creek and the Cherokee—and counseled together on

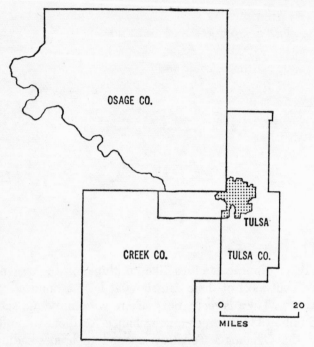

Standard Metropolitan Statistical Area.

matters of common interest. It makes the purchase of real estate different in Tulsa from apparently similar transactions elsewhere. The title search takes you back to the Louisiana Purchase, treaties with Indian nations and finally the first transactions registered (sometimes on God knows what basis) in the usual courthouse manner.

The newness of Tulsa has had conflicting influences on the city's growth. This was Populist country, with strong views on honest municipal government; so Tulsa got a city commission plan of government as early as 1908. According to the city's charter, mineral rights were reserved to the municipality, so there are none of the downtown oil derricks which disfigure neighboring Oklahoma City.

326

The city grew most rapidly in the 1920's, when high-density downtown construction was much in vogue, so downtown is compact, set safely several blocks in from the river, and just south of the railroad tracks. But the 1920's were careless about transit, access roads and parking, and the little downtown grid was stuffed with all the building it could conveniently handle when the postwar boom began. Postwar expansion has been mostly to the south, at the bottom

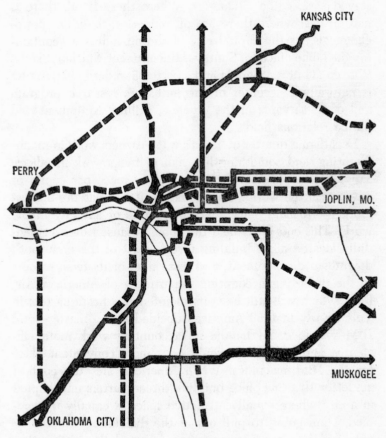

Highway Arterial System.

of the grid or below. The biggest of the city's postwar skyscrapers, the First National Bank of Tulsa, went up, facing south, in the southern part of the grid. Building below the grid is not like redeveloping a blighted inner ring; it's more like opening up new countryside.

All the oil that was reasonably easy to get was taken out of the ground, but most of the oil companies remained. The big refineries stand across the river with land around them for expansion (commercially and residentially, Tulsa has stayed east of the Arkansas). Where there is oil, there is natural gas; where there are oil refineries, there are petrochemicals. As the capital city of the oil industry (containing the home offices of Sunray–Midcontinent, Sinclair, Skelly, Warren (Gulf), Amerada and assorted Standard Oils), Tulsa is naturally the center of the industry's research program and of its servants in the pipeline, drilling equipment and public relations fields.

Less than a quarter of Tulsa's wage earners work in manufacturing, and something like half of them work in offices. Tulsa has the highest footage of office space per capita of any city in the world. Unfortunately, it also has the highest footage of *vacant* office space per capita of any city in the world. This cuts fairly near the bone, because I own a splendidly located office building in the heart of the new south downtown development, and lease nine of its twelve floors to the departing accounting department of American Airlines, which will still have its maintenance headquarters in Tulsa. Early in 1960 American decided that a master-brain IBM system could handle its accounting work more efficiently, and New York would be a more convenient place for the IBM machines. When American flies the coop, I am left with a fine office building three-quarters unoccupied in a city where equally attractive space is equally unoccupied. I am going to pull out of the difficulties rather than out of Tulsa—but I cannot entirely avoid the feeling that everybody would have been a little better off if there had been perhaps a dozen rather than seventeen major buildings added to the city's skyline during the 1950's. Certainly the city had no need for all those showplace, single-purpose headquarters buildings.

Urban renewal has come to Tulsa only in the last few years, spurred by the prospect of a big Civic Center (complete with theaters, museums and sports facilities) just west of downtown. A complete plan for "Tulcenter" and its adjacent streets has been drawn up by Harold F. Wise, Inc., architect Richard Neutra and consultant Larry Smith. Tied to approved expressways and an inner loop, the plan is ambitious but not inconceivable. It calls for the closing off of the major downtown streets (Main and Boston, Third, Fourth and Fifth), with garbage pickup, goods deliveries and such to be made through the city's extensive back-alley system. Along the pedestrian malls the landscape architects, the building architects, the planners and the city's retailers would combine to create tree-shaded colonnades, little swirls of foot traffic to be drawn into the shops as water is drawn down a narrow drain.

In addition to the downtown malls (and the garages and one-way streets necessary to service it), the plan proposes a Transportation Center to the north, built around the existing Union Station; a permanent Oil Mart beside the Center; and a special parking-and-shopping structure adjoining the old Courthouse Square at Sixth and Boulder, now a decaying block which would tend to barricade downtown from the projected Civic Center due west. Between the railroads and the new Route 244 expressway, which will make a nose just north of downtown, the plan foresees a revitalized wholesale and distributive center. Adjacent to the Civic Center both north and south, the planners want a large group of middle-income apartment houses, the land to be put together with urban-renewal authorizations and developed with the help of FHA. South of downtown, in the area where the new office buildings have been encroaching, the planners would like to see a "Cathedral Square," a parklike area to house the city's large churches, four of which are already *in situ;* plus more middle-income housing beside it, adjacent to the southern line of the inner loop.

As lagniappe, the planners throw in the idea of a Marina on the Arkansas River (to be made safe for boating and more attractive generally by a series of dams under construction). The Marina would be something less than a mile south of the heart of town; and it very likely would, as the planners suggest, "make living in central Tulsa the envy of every western city dweller."

At present it is hard to predict how much we shall actually see of this ambitious program (which carries on it the names of the City Commissioners, the County Commissioners, the members of the Planning Commission and the Central Business District Master Plan Committee). No windfall boom is in prospect to pay for it. On the other hand, action could come simply from the fact that the inner loop, part of the federal highway program, will doubtless be realized and must generate action in a city which faces a long siege if nothing is done. I have yet to see an instance where major transportation improvement failed to generate real estate development.

Geographically, Tulsa is one of the belt of "mid-continent" cities which will be the greatest beneficiaries of the nation's increasing population. There is vacant land all around it (indeed, adjacent Creek County, now part of the city's Census Bureau metropolitan area, lost population in the 1950's). American Airlines projected electronic monsters may have stabbed me in the back, but its maintenance headquarters is permanently in Tulsa and must expand, now that the jet repair facilities are completed. The city's road and rail transportation picture is also excellent. What has held Tulsa back, and will probably prevent forever its development into a major metropolitan center, is a position equidistant from and rather near to Kansas City and Dallas.

Economically, Tulsa is safer than its rival Oklahoma City, which is appallingly dependent on government employment (especially at the Tinker Air Force Base). While the oil industry seems unlikely to enjoy the 1960's as much as it did the 1950's, any tendency for the industry to pull in its horns will further concentrate it in Tulsa. Like most western cities, Tulsa has a big aircraft plant, in this case Douglas repair and maintenance, with seventy-five hundred employees.

One stimulus to downtown, and to the city as a whole, must be the growth of a greatly improved restaurant business, now that prohibition is no longer the law of Oklahoma. Actually, consumption of liquor per capita will probably decline (it could scarcely go up), and the loss of profits from bootlegging will be severely felt by many, as once the wildcatters felt the drying up of the oil reserves. Still, a city can only gain when a change of law makes possible a more civilized system of distribution and consumption.

On the whole, then, Tulsa's future seems secure, though no longer gold-plated guaranteed-or-your-money-back. Now that the overbuilding phase is past, things should presently be looking up again—provided enough is torn down. Tulsans have the robust spirit to do it. Construction and transformation is easier for young cities, especially when they are flush with the wealth of our natural resources and blessed with a "must-thrive" location.

# 24.  *San Francisco*

And here we are in the best of all possible worlds, where for once you need not add the Britisher's complaint that everything in it is a necessary evil. Fortunate in almost every way (one cannot regard the San Mateo fault as an advantage), San Franciscans have done remarkably little to destroy their luck. Other cities may have a more certain future than San Francisco itself (as distinguished from its gold-plated region, the wine counties which make up the San Francisco Bay area). It is an enormous job to maintain forty-five square miles at the tip of a peninsula as undisputed urban headquarters for so violently expanding a region. But San Francisco's *present* is more cheerful than that of any other major American city. *Omnis Habitare in Urbe Sancti Francisci Volunt* reads the motto of the city's redevelopment agency: "Everybody Wants to Live in San Francisco." Which is very nearly true—and must be a great asset to the city.

The hills run virtually the length of the California coast, blocking the sea winds from the stifling interior valleys and permitting few safe anchorages. They open briefly at the

Standard Metropolitan Statistical Area.

Golden Gate, a treacherous gap about two-thirds of a mile wide. Behind the gate, a bay seventy miles long—accessible to a large hinterland by its very size, becoming convenient to a still larger hinterland by current dredging operations in the Sacramento River—makes a natural harbor the equal of any in the world. An inevitable center for intercoastal shipping along the Pacific shore, San Francisco first grew as the port of entry for the clippers coming round the Horn from the East, or competing with Europeans for the China trade; raced forward with the opening of the Panama Canal (which sparked an exposition still remembered by old-timers); and now, with the steady expansion of trade between America and Hawaii and Japan, comes into the greatest period it has ever known.

The wealth of the port, the incredible richness of the sur-

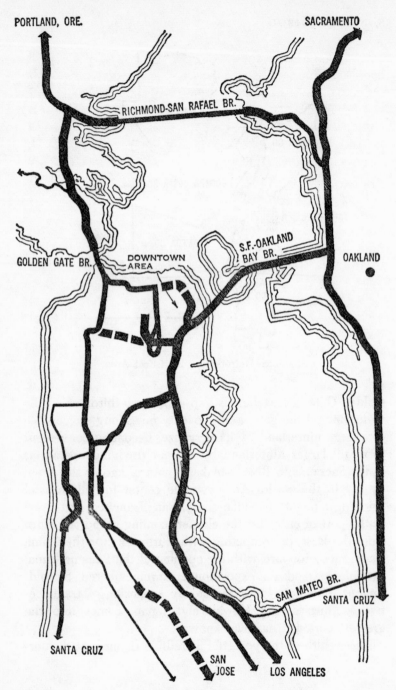

PORTLAND, ORE.

SACRAMENTO

RICHMOND-SAN RAFAEL BR.

S.F.-OAKLAND
BAY BR.

OAKLAND

GOLDEN GATE BR.

DOWNTOWN
AREA

SAN MATEO BR.

SANTA CRUZ

SANTA CRUZ

SAN
JOSE

LOS ANGELES

Highway Arterial System.

rounding farmlands, the gold in the hills (some of it still there—adventurous San Franciscans amuse themselves by climbing hills and panning a little dust uneconomically) built beside the Gate what was until the early years of this century the largest city in California. Because the peninsula was almost as inconvenient to railroads as Manhattan Island, a sister city Oakland grew up on the inland side of the bay to serve as land shipping terminal for the area and the center of its industrial production.

Connected only by a lengthy ferry ride until well on in this century (the bridge that finally linked them runs eight and a quarter miles), San Francisco and Oakland developed more or less independently. It is broadly true to say that San Francisco became the commercial, cultural and upper-income residential center, while Oakland grew into an industrial, blue-collar, lower-middle-class appendage. But Oakland has its own downtown, containing corporate head-quarters (most notably the spanking new Kaiser Center, on the north edge of Oakland's core, the largest industrial head-quarters west of the Mississippi); and in its own hills and those of adjoining Berkeley, by the University of California, Oakland has residential districts as wealthy as any in America. On the other side, San Francisco has its industries (especially in the stretch south along the shallow, smelly bay culminating in the vast self-contained municipally independent complex of South San Francisco)—and its slums, Oriental and otherwise.

As part of the coast range, San Francisco's peninsula is appropriately hilly, not to say mountainous. The hills gave the city an automatically successful zoning pattern; business had to go into the valleys, where people and goods could come in and out relatively easily. Residences, therefore, were to be built on the slopes and the hilltops, where the air was luxuriously clean and the views magnificent. The port inevitably grew up along the curve of the peninsula facing the bay, and the northeasterly hills—Telegraph, Russian and Nob—were the first to be built up. Socially as well as topographically, they have had their ups and downs, but today even Telegraph, once a slum (the steepest of them all, and the only one the grid pattern respects, the streets breaking off and re-forming on the other side), is a highly desirable residential quarter. San Francisco can use and will receive some new inner-ring apartment houses. San Franciscans like to live in apartment houses, and most of those three-story, bay-windowed wooden residences were built for several families. But no city in America can claim, in proportion to its size, so much existing good inner-ring housing. Which figures: no city in America has so high an average per capita income.

South of these hills is the city's largest single expanse of flat land (much of it swamp before there was a city here). On this flat—mostly in a strip about Market Street, running southwest from the old ferry terminal, now a heliport—San Francisco built its distribution, commercial, financial, retail and entertainment centers. Finance and shipping are, as usual, nearest the water; then comes the mixture of commercial and retailing; and finally popular entertainment, well out on Market Street—theoretically bolstered by the splendid post-World War I Civic Center, complete to Baroque-domed City Hall, Florentine opera house and art museum, actually an area in great danger of going to seed until recent private development began dressing it up. The city's largest urban renewal project, the Western Addition, already past the clearance phase, will permanently guard the neighborhood against blighted residential encroachment from the north.

San Francisco harbor was easily defensible by guns on the hills over the sea gate, and since the Spanish days the northwest tip of the peninsula has been given over to a fort—still named the Presidio, as the street by the docks is

336

named the Embarcadero, in honor of Spain. The approaches
to the Golden Gate Bridge run through the hills of the
Presidio, undoubtedly the most attractive berth the regular
Army can give an officer. Between the Presidio and Russian
Hill, along the water, runs a residential area plus yacht
clubs for brave and good sailors who can swim (this is
rough-water country). Behind the Presidio is another residential district, run-down once upon a time, now a hotbed
of private remodeling, another demonstration of the city's
remarkable ability to renew itself.

The ridge that made the peninsula contributes several
high peaks to the center of the city, among them Twin
Peaks, visible from all over town, and Mount Davidson and
Mount Sutro, rising nearly a thousand feet over dock level.
The city hesitated a long time before jumping the ridge into
an area where what was not hill was mostly sand dune.
When the jump came it was rapid, and San Francisco built
a middle-income residential community in rectangular rows
in the stretch between the Presidio and the very large, man-
made Golden Gate Park. South of the park, convenient to
downtown via the transit tunnel dug through Twin Peaks,
another residential area runs down from the hills (where
the streets, for once, are cut on contour lines rather than
straight up and down) to the beach on the Pacific and the
Zoo. South again along the ocean is the Merced district
with its lakes and golf course (genuine links in the Scotch
sense), and what may be Metropolitan Life's most elaborate
set of middle-income apartment houses. The city limits cut
the golf course, appropriately, for what lies south along the
ocean is suburb of the vintage and quality of Winnetka or
Scarsdale or Pasadena.

On the bay shore of the Peninsula, the march south is
broken by the Southern Pacific tracks and the industry and
distribution associated with them. Settlement resumes when
the hills begin again—light industry in the valleys, and on

the hills housing which would be slum elsewhere but which seems livable enough here because of its setting and the general, rather remarkable cleanliness of the city. Finally a range of real mountains—not yet built upon, though doubtless their time will come—separates the city from the bay shore of San Mateo County. Just before the mountains stands the monstrous Cow Palace, a convention center with a floor space occupying almost two acres of land. And where a northeast cropping of the hills reaches the bay, the former New York Giants have built Candlestick Park, a handsome stadium which serves its purpose well despite its odd location in a natural wind funnel. (Then again, the Giants were used to working in the shadow of a bluff.)

Very little of San Francisco is blighted in the way that large stretches of other cities are blighted. Proximity to Nob Hill and Telegraph Hill has limited the deterioration possible in the old Chinatown and Barbary Coast. The Oriental immigrants as a community have achieved comfortable middle-class incomes. The worst of the existing residential slums will be taken care of by the Western Addition and other private improvements down from Marina and the Presidio section. (Not the least of San Francisco's advantages is the fact that most of the good areas near downtown and most of the not-so-good areas were built about the same time, shortly after the earthquake and fire, and in more or less the same style.) The new Jack Tar Hotel on Van Ness, fronting the Western Addition, will probably help that project, though it is an ugly building, a kind of monument to the oft-forgotten fact that San Francisco is in the same state as Los Angeles.

The city's next big renewal project will come beside the bay, between Market Street and Telegraph Hill, where the old distribution center is slummily fading away. Publicity has given the project the name Golden Gateway, which is fine, but even without names there would have been no difficulty finding private money for this one. San Francisco needs new office buildings and high-rise apartment houses, and the location—3.2 acres along the bay, beside and behind the financial district—could not be improved upon. Indeed, the land adjacent to this deteriorated patch has been coming up rather than down, as interior decorators, advertising agencies and the like remodel the quaint to make the chic. Not far away are the city's most remarkable new office buildings—the granite cube of the new John Hancock offices, and the Crown-Zellerbach Building, taking up only one-third of a full-block odd-size lot, with a charming little carousel of a bank office sitting by itself in the northwest corner.

On the other side of Market Street, dilapidation is worse. This is old San Francisco, including survivals from the fire; it is hard to say whether the area *is* more deteriorated because it is flat, or *looks* more deteriorated because it is flat. The railroad tracks, which are on grade, are no help; and neither is the elevated expressway. Skid Row is here, much-dilapidated commercial and what is by far the city's worst housing; though, fortunately, there isn't much of it. As the distance widens between Market and the bay, the strip of good commercial area south of Market grows wider; once you get southwest of Fourth Street you even find some new building, neat and clean if not unusually good-looking. This area must be redeveloped eventually, but certainly one could argue that San Francisco is wise to wait a while, until the future direction of the city becomes more certain.

For great changes must be coming to San Francisco. It is a headquarters city, with much more office space per capita than any other city its size in America. The nation's largest bank has its main office here (Bank of America), and there are three other San Francisco banks in the exclusive, twenty-one-member billion-dollar club. Shipping lines are concentrated near the Embarcadero—American President, Matson, others; the Southern Pacific calls Market Street home; Pacific Gas and Electric centers here, as does Standard Oil of California, the nation's third largest producer, and the Pacific Stock Exchange, the most important west of Chicago. Nearly every major company has at least a branch here, and a number, like Bethlehem Steel, have set up independent or locally run subsidiary operations.

Industrially, this region is expanding more rapidly than any other in the United States (*much* more rapidly, if the nearby Sacramento Valley is included). The farmland is disappearing to make way for factories and parking lots, subdivisions and houses. Stanford and California, the Coast's two great universities, have drawn the research operations, the electronics industry, the drug producers. To maintain its role as the area's heartland, San Francisco must continually increase its commercial density, and that density is already overstraining the available traffic and transit facilities. Residential density will probably continue to decline; the 1960 Census showed a steep drop for center city, a steep rise for suburbia. The city fathers refuse to believe it.

There are garages in San Francisco, including the earliest and most luxurious of the invisible garages—three decks of it under Union Square between Market Street and Nob Hill in the heart of the retail district. Except in the financial district, where double-parking (let alone curb parking) is insufficiently policed, the traffic problem is not severe. Cars still move, however slowly at rush hours, on the Golden Gate Bridge to the north, the Bay Bridge to the east and the Bayshore Freeway from the south, feeding the Bay Bridge, riding into the city on big concrete stilts and dumping its elevated traffic into both the Civic Center area and the financial district. A project already under construction will link this freeway to the west end of the city and the traffic coming up from the luxury suburbs. When the connection is completed, traffic on the freeway between Silver

Avenue and downtown may begin moving a little more slowly than traffic in some of the wide one-way streets of the grid, at least during rush hour.

But San Francisco cares deeply for the looks and livability of its neighborhoods (the invitation to bid on the Golden Gateway project stated that those development proposals would be favored which called for different architects to design different buildings, in keeping with the diversity of the city). No one in a responsible position is willing to chew up the city and grind out concrete ribbons, or shadow it with too many elevated highways. Express roads and grade interchanges cannot answer San Francisco's problem anyway, because this compact downtown simply cannot park that many cars. There is a little public transit now, most of it busses despite the glamor of the cute little cable cars and their friendly grips. There is good metropolitan-area mass transit to the south, on the Southern Pacific's commuter service to the peninsula. But if San Francisco is to maintain itself, it must build today what New York and Chicago built so inexpensively fifty and sixty years ago—a true rapid-transit system, much of it underground. Otherwise, the city's vitality will leak off to Oakland and Redwood City and San Jose and Sacramento. The last two are metropolitan areas in their own right, and among the fastest-growing in the country.

San Francisco plans to build a subway. It has rejected good, odorless state money for the construction of new urban expressways, and received somewhat less but still substantial state aid for engineering studies on rapid transit. Eighteen months ago San Francisco's subway seemed relatively certain, but today the doubts are greater. The bond issue referendum scheduled for November, 1960, has been postponed, at least until summer, 1961. Marin County, across the Golden Gate Bridge, has pulled out of the Bay-Area authority which was to unite all the counties in sponsoring the program. (The Marin County people were afraid they would have to pay taxes to support the transit system that would make their homes convenient to their area's cultural and commercial center.) Cynics have been remembering how conservative a city San Francisco really is—an aristocratic community, more than a little like Boston, moving only when really pushed. The conservatism has served the city well, maintaining a much more *human* ambiance than any other American urban center can display. But the days are past when conservatism was useful to San Francisco—and nowhere on the San Francisco scene does one see the man who will light the necessary fire.

But this is still the Gateway Center, where character and environs, diversity and climate draw much of the nation's best potential. More beautiful than Washington, more cosmopolitan than New Orleans, a better market place than Atlanta, industrially sounder than Houston or Dallas, wealthier and more civilized than Los Angeles or San Diego, San Francisco offers to the next generation much of what New York offered to the last generation. Given a continuation of the exuberance that is the legacy of this coastline, San Francisco could become the City of the Future.

# Epilogue

One thing is certain: between this moment of writing and the time when you read this book, the cities will have changed. We are dealing here with an organism, which cannot be held in one place while you examine it. The city has a life of its own—grows and decays, and then, if the reason for its growth was a good one, it adapts to its environment and grows again. Its root structure is its economic function, and what you see cannot be larger and healthier than what the economic roots will support and nourish. And therefore the measure of its functional quality is basic to the understanding of its role.

Most larger American cities are soundly planted. They grew where they are because their site was economically rich, usually in natural transportation advantages combined with a proximity to our mineral wealth and sources of power. A few, most notably Washington and the state capitals, have been nourished artificially—but in a sense their roots spread out through the state or the country: they both serve and reflect the means by which we enjoy the wealth of the land as a whole. Some, like Boston and Pittsburgh (and perhaps Baltimore, despite its renewal plan and a metropolitan population growth of more than twenty per cent since 1950), have lost or are losing the eminence of their economic function, and will be pruned or externally stimulated before they can grow again. A few, like Denver and Phoenix, have grown too lush for the relatively barren soil on which they stand. Others, such as Seattle, Oklahoma City, or Miami, stand on the thin soil of a single dominating service and could topple in a regional setback. But most of the cities we have discussed need fear the future only if they distort their own growth by ignoring history.

Metropolitan area and city are different entities, socially and economically. As a metropolitan area, Los Angeles is safe—but as a city it hardly exists. Logically, one would say that a healthy metropolitan area cannot grow around a diseased core, but Los Angeles has proved that such freaks of nature can occur. They are disgusting, but they are viable. Over the long run, of course, the cost of maintaining such hydra-headed monsters will be enormous. A look at the state and municipal finances of cities like Los Angeles and Phoenix —and the very minimal public services paid for by those finances—demonstrates the dangers of "spread-out density." But when the costs of such inefficient organization grow too great, Los Angeles will be able to rebuild—because its soil is rich.

Eventually, the growth of the metropolitan area must benefit the central city. People may want a back yard for the kids, but for themselves they like much about the urban existence. They like the excitement of working at the heart of the machinery, of browsing past the shop windows, of eating out, of being where interesting things are getting done. And during the next decade, unless all the signs are wrong, central city will grow more attractive while the nearer suburbs—overdeveloped in the years since the war and still without master planning, growing less green, changing in economic function as industry and distribution move out from the core—begin to suffer the effects of the aging process. Urban housing will expand, and again New York, traditionally the leader in all matters urban, has shown the way with the Mitchell-Lama law, a state improvement on federal legislation. Under the terms of this law, middle-income apartment construction quite near the core has become attractive to builders and investors.

All over America, central cities have been awakening with a sense of shock—at best, of anger—to the significance of their own mistakes. Streets, buildings, whole neighborhoods are being refurbished; transportation to the core is being improved, either by express roads built with federal money or (in too few cases) by rapid transit systems. The commuter railroads will be saved, probably by state governments. New York State, again, recently put into effect a plan which curbs municipal taxation of the railroads, avoiding a strangulation otherwise inevitable. Some of what the localities lose in revenue will be refunded to them from the state treasury.

To me, real estate is a business of markets, not of rent rolls. Often my associates come to me with the details of an offer which seems extremely profitable when you simply add up the income and subtract the running and maintenance costs, interest and amortization. Often, I wouldn't touch the deal with a pole, and the people who do want to go in on it make a joke: "He doesn't buy figures, he buys basics." But it isn't a joke. The purchases I am most proud of are buildings where the figures were poor, but the basics were good. They could be bought inexpensively because they were not as profitable as sound management could make them. With work and modernization, they became safer and more profitable, in every way more competitive. They were located where the city was moving, or where renewal was essential, and the city itself was certain to prosper. If the basics are right, the current figures are almost irrelevant, if not downright deceptive in terms of the investor's yardstick—risk. The right man can always move the figures, at least some small distance; but only God can make a tree.

What central city means to me is, most simply, the market place—the market for capital and labor, for dry goods and recreation, for experiment and innovation. The market functions most efficiently at the core, and if artificial restraints are not interposed gravity will pull to downtown. The job of urban renewal, first of all, is to eliminate the blocks that stand between the market and its natural site. Shopping centers and strip developments are often artificial: they exist to catch the customer on his way to the big market, and by offering extra convenience to keep him from achieving the natural end of his journey. The objection does not hold against all shopping centers—some are natural subcores, secondary markets in an area too large to be served efficiently by the central district. They alone will survive because they draw from their immediate community much as central city draws from the metropolitan area. The others would wither before a challenge from a reconstituted, convenient central business district.

When we speak of markets, we are inevitably dealing with *regions*, not just with the artificial boundaries of a census definition. Kansas City is strong not only because its metropolitan area is growing, but because it is the center of a region which is only beginning to be developed. Short, medium, and long-haul transportation are important, all three; the distribution trades serve more than the immediate suburbs. The economic potential of a site may be determined by its distance from other cities. Denver's remoteness, for example, is an inescapable weakness: why should anyone assemble cars in Denver, when there is nothing that goes into a car which can be shipped more cheaply to Denver than to already existing assembly plants? The integrated industrial area—the Gary-Chicago-Milwaukee complex, the Philadelphia-New York megalopolis, the Buffalo-Youngstown-Akron-Cleveland-Toledo-Detroit crescent, all assure their own future by the sheer variety of their industrial production, though none of these areas is particularly strong in raw materials. Transport routes are there in dazzling quantity, though the railroads must merge to make them efficient competitors against the new superhighways and the waterways, both the beneficiaries of federal largesse, which has given them the fixed assets the railroads must pay for by themselves. On the other side, the New Orleans-Baton Rouge strip grows on the strength of its convenience to mineral wealth. And the San Francisco Bay area swells on newly established convenience—just look at the airline route map and you see the role of San Francisco in the perspective of the continent and of the world.

If the market is central and the market is large, the core *must* be dense. The skyscraper and the high-rise apartment house are not decorative frills on the modern city; they are its essentials. But when you have great density, you must also have clear channels through which the traffic in people and ideas, words and goods, can move without delay. Hence, planning—and, at last, the cities know it. According to the *Wall Street Journal,* American cities are now spending $30,000,000 a year on planning, and as more and more able, angry men come into the field both expenditure and effectiveness will rise.

By habit of mind, I look for analogies, and the analogy to my business is near at hand: radio. Radio, too, depends on the market, and on the strength of the core. It reaches a region rather than a geographical faction, and where the central market is strong the radio station prospers. Not the least of the factors to consider when examining a city is the strength of the central broadcasting stations. The television station is inescapably part of a national network; the local newspaper fights fire with soft soap, offering special pages on each suburb to hold readers; but the radio station stands for a core.

Numbers are important. I can demonstrate the success of what I have done because the numbers turn out right. But in the great debate between the statistician and the philosopher, I go with the philosopher. He is the truer mathematician, the analyst of the significant, the causal rather than the coincidental relationships. The organism changes, not because the numbers hit bottom and bounce, but because change has become necessary in philosophic terms. Urban renewal occurs, not because altruists or capitalists impose themselves on a situation, but because each organism seeks survival and ultimately reacts massively to a massive danger. Economic philosophy makes its public appearance these days mostly as the theoretical arm of brainless propaganda, right or left. I have no interest in that. But I would argue that economic philosophy based on understanding of history can tell us better than any amount of statistics where we are and what we should do about it. I hope this attitude has informed and where necessary excused what I have said about our cities. I know that it has made possible the work I have done in the last ten years.

# Index

Action, 106, 246, 280

Agle, Charles, quoted, 243

Agriculture. *See* Farms

Aircraft: commercial routes of (map), 172; influence on cities by, 29–30; scheduled departures of (chart), 172

Akron (Ohio): Cleveland and, 312; "downtown" in, 313–17; future of, 317, 347; history of, 309; industry in, 43–44, 63, 309, 312–13, 316; maps of, 189, 310–11; railroads and, 311; real estate taxes in, 316; transportation in, 311, 313–16

Alaska, 111

Aluminum Company of America (ALCOA), 158

American myth, 15–16, 81–32

American Revolution, 83

*American Skyline*, 68

Anaheim (Calif.), 157

*Anatomy of a Metropolis*, 20, 278

Anderson, Perry, 234

Apartment houses, 57–58, 69, 112, 249–50; as essentials for modern city, 347; zoning and, 94, 264

Arizona, 32

Arkansas River, 112, 328, 330

Assessed valuations. *See* Real Estate

Atomic energy industry, 42

Atlanta (Ga.), 106, 342; airport of, 218–19, 223; "downtown" in, 218, 221–22; future of, 112, 220–21, 224–25; industry in, 39, 220, 223–24; maps of, 179, 218–19; Negroes in, 223; population increase in, 196; railroads and, 218–21; schools in, 224; South and, 217; transportation in, 218–20, 222; urban renewal in, 222–25

Automobiles, 6–7, 53, 118; city growth and, 29–30, 50; driving to work in, 59–61; increase of ownership of (chart), 170. *See also* Parking, Roads, Traffic, Trucks

Baltimore (Md.): future of, 111, 344; planning of, 97; "row" houses in, 70; transportation in, 59–60; urban renewal in, 246

Baton Rouge (La.), 291, 347; "downtown" in, 298–99; growth of, 294; industry in, 44, 292, 294–95; maps of, 187, 293–94; as port, 294–95

349

Denver (Colo.): finances of, 88, 229–30; future of, 234–35, 344, 346; government of, 229–30; industry in, 226–27; maps of, 180, 227–28; real estate taxes in, 88; transportation in, 59, 232–34; urban renewal in, 230–35. *See also* Mile-High Center

Depression, future possibility of, 110–11, of 1920–21, 34

Des Moines (Iowa), 19, 111

Detroit: as automobile center, 39, 43, 63, 111, 310; future of, 111, 347; Negroes in, 72, 75; planning of, 94; slums in, 168; transportation in, 60. *See also* Northland, Willow Run

Dilworth, Richardson, 244

Discrimination against Negroes, history of, 74

Douglas, William O., quoted, 121

Downey (Calif.), 157

"Downtown": advantages of, 46–47; decay of, 23, 26–27, 118–19; entertainment in, 130–31, 159; future of, 114; industries normally located in, 45; planning of, 129–34; retail stores in, 64–67; skyscrapers and, 200–1; tax discrimination against, 88; transportation and, 55–57, 132. *See also* Central city areas

Duluth (Minn.), 24; as port, 19

East St. Louis (Ill.), 66

Ebasco (consulting firm), 323

Elevated railways, 50–52, 58; in Chicago, 54; in New York City, 53, 274

Elizabeth (N.J.), 272, 287; Negroes in, 79

Erie Canal, 19–21, 271

Ethnic communities (Ghettos), 32, 71; in suburbs today, 72. *See also* Mexicans, Negroes, Puerto Ricans

Europe: cities in, 15–17; myth that it was urban, 15–16

Evanston (Ill.), 143

Expressways, 114, 345; in Stock-

holm, 108; urban renewal and, 121. *See also* Freeways

Farms: dependence of cities on, 31; immigration and, 31–32; legislative influence of, 106; movement from, 35–36, 102

Farnsley, Charles, 258, 264

Federal Housing Administration, 68

Financial business, 45; in Atlanta, 200, 293; in Chicago, 142; in Dallas, 200–1, 204–5, 293; in New York City, 37, 42, 92, 272–73; in Philadelphia, 248

Financing: of municipal services, 107–8; by special assessment, 107; of subways, 54–56; taxes and, 87–93; of transit lines, 52

Fire departments, 98, 107

First International Seminar on Urban Renewal (The Hague), 122, 127

Fischer, Robert, 234

Floods, 21, 112, 320; in Dallas, 203, 206; in Louisville and Cincinnati, 262

Florida, urban renewal and, 121

Ford, Henry, 39, 57

Fort Worth (Tex.), 111; Dallas and, 206–7; industries in, 206; transportation in, 108, 202; urban renewal in, 206–7

*Fortune:* city government survey, 258–59; traffic survey, 56, 59–60, 197, 202

France, 16, 22

Frankfurt (Germany), 148

Freeways, 61, 94, 109, 160; in Kansas City, 209; real estate valuation and, 62

Frontier, American, 16, 20, 31–32

Galveston (Tex.), as port, 19

Garages. *See* Parking

Garbage collection, 91; through back alleys, 329; financing of, 107

Garment industry, 45, 126–27; in Dallas, 205; in Los Angeles, 38, 154; in New York City, 38, 282

Garst, Roswell, 31

168; transportation in, 59–61, 94, 132, 168, 195–97; zoning laws in, 94, 167, 196–97. *See also* Pentagon

*Washington Square,* 27

Water supply, 91; in Dallas, 203; in Denver, 229; financing of, 107; obsolescence of, 117; sewage disposal and, 97; special districts for, 85–87

Webb & Knapp, 158

Welfare services, 91, 98; taxes for, 107–8

Western Electric, 215

Westchester County (N.Y.), 52

White Plains (N.Y.), 113, 287

Whittier (Calif.), 157

Wichita (Kans.), 111, 325

Willow Run, 64

Wisconsin, 31, 82

Wood, Robert C., 98, quoted, 87

Woodward, August, 94

Wright, Frank Lloyd, 163

"Wrong side of the tracks," 25

Wyoming, 32

Yonkers (N.Y.), 287

Young, Robert, 138

Youngstown (Ohio), 347

Zeckendorf, William, 260

Zoning laws, 93–94, 96–97, 104, 282, 284, 323. *See also* Building codes